D0485746

WORDSWORTH CLASSICS
OF WORLD LITERATURE

General Editor: Tom Griffith MA, MPhil

SYMPOSIUM AND THE DEATH OF SOCRATES

Plato

Symposium and
the Death of Socrates

❖

Translated by Tom Griffith
With an Introduction
by Jane O'Grady

WORDSWORTH CLASSICS
OF WORLD LITERATURE

This edition published 1997 by Wordsworth Editions Limited
Cumberland House, Crib Street, Ware, Hertfordshire SG12 9ET

ISBN 1 85326 479 2

© Wordsworth Editions Limited 1997

Wordsworth® is a registered trade mark of
Wordsworth Editions Ltd

Typeset by Antony Gray
Printed and bound in Great Britain by
Mackays of Chatham plc, Chatham, Kent

CONTENTS

INTRODUCTION

Plato's Immortality

'Philosophy is a series of footnotes to Plato', said the twentieth-century philosopher Whitehead, and in the nineteenth century Ferrier wrote: 'All philosophic truth is Plato rightly divined; all philosophic error is Plato misunderstood'. Though Plato was born almost 2,500 years ago, many would agree. Similar tribute could hardly be paid to other great forerunners in learning. It would be absurd to say that astronomy is a series of footnotes to Copernicus, or that medical errors are Galen misunderstood. That this is so is partly due to the nature of philosophy, which is less amenable to proof and progress than are other areas of knowledge, and which need not therefore be superseded. Yet philosophy, like science, relies on cumulative building, for it consists of argument and counterargument. Plato set the agenda for all subsequent philosophy, asking questions that are still unsolved, and creating the framework in which they would be tackled. His thought contains in embryo the whole of Western philosophy. His own answers may ultimately be wrong, as are most philosophical answers, but they are compelling, tantalising, and seminal in their wrongness. Most great philosophers have engaged with him, whether as ally or antagonist.

What Plato is probably most famous for is his theory (in so far as it actually is a theory) of Forms (sometimes called 'Ideas'). Briefly (I'll say more about it later), this is the theory that each of the changing, multiple objects or qualities in the perceptible world only is what it imperfectly is because of its resemblance to an archetypal essence or Form, which is its underlying reality. It is the Forms alone that truly exist beyond our world of becoming. To acquire knowledge and virtue, we must discover them through their reflections here; or rather rediscover them, since we already knew them before being born. 'Learning is recollection.'

Powerful and beautiful, if wrong, the idea of the Forms permeates the metaphysics of Kant and Schopenhauer. Nietzsche, Heidegger and Wittgenstein fruitfully repudiate it. It is partly a response to, and articulation of, the problem of how exactly objects or qualities designated by a certain name (for instance, 'cat' or 'red') all manage to be so designated; to which the obvious answer – because they all have something in common, being cats or being red – proves circular in that it makes use of the very name that needs to be explained. This problem, the problem of universals, is still debated by philosophers, and from it have ramified most of the issues – of knowledge, metaphysics, conceptualisation, the mind and language – that comprise philosophy. Plato's Forms were also important (though misunderstood) in the creation of Christian theology, and for many psychologists, artists and writers – notably Freud, Jung, Claude, Dante, Herbert Vaughan, Wordsworth, Proust and John Cowper Powys. Plato's analysis and hierarchical, tripartite division of the human personality was echoed by Freud, and the idea of Platonic love, as adumbrated in the *Symposium*, is (though often misinterpreted) highly significant in art, life and thought. So, for good or ill, is Plato's ideal city as portrayed in the *Republic*.

Yet oddly, apart from the thirteen Letters which are considered only questionably his, everything that survives of Plato's writings – the twenty or more philosophical dialogues – purports simply to be recording the words of his teacher Socrates, who lived from 469 to 399 BC. 'There is no writing of Plato nor will there ever be,' says Plato's Second Letter. 'What goes by that name really belongs to Socrates turned young and handsome.' There is much controversy over how far Plato's dialogues represent Socrates' views or his own, and a lot of support for the belief that the early dialogues, which include the *Apology* and the *Crito*, represent Socrates' teachings, but that, while Socrates continues to be the spokesman in the dialogues of the middle and later period, Plato was in fact using him as a mouthpiece for his own views as they developed. Whatever the truth, it is clear that the style of thought instigated by Socrates and represented – in spirit if not literally – by Plato in his dialogues was a huge leap forward from the primitive cosmological deductions of his predecessors over the previous two centuries.

The Pre-Socratics

Socrates was ground-breaking in his capacity for subtle distinctions, but Thales, living about two centuries earlier, is rightly called the first philosopher, for he created the most fundamental distinction of all – that of the human mind from its surroundings. He hewed intelligibility out of the sheer cliff-face of reality, and drew form out of the void. Some time at the turn of the sixth century BC, he asked the question 'What is the world made of?' Until then, for all the great technological and mathematical achievements of Egypt, China and Babylon, the world had been manipulated and measured piecemeal, but not described or explained as a whole, except in terms of myth. Myth does not analyse reality, but projects human concerns on to it, investing organic and inorganic matter with gods created in our own image. Thales, however, was trying to deal with reality as it is in itself, irrespective of observation, leaving himself out. He wanted to explain the seen world – and how it came into being – in terms of its seen constituents. As Aristotle commented almost three centuries later, Thales and his successors assumed 'there must be some natural substance, either one or more than one, from which the other things come-into-being, while it is preserved.' Thales said this natural substance was water; Anaximander that it was the conflict and reconciliation of opposites; Anaximenes that it was air, which becomes fire, wind, cloud, water, earth and stone; Heraclitus that it was eternal flux, underpinned with fire; Parmenides that it was indivisible, changeless being; and Democritus (Socrates' contemporary) that it was unsplittable particles (atoms) combining, disintegrating and re-combining.

That these pre-Socratic philosophers relied more on logical deduction than experimental research to establish their hypotheses, and that these hypotheses were wrong, is unimportant. What was important was the questions they were asking and the ways they were thinking. Taking the whole of reality as their subject-matter, they were 'thinking without headings', as Heidegger was to say more than twenty centuries later. Yet they were doing cosmology, physics, chemistry, biology, logic, epistemology and metaphysics all at once, and all the disciplines of knowledge were to be constructed from their preliminary excursions into thought.

Socrates

According to Aristotle in the *Metaphysics*, Socrates 'disregarded the physical universe'. It might be true to say that instead of trying to describe the world, as his predecessors had done, he wanted to determine what we could truthfully say about it. He concentrated less on the objects of knowledge than on knowledge itself, and on how we are to live. By all accounts (and as well as Plato's we have those of Xenophon, another of his pupils) he was an eccentric character – given to collaring people in the Athenian market place and doggedly questioning them. He went barefoot and often fell into ecstatic trances. Of humble origins, he was ugly and maladroit, though with enormous charm and charisma, as Alcibiades attests in the *Symposium*. His wisdom was legendary, and one of his friends (according to the account in the *Apology*) asked the Delphic oracle if there was anyone wiser than Socrates, getting the answer no. Socrates himself professed amazement at this, but after quizzing those he had supposed wiser than he, he found that in at least one respect he knew more – in knowing that he knew nothing. And he decided he should convince others that they were ignorant too, so putting them on the path to knowledge and virtue. 'I have never been anyone's teacher', says Plato's Socrates in the *Apology*; and in the early (so-called Socratic) dialogues he never explicitly teaches, merely asks questions ('What is virtue?' 'What is courage?', etc). Seeking definitions from his interlocutors, he showed that their proposed definitions were inadequate because either not sufficiently specific or not sufficiently general. He dubbed himself (referring to his mother's livelihood) a midwife to knowledge.

From his childhood, according to his speech in the *Apology*, a divine voice had guided Socrates, telling him at important moments what not to do, and debarring him from entering public life. However, he was chosen by lot to be a member of the council in Athens, and took principled and dangerous stands against abuses by both democratic and oligarchical governments. He fought in the Peloponnesian War, and, by Alcibiades' account in the *Symposium*, was exceptionally brave. In 399 BC, at the age of seventy, Socrates was accused of impiety and of corrupting the minds of the Athenian youth (an accusation that was never spelt out but which was certainly quite exempt from sexual connotations, centring mainly on the political and religious subversiveness of Socrates' teaching). It is at first sight surprising, to a modern mind, that he was given the death penalty for these charges. Several of his philosophical predecessors had also been accused of heresy, but only four had actually ben prosecuted, none of these suffering the death penalty. Athens had of course been through major political upheavals, and three of Socrates' closest followers had been members of the tyrannical government recently ousted by his democratic accusers. He could have avoided the death penalty by proposing, as Athenian law entitled him to do, an appropriate alternative sentence of exile or a heavy fine. But, in Plato's portrayal, his principles forced him deliberately to embrace death. As far as we know, he left no writings at all.

Plato

Plato knew Socrates for at least eight years, and is clearly supposed to have witnessed the conversations he reports. Yet he himself plays no part in the dialogues, apart from being mentioned (in the *Apology*) as being present at Socrates' trial and offering to help pay his proposed fine, and (in the *Phaedo*) as being absent, due to illness, during his last hours. He was more than forty years younger than Socrates. Born in 428 BC of an aristocratic family (on his father's side, it was claimed, going back to the god Neptune!), and well educated, he was primed for a political life. But he was deflected from any desire for office by the influence of Socrates' teachings and still more of Socrates' death when he himself was twenty-eight. 'I was disgusted,' the Seventh Letter records, 'and withdrew myself from the evils of the time.' He realised, he said, that 'all government is without exception bad' and that the only salvation was to put philosophers in political control. Either at this point or, some scholars say, later, Plato began many years of worldwide travel, and over the course of three visits to Sicily he became closely involved with the

Syracusan tyrant Dionysius the Elder (who is said to have had him sold into slavery), and later with his son Dionysius the Younger whom he tried, unsuccessfully, to make into one of his ideal guardians, or philosopher-kings, as described in the *Republic*.

On one of his returns to Athens Plato bought a piece of land just outside the city boundaries, and some time around 387 BC founded what could be called the world's first university, the Academy. It was intended to turn its students into philosopher-kings – legislators and administrators of the state, who would first have been trained in the disinterested pursuit of truth. This is, in a sense, what medieval and modern universities would later do. It replaced the teaching of the wandering philosophy teachers, or sophists, whom Plato's dialogues so constantly condemn. Instead the students gathered from far afield to study a set of courses presumably approximating to the educational programme outlined in the *Republic* – mathematics, dialectic, political theory, astronomy, natural science, biology, harmonics, and of course philosophy. The Academy's most famous product was Aristotle, who studied there for nineteen years, and it lasted for about nine centuries. For twenty years (he lived to be eighty), Plato himself lectured, mostly to an elite group. Like Socrates before him, he did so unpaid. The twenty or so dialogues, most of which are certainly authentic, were probably written as easy learning devices, but sadly no fragment of his serious lectures, nor any of his students' lecture notes, survives.

Euthyphro, Apology and Crito

The *Euthyphro*, *Apology* and *Crito* are interesting less for their philosophical import than for their portrayal of Socrates. *Euthyphro* is a typical early dialogue, asking the question 'What is the holy, or holiness?' Socrates poses what is now called the Euthyphro dilemma: is the holy loved by the gods because it is holy, or is it holy because it is loved by the gods? He rejects the latter alternative, while the former has the consequence that the gods (or God) are not indispensable for morality, and also that their own holiness or otherwise remains an open question. Showing that each alternative is problematic, Socrates gently but firmly exposes the pretensions to moral knowledge of the soothsayer Euthyphro.

The *Apology* is one of Plato's early dialogues, and for the most part not a dialogue but a monologue. It consists of Socrates' speech in his defence at his trial, and a final address, together with, between these, the counter-proposal to his sentence. Socrates proposes an absurdly small fine, which is inevitably rejected. He makes it clear that it is not just a matter of his refusing to accept an accusation which he considered unjust, but that he could not agree to stop teaching (or rather cross-examining). He felt that he had been deputed by the gods to live the philosopher's life, continually examining himself and others. For, and this surely applies also to those who are not divinely inspired, 'the unexamined life is not worth living'.

Crito, also an early dialogue, is set in prison, and shows us Socrates refusing to agree to his friends' offers to help him escape. He says he cannot try to escape, because that would mean breaking the laws of Athens, and this would be unjust. Although the trial scene is probably accurate, both it and the more fanciful prison scene are tendentious. They have encouraged an idealisation of Socrates in which Christians and humanists tended to exalt him into the prototype of the innocent martyr Jesus. While perhaps more or less faithful to Socrates' words, the *Apology* plays down the grounds for the charge of corrupting the youth, and only the well-informed would catch the passing reference to Socrates' connection with three of the Thirty Tyrants. If he is correctly recorded in the *Republic*, the *Gorgias* and elsewhere, Socrates condemned democracy and disparaged democratic leaders, including Pericles. The ideal state he advocated has been branded by commentators like Karl Popper as totalitarian. His democratic accusers did therefore have grounds for seeing him as politically subversive.

Phaedo: the soul

In the *Phaedo*, a dialogue of the middle period, the imprisoned Socrates seeks to console his friends for his impending death. He begins with the assertion that the true philosopher has been practising being dead throughout his life. By continually spurning physical pleasure and the body's demands, he has been trying to dissociate his soul from his body, which is exactly what death will do; so he can hardly repine now. In a further paradoxical twist, he says that the soul lives on after dying, suggesting that death itself need not be death.

For modern readers, talk of the immortality of the soul, overlaid by subsequent echoes and accretions of theology, is a stale antidote to grief or fear. For Socrates' hearers or Plato's readers, such talk was much more of a novelty – though not, as the *Phaedo* makes clear, a complete novelty. To most ancient Greeks, as to most primitive societies, the soul or psyche was the principle of life, which is dispersed by death. In the commonsense view it was what accounted for the difference between people you see walking upright in the street and the corpses you see lying in the gutter, as the puppeteer's hand accounts for the difference between the puppet moving and the puppet collapsed. Already in Homer's tales, and even in some of the pre-Socratic philosophers, this galvanising force had assumed some of the characteristics of a human, becoming, as in so many of the societies described by anthropologists, a mannikin within the man. Homer's Hades was peopled by bloodless shades – but this still hardly counted as life. Plato, following the tentative steps in that direction by Anaximenes and Heraclitus, made the soul not just the self-mover but the seat of consciousness, reasoning and moral decision. In fact, the soul is given independent full-blooded life, and the body, with its 'deceptive senses', becomes a 'hindrance', a prison from which the soul looks out. Following the logic of this metaphor (which will become the more fleshed-out parable of the Cave in the *Republic*), Plato produces the paradox that we are freer and more clear-sighted when we are dead. Realising more explicitly than his predecessors that pure knowledge of the world is vitiated by the knower, he suggests that we will know more easily when unhampered by the body's interference. Death, then, will be a release in the most triumphantly literal and optimistic sense.

Arguments for immortality

There are various arguments for the soul's immortality throughout the *Phaedo*, none of them very good. First, what is often called the argument from opposites – that nothing can increase in one quality without decreasing in another. Just as sleeping comes from waking, and waking from sleeping, so, if death follows life,

life must follow death, as part of a 'complementary process' without which everything would, in the end, be asleep or dead. The second argument is the argument from recollection (see *The Forms*, below). Third is what I shall call the argument from two types, which attempts to rebut Cebes's fear that the soul will be scattered to the winds at death. Only composite things (like the body) disintegrate, says Socrates. Anything in the non-composite class of things (to which the soul must surely belong) is more likely to be constant and unchanging, invisible, essentially divine and masterful, ruling the body, immortal, indestructible, and forever true to itself. Fourthly, there is an argument against a new model of the soul proposed by Simmias, which foreshadows Aristotle's theory that the soul, rather than being an insubstantial substance, is the functional states of the body. (This in turn foreshadows functionalism, one of the twentieth-century theories of mind.) Simmias points out that invisibility, incorporeality, beauty and divinity, which Socrates claims essentially belong to the soul, belong also to the tuning of a lyre. May not the soul be the body's tuning? And, if so, is it not as liable to destruction as the body-lyre on which it depends? Socrates replies that what is true of an attunement is not true of a soul. An attunement can be less or more in tune; a soul cannot be less or more a soul. What is more, if goodness is like attunement and badness is like non-attunement, then the soul cannot be bad without ceasing to be a soul.

Socratic progress

When Cebes still professes himself dissatisfied, Socrates drops the dialectical mode and, as an introduction to an account of the Forms, gives a disquisition on his own philosophical development. He began by wanting to know the causes of everything, how things come into being, exist and die. He asked questions such as: 'Is it blood that enables us to think? Or air? Or fire? Does the brain give rise to hearing, sight and smell, and do these sensations engender memory and opinion?'

But once he began thinking about the decay of these faculties and about cosmology, he realised he was not suited to natural science. In an apparently irrelevant transition, he describes how things he had previously thought self-evident became puzzling.

For instance, seeing a tall man standing by a smaller, he had once thought it obvious that the tall one was taller – and the small one smaller – by a head. But how can the same thing be the cause both of tallness and smallness?

Or again, two things become two by being brought together. And yet two can also arise from the opposite reason – when one thing is divided and the two halves separated. Confused, and despairing of ever knowing the reasons for birth, life, or death, Socrates was delighted by Anaxagoras' claim that Mind was the cause and underlying principle of everything. But, on reading him, he was disappointed. Anaxagoras was merely doing natural science like the rest of them, omitting 'the good that binds everything together'. The mere disposition of bones and muscle was no explanation of his (Socrates') being in prison, any more than movements of the air, hearing, and so on, satisfactorily explain their present conversation. Such explanations confuse causes and basic conditions. The 'real reason' for his sitting there was that the Athenians thought it right to condemn him, and he to submit to their penalty. He wants to find 'the thing which makes it possible for the reason to be a reason'. So he proposes his own theory of causation – the Forms.

The problem of knowledge

In his progress from natural science, through maths and logic, to patterned metaphysics, Socrates seems to be grappling with a problem that had only begun to be apprehended by Heraclitus, and after him by Parmenides. The early pre-Socratics had assumed that the world could be transparent to them, and they to the world. But even to ask what is the One (cause or principle) originating, galvanising or underlying the Many involves differentiating between what things really are in themselves and what they merely seem, involves distinguishing between appearance and reality. Appearance to whom? We are led back to ourselves, the appeared-to. However strong our desire for a dispassionate, self-divested view of the world, we cannot leave ourselves out of the picture.

The problem inevitably becomes: how far and in what guises reality can appear to us. Our mind, said Heraclitus, a hundred years before Plato and his cave, 'peeps out through the channels of perception as though through a kind of window'. The senses can be regarded as the medium through which reality is glimpsed, or as instruments to seize it. But whichever metaphor one uses, reality, whether sucked in or grasped by the senses, is inevitably not transparent to us, but richer than revealed by our sensory inlets, which are often unreliable. For Socrates in the *Phaedo*, they dizzy and confuse knowledge, obscuring its clarity.

Equally unreliable, for any fixed and steady reasoning upon it, is the shifting, kaleidoscopic world. For, as in Socrates' size and counting examples, what can truly be said of anything depends on its context and its relation to other things. Simmias is smaller than Phaedo and taller than Socrates. Everything is in flux, said Heraclitus, so full of change and decay that 'we cannot step twice into the same river.' Or rather 'we step and do not step into the same rivers', for 'on those who step again into the same river, different and different waters flow'. To which Cratylus (another pre-Socratic) answered that we cannot step into the same river even once. For the sake of accuracy, we should really only point at things, not name them. We cannot even think them, said Parmenides. Anything that comes into existence, anything that grows, decays and dies, never completely and forever is. And since we cannot think or know what is not, and since thought and knowledge must correspond to something, 'the only thing that exists for thinking is the thought that it is' – a log-jam of logic. True reality must be unitary and unchanging is-ness, change and multiplicity merely an illusion. Although Socrates' contemporary Democritus, with his theory of atoms, would revert to the original impulse to describe perceptible reality, knowledge, with Parmenides, had ceased to be knowledge of the world.

The Forms

Plato combines the two conflicting theories of Parmenides and Heraclitus. He agrees with Heraclitus that, like the river stepped into twice, the sensory world is forever changing. He agrees with Parmenides that what changes never totally is anything, and is therefore unknowable. As he makes Glaucon ask in the *Republic*, 'How could a man know something that was not?' Like Parmenides, he doesn't dispute the possibility of something being known, but the something he postulates is not congealed is-ness.

Instead, it is Heraclitean multiplicity at another, changeless level – Forms appropriate to each type of thing, which make each thing of that type the type it imperfectly is. Thus he sees reality as comprising two sorts of realm, a world of being and a world of becoming (though this terminology can be misleading – the world of being is not, like religious heavens, an aethereal earth).

Phaedo is the first dialogue to express the idea of the Forms. In earlier dialogues Socrates had searched for what same-named things (for instance, 'courageous') had in common among themselves. Here Plato argues that what same-named things had in common was outside themselves. He uses a similar sleight of hand to that of the ontological argument, which says that since our idea of God is that of an all-perfect being, and since to exist is more perfect than not to exist, God must necessarily exist. A beautiful, odd idea that our idea of God forces him to exist, and Plato similarly presses reality out of logic. It is from seeing sticks that are the same size as other sticks, he says, that we get the notion of equality, and yet not from the pair of sticks themselves. For we recognise that a pair of things may be equal to one another yet not equal to other things, and that equality itself is something over and above equality in that particular case, which is anyway not absolutely equal.

Similarly we know that beautiful things fall short of perfect beauty, and that good things are not perfectly good. How could we recognise this falling short unless we were reminded of an absolute reality – an absolute equality, beauty and goodness, which the particular instances of each are striving, however fruitlessly, to achieve? Just as the ontological argument 'proves' that our concept of God necessitates his existence, so our ability to use a general term for many particular things necessitates a reality of which those particulars partake.

It is important to avoid a popular misconception – that the Forms are subjective, mental, conceptual, the product of thought. Obviously they are the product of Plato's (or Socrates') thought, but he intended them to be objective, existing irrespective of whether we exist, and whether we conceive them. This is why scholars since the 1930s have translated Plato's *eidos* (and sometimes *idea*) as 'Form' rather than the earlier 'Idea'. Nonetheless, as shown above, Plato's epistemology (theory of knowledge) is closely entwined with his metaphysics (theory of what there is), and his first explicit formulation of the Forms – in the *Phaedo* – occurs interdependently with establishing the soul's immortality and the doctrine of recollection. He claims that when we recognise the perfect original in its imperfectly resembling particular, we rekindle a now-dormant knowledge.

This knowledge of the Forms cannot be derived from the senses, since it forestalls and informs our sensory experience. Our sensory experience begins at birth, and therefore this knowledge must have occurred before we were born. In Plato's *Meno*, the slave-boy, who is quite untutored in maths, proves to understand geometry when Socrates questions him. And as in maths, so in metaphysics, what we call learning is simply the recovery of what we already knew.

But it is not just that our capacity for knowledge entails the existence of the Forms, and that it is the Forms that make our knowledge possible. It is the Forms that enable everything to be what it is, in so far as it is. Things are what they almost are by copying, resembling, following the pattern of, and partaking in, their appropriate Forms (the *Phaedo* has several different terms for the Form/particular relation, and they are not all compatible). Here, finally, are the causes that Socrates was seeking. Cryptic, mystical, and supplying ample scope for scholarly debate, his 'safe answer' is that 'it is the beautiful that makes all beautiful things beautiful' and that 'by bigness big things are big, and bigger things bigger'. The sole explanation, he says, for any given thing's coming into being is that it shares its Form's reality.

The Symposium: ladder of Platonic love

The *Symposium* is a dialogue of Plato's middle period, thought to have been written later than the *Phaedo*. Whereas the *Phaedo* portrays Socrates' last hours, the *Symposium* is a banquet at which Socrates is enjoying the company of his friends.

It is not really a dialogue, any more than the *Apology* is. It is a collection of speeches, in which each guest undertakes to make a speech in praise of Eros, the god of love. The early speakers offer more or less conventional panegyrics, whose interest lies both in the picture they give us of the social life of upper-class, intellectual Athenians, and in the skill with which Plato picks up these conventional ideas when he comes to Socrates' speech. Eros, according to Diotima (the wise woman from whom Socrates says he learnt about love), is not a god, and not beautiful or good, yet he is not automatically the opposite of these either. He is something intermediate between divinity and humanity, beauty and ugliness, badness and goodness, wisdom and ignorance. The idea of an intermediate state between wisdom and ignorance foreshadows Plato's threefold model of cognition (as knowledge, opinion and ignorance) in the *Republic*, which replaces the *Phaedo*'s straight choice between knowledge and ignorance. In the *Symposium*, however, the middle position is lover of wisdom rather than believer.

Love, says Diotima, is the desire for permanent goodness and happiness. Its method of pursuit is the use of what is beautiful for producing immortal offspring. Socrates is happy to countenance love at its most basic level, as sex and the raising of children, which involves extraordinary and irrational unselfishness. However, though accepting 'sexually creative' love, Socrates prefers the mentally creative, including in 'artistic reproduction' thought in general, composing music and political theory and practice. What is thought by some scholars to be a third level to these other two levels of love, but which is surely of a different kind from them (since they are self-enclosed and mutually exclusive, and it is fluid and progressive), is the love-ladder of the young initiate lover.

The lover starts out in pursuit of physical beauty, and if properly taught, will be attracted to one person, producing the progeny of beautiful discourse. He then sees that his beloved's physical beauty is akin to any other physical beauty, and all physical beauty now appears interchangeable to him. At the next ascent, greater value becomes attached to mental than to physical beauty, so that, as with the beautiful Alcibiades and the ugly Socrates later in the dialogue, the lover is kindled to love by beauty of soul, whatever the beloved's appearance. The lover next graduates to contemplating the beauty of customs and institutions, dismissing physical beauty as insignificant; and next from practice to knowledge – contemplating the beauty of different kinds of knowledge and engendering inspirational ideas as he concentrates on philosophy. Finally he beholds beauty itself, the 'final revelation'.

Unlike instances of earthly beauty, which are partly beautiful and partly ugly, sometimes beautiful and sometimes not, accepted as beauty by some and not by others, the Form of Beauty is wholly and forever beautiful. From it all other beauty is derived, and it inspires the lover to produce 'not likenesses of goodness (since it is no likeness he has before him), but the real thing'. And yet, in a radical departure from the *Phaedo*, he has only ascended to the Form of Beauty by a ladder of particular beauties and the feelings fitted to them, all of them to some degree valuable.

In the *Phaedo*, Plato denigrates what would normally count as the instrument of knowledge (the body) and what would normally count as the objects of knowledge (particular things). He urges us to have as little to do with either as possible. This harsh dichotomy echoes the way Socrates' soul, immortal or not, is about to be severed from his body. In the *Symposium* the attitude to corporeal and sensory things is more tolerant. Soul and body more comfortably interact. The soul is no longer pure intellect, but the seat of love, desire, aesthetic appreciation, delight. The body is no longer the soul's prison but its vehicle, though Socrates does still speak of human flesh as clogging, and lumps it with 'other worthless and corruptible matter'. The model of the human character portrayed in the *Symposium* widens the scope and character of both soul and body. It is more fleshed out, more recognisably human. It is still, however, a unit. In the *Republic* and the *Phaedrus*, the soul will be tripartite. Though inevitably hierarchical, its three parts will be required to work harmoniously together, with the element intermediate between intellect and appetite (and variously translated as 'spirit', 'passion', 'will', 'indignation', or 'feelings') able to be co-opted by either the higher or lower level.

Any model of a divided or physically mediated soul would fail to square with the 'two types' argument for immortality, which requires that the soul be non-composite and unitary. On the other hand, the antagonism found in the *Phaedo* between soul and body, and between knowledge and perception, is ultimately inconsistent with the doctrine of recollection in the same dialogue. We need knowledge (of particular things) by means of the senses. Or rather, since this cannot count as knowledge, we need opinion, to trigger our recollection (and restoration) of true knowledge – knowledge of the Forms by means of reason or the soul. If the realms of becoming and being were entirely separate, or if we dispensed with the bodily realm of becoming, the knowledge we can rekindle of the Forms and Being would be impossible. We need the disparaged entities – of body, opinion and sensory particulars – as stepping-stones to the exalted ones. The *Symposium* abandons dichotomy in favour of gradualism, and outlines a ladder relationship which enables the separate realms to interact.

JANE O'GRADY

SUGGESTIONS FOR FURTHER READING

Richard Kraut (ed.), *The Cambridge Companion to Plato*, Cambridge University Press, 1992

J. E. Raven, *Plato's Thought in the Making*, Cambridge University Press, 1965

G. S. Kirk, J. E. Raven, M. Schofield, *The Pre-Socratic Philosophers,* Cambridge University Press, 1983

R. M. Hare, *Plato*, Oxford University Press, 1982

G. M. A. Grube, *Plato's Thought*, Hackett, Indianapolis 1980

SYMPOSIUM

THE SPEAKERS IN THE DIALOGUE

AGATHON	a writer of tragedies
SOCRATES	a truth-loving eccentric
PHAEDRUS	an idealist
PAUSANIAS	a realist – Agathon's lover
ARISTOPHANES	a writer of comedies
ERYXIMACHUS	a doctor
ALCIBIADES	a politician and playboy

APOLLODORUS You couldn't have asked anyone better. I live in 172
Phalerum, and the day before yesterday I was going up to town
when a man I know caught sight of me disappearing in the
distance. He gave me a shout, calling me (a little facetiously)
'You there! Citizen of Phalerum! Hey, Apollodorus! Wait a
moment.'

So I stopped and waited.

'Apollodorus,' he said, 'I've been looking for you for ages. I
wanted to ask you about the time when Agathon and Socrates
and Alcibiades and the others all met for dinner. I want to know b
what was said about love. I was told about it by a man who had
talked to Phoenix, son of Philippus; he said you knew about it
as well. He wasn't much help – couldn't remember anything
very definite. Can you give me your version? After all, who
better than you to talk about Socrates' conversations? For
instance, were you at the dinner-party yourself, or not?'

'You must have been given a pretty garbled account, if you
think the party you're asking about took place recently enough c
for me to have been at it.'

'Oh! I thought you were.'

'Really, Glaucon, how could I have been? It's ages since
Agathon last lived in Athens, and less than three years since I
became friends with Socrates, and got into the habit of keeping
up with what he says and does every day. Before that my life
was just a random whirl of activity. I thought I was extremely 173
busy, but in fact I was the most pathetic creature imaginable,
just as you are now, doing anything to avoid philosophical
thought.'

'Very funny. When *did* the party happen, then?'

'It was when we were still children, when Agathon won the
prize with his first tragedy, the day after he and the members of
the chorus made the usual winners' thanksgivings.'

'Oh, I see. It *was* a long time ago, then. Who told you about it? Was it Socrates himself?'

b   'God, no. I got it from the man who told Phoenix, a man called Aristodemus, from Cydathenaeum. Small man, never wears shoes. He'd been at the party; in fact, I think he must have been one of Socrates' keenest admirers in those days. But I've also asked Socrates about some of the things he told me, and his version agreed with Aristodemus'.'

'You must tell me all about it, and walking into town is an ideal opportunity. You can talk, and I will listen.'

c   So we discussed the party as we went along, and that's why, as I said originally, I'm a good person to ask about it. And if I've got to tell it to you as well, I'd better get on with it. In any case, I get tremendous pleasure out of talking about philosophy myself, or listening to other people talk about it, quite apart from thinking it's good for me. Other conversation, especially your kind, about money or business, bores me stiff. You're my friends, but I feel sorry for you, because you think you're

d   getting somewhere, when you're not. You in turn probably think me misguided, and you may well be right. However, I don't *think* you are misguided; I know for certain you are.

FRIEND Still the old Apollodorus we know and love. Never a good word for yourself or anyone else. As far as I can see, you regard absolutely everyone, starting with yourself, as a lost cause – except for Socrates, that is. I don't know where you picked up the nickname 'softy'; it certainly doesn't fit your conversation – always full of fury against yourself, and everyone else apart from Socrates.

e   APOLLODORUS And if that's my opinion of myself and the rest of you, then obviously I'm crazy, or mistaken, I suppose.

FRIEND Let's not argue about that now, Apollodorus, just do as I ask, and tell me what was said at Agathon's party.

APOLLODORUS The conversation went something like this . . . or

174   better, let me try to tell it to you right from the beginning, as Aristodemus told it to me.

ARISTODEMUS' ACCOUNT

I met Socrates, all washed and brushed, and wearing shoes (a thing he hardly ever did). I asked him where he was going looking so elegant.

'I'm going to dinner with Agathon. I avoided the first celebration last night; I couldn't face the crowd. But I said I'd come this evening. I'm looking elegant, because Agathon always looks elegant. What about you? How do you feel about coming b to dinner uninvited?'

'I'll do anything you tell me.'

'Come on then. Let's ignore the proverb, "good men come uninvited to lesser men's feasts", or rather let's change it, to "good men come uninvited to Agathon's feast". After all, Homer does worse than ignore it; he completely contradicts it. His Agamemnon is an outstanding warrior, while his Menelaus is a man of straw. But when Agamemnon is sacrificing and c feasting Homer lets Menelaus come to the feast without an invitation, though that's a case of a lesser man coming to dinner with a better.'

'I'm afraid, in my case, that Homer is likely to be nearer the mark than you, Socrates. It'll be a question of a nonentity coming to dinner uninvited with a wise man. You'd better decide what you'll say if you do take me. I'm not coming uninvited – only as your guest.'   d

'Two heads are better than one. We'll think of something to say. Come on.'

So off we went. But Socrates, absorbed in his own thoughts, got left behind on the way. I was going to wait for him, but he told me to go on ahead. So I turned up at Agathon's house by myself, and found the door open. In fact, it was slightly e embarrassing, because one of the house-slaves met me, and took me straight in, where I found the others had just sat down to dinner. Agathon saw me come in, and at once said, 'Aristodemus, you're just in time to have dinner with us. I hope that's what you've come for. If not, it'll have to wait for another time. I tried to get hold of you yesterday, to ask you, but couldn't find you. How come you haven't brought Socrates with you?'

I turned round and looked behind me, and couldn't see

Socrates anywhere. So I explained that I had come with Socrates.
In fact, but for his invitation, I wouldn't have come at all.

'I'm glad you did. But where is he?'

175   'He was right behind me just now. I've no more idea than
you where he could have got to.'

Agathon turned to a slave. 'Could you go and look for
Socrates, please, and ask him in? Aristodemus, why don't you sit
over there by Eryximachus?'

While one slave was giving me a wash, so I could sit down to
dinner, another slave came in: 'That Socrates you asked me to
look for has gone wandering up to the front door of the wrong
house. He's just standing there. I asked him to come in but he
won't.'

'How odd. Still, don't give up. Keep on asking him.'

b   But I said, 'No, leave him alone. He's always doing this. It
doesn't matter where he is. He just wanders off and stands there.
I don't think he'll be long. Don't badger him; just leave him.'

'Well, if you say so, I suppose we'd better.' He turned to the
slaves. "The rest of us will eat now. Serve the meal just as you
like. No one's going to tell you how to do it, any more than I
c   ever tell you. Imagine we're all your guests, and try to give us a
meal we'll enjoy.'

So we started having dinner, though still no sign of Socrates.
Agathon kept wanting to send people to look for him, but I
wouldn't let him. When he did turn up, he hadn't been long by
his standards, but even so we were about halfway through dinner.
Agathon, who'd sat down last, at a table on his own, said 'Come
d   and sit next to me, Socrates. Then perhaps I shall absorb whatever
it was you were thinking about outside. You must have found
the answer, or you wouldn't have come in to join us.'

Socrates sat down. 'Wouldn't it be marvellous, Agathon,' he
said, 'if ideas were the kind of things which could be imparted
simply by contact, and those of us who had few could absorb
them from those who had a lot in the same sort of way that
liquid can flow from a full container to an empty one if you put
a piece of string between them? If that's the nature of ideas, then
I think I'm lucky to be sitting next to you, and getting a nice,
e   substantial transfusion. My ideas aren't much use. They have an
ambiguous, dreamlike quality, whereas yours are brilliant, and

with so much scope for further improvement. You're only young, and yet they were particularly brilliant the day before yesterday, as more than thirty thousand Greeks can testify.'

'Don't be sarcastic, Socrates. And let's settle this question of ideas a bit later. We'll give Dionysus the casting vote, but you'd better have dinner first.'

So Socrates sat down and ate, with the others. We poured 176 offerings, sang hymns, and did all the usual things. Then our thoughts turned to drinking, and Pausanias made a suggestion. 'Well, gentlemen, how can we make things as painless for ourselves as possible? I must admit to feeling rather frail after yesterday evening. I need a breather, and I expect most of you do, too. After all, you were there as well. So, how can we make b our drinking as painless as possible?'

ARISTOPHANES I couldn't agree more, Pausanias. Whatever else we do, we don't want to let ourselves in for another evening's hard drinking. I'm one of those who sank without trace last night.

ERYXIMACHUS I'm glad you both feel like that. But we ought also to consider how strong Agathon is feeling.

AGATHON Not at all strong.

ERYXIMACHUS It would certainly be a stroke of luck for people c like Aristodemus and Phaedrus and me, if you hard drinkers are prepared to take an evening off. We're not in your league. I'm not worried about Socrates – he's equally happy either way, so he won't mind what we do. But as far as I can see, no one here is all that keen on drinking a lot, so perhaps I can tell you the truth about getting drunk without causing too much offence. My experience as a doctor leaves me in no doubt that getting drunk is bad for you. I'm not keen on drinking to excess myself, d and I wouldn't advise anyone else to, especially anyone who still had a hangover from yesterday.

PHAEDRUS Well, I generally follow your advice, especially on medical matters. So will the others, if they have any sense.

So we all agreed just to drink what we felt like, rather than e treating it as an opportunity to get drunk.

ERYXIMACHUS Good, that's settled then. We'll all drink as much as we feel like, and there's no compulsion on anyone. And since we've got that sorted out, I've another suggestion to make. I don't think we need this flute girl who's just started playing. She can play to herself, or to the women upstairs, if she feels like it, but for this evening I suggest *we* stick to conversation. And I've an idea what we might talk about, if you want to hear it.

177 Everyone said they did want to hear it, and urged him to make his suggestion.

ERYXIMACHUS: Well, it arises out of Euripides' *Melanippe*. And it isn't really my idea. It's Phaedrus'. He gets quite worked up about it. 'Don't you think it's odd, Eryximachus,' he says, 'that most of the other gods have had hymns and songs of praise

b written to them by the poets, but never a word in praise of Eros, the oldest and greatest god? And it's not for want of good poets, either. Or think of the great teachers – they've recorded the exploits of Heracles and other heroes, in prose. Prodicus, for example, does that sort of thing beautifully. Now maybe that's not very surprising, but I came across a book the other day, by a well-known writer, with an extraordinary eulogy in it on the value of salt. You can find any number of things singled out for

c praise in this way. What is surprising is that there should be so much enthusiasm for that kind of thing, and yet no one, up to the present day, has ever found himself able to praise Eros as he deserves. He is a remarkable god, but he has been totally neglected.'

I agree with Phaedrus. I'd like to do him a favour and make my contribution. What's more, the present gathering seems an

d ideal opportunity to praise the god. So, if you agree, we can quite happily spend our time in talk. I propose that each of us in turn, going round anticlockwise, should make a speech, the best he can, in praise of Eros. Phaedrus can start, since he is in the position of honour, and since the whole thing was his idea.

SOCRATES: I don't think anyone will vote against you, Eryximachus. I'm certainly not going to refuse, since love is the only thing I ever claim to know anything about. Agathon and

e Pausanias won't mind – still less Aristophanes, since his only interests in life are Dionysus and Aphrodite. In fact I can't see anyone here who *will* object. It's a little unfair on those of us sitting here in the last positions. Still, if you first speakers speak well enough, we shan't have to worry. Good luck, Phaedrus. You go first, and make your speech in praise of Eros.

They all agreed with Socrates, and told Phaedrus to start. Aristodemus couldn't remember the exact details of everybody's 178 speech, nor in turn can I remember precisely what he said. But I can give you the gist of those speeches and speakers which were most worth remembering.

Phaedrus, as I said, began – something like this.

PHAEDRUS

Eros is a great god, a marvel to men and gods alike. This is true in many ways, and it is especially true of his birth. He is entitled to our respect, as the oldest of the gods – as I can prove. Eros b has no parents, either in reality or in works of prose and poetry. Take Hesiod, for example. All he says is that in the beginning there was Chaos. '. . . and then came the full-breasted Earth, the eternal and immovable foundation of everything, and Eros.' Acusilaus agrees with Hesiod, that after Chaos there were just these two, Earth and Eros. And then there's Parmenides' theory about his birth, that 'Eros was created first of the Gods.' So there is widespread agreement that Eros is of great antiquity. And c being very old he also brings us very great benefits. I can see nothing better in life for a young boy, as soon as he is old enough, than finding a good lover, nor for a lover than finding a boyfriend. Love, more than anything (more than family, or position, or wealth), implants in men the thing which must be their guide if they are to live a good life. And what is that? It is a d horror of what is degrading, and a passionate desire for what is good. These qualities are essential if a state or an individual is to accomplish anything great or good. Imagine a man in love being found out doing something humiliating, or letting someone else do something degrading to him, because he was too cowardly to stop it. It would embarrass him more to be found out by the boy he loved than by his father or his friends, or anyone. And you can see just the same thing happening with the boy. He is e more worried about being caught behaving badly by his admirers than by anyone else. So if there were some way of arranging that a state, or an army, could be made up entirely of pairs of lovers, it is impossible to imagine a finer population. They would avoid all dishonour, and compete with one another 179 for glory: in battle, this kind of army, though small, fighting side by side could conquer virtually the whole world. After all, a lover would sooner be seen by anyone deserting his post or throwing away his weapons, rather than by his boyfriend. He would normally choose to die many times over instead. And as for abandoning the boy, or not trying to save him if he is in danger – no one is such a coward as not to be inspired with courage by Eros, making him the equal of the naturally brave b man. Homer says, and rightly, that god breathes fire into some of his heroes. And it is just this quality, whose origin is to be found within himself, that Eros imparts to lovers.

What is more, lovers are the only people prepared to die for others. Not just men, either; women also sometimes. A good example is Alcestis, the daughter of Pelias. She alone was willing c to die for her husband. He had a father and mother but she so far surpassed them in devotion, because of her passion for him, that she showed them to be strangers to their son, relations in name only. In so doing she was thought, by men and gods alike, to have performed a deed of supreme excellence. Indeed the gods were so pleased with her action that they brought her soul back from the underworld – a privilege they granted to only a fortunate handful of the many people who have done good d deeds. That shows how highly even the gods value loyalty and courage in love. Orpheus, the son of Oeagrus, on the other hand, was sent away from the underworld empty-handed; he was shown a mere phantom of the woman he came to find, and not given the woman herself. Of course Orpheus was a musician, and the gods thought he was a bit of a coward, lacking the courage to die for his love, as Alcestis did, but trying to find a way of getting into the underworld alive. They punished him further for that, giving him death at the hands of women.

e   In contrast, the man whom the gods honoured above all was Achilles, the son of Thetis. They sent him to the Islands of the Blessed. His mother had warned him that if he killed Hector he would himself be killed, but if he didn't, he would return home and live to a ripe old age. Nevertheless out of loyalty to his lover

Patroclus he chose without hesitation to die – not to save him, 180
but to avenge him; for Patroclus had already been killed. The
gods were full of admiration, and gave him the highest possible
honour, because he valued his lover so highly.

Incidentally, Aeschylus' view, that it was Achilles who was in
love with Patroclus, is nonsense. Quite apart from the fact that
he was more beautiful than Patroclus (and than all the other
Greek heroes, come to that) and had not yet grown a beard, he
was also, according to Homer, much younger. And he must
have been younger, because it is an undoubted fact that the
gods, though they always value courage which comes from love,
are most impressed and pleased, and grant the greatest rewards, b
when the younger man is loyal to his lover, than when the lover
is loyal to him. That's because the lover is a more divine
creature than the younger man, since he is divinely inspired.
And that's why they honoured Achilles more than Alcestis, and
sent him to the Islands of the Blessed.

There you are then. I claim that Eros is the oldest of the gods,
the most deserving of our respect, and the most useful, for those
men, past and present, who want to attain excellence and
happiness.

That was the gist of Phaedrus' speech. After him, several other c
people spoke, but Aristodemus couldn't really remember what
they said. So he left them out and recounted Pausanias' speech.

PAUSANIAS

Phaedrus, I don't think we've been very accurate in defining
our subject for discussion. We've simply said that we must make
a speech in praise of Eros. That would be fine, if there were just
one Eros. In fact, however, there isn't. And since there isn't, we
would do better to define first which Eros we are to praise. I am d
going to try to put things straight – first defining which Eros we
are supposed to be praising, and then trying to praise the god as
he deserves.

We are all well aware, I take it, that without Eros there is no
Aphrodite. If there were only one Aphrodite, there would be
one Eros. However, since there are in fact two Aphrodites, it
follows that Eros likewise must be two. There's no doubt about

there being two Aphrodites; the older has no mother, and is the daughter of Heaven. We call her Heavenly Aphrodite. The younger is the daughter of Zeus and Dione, and we call her
e Common Aphrodite. It follows that the Eros who assists this Aphrodite should also, properly speaking, be called Common Eros, and the other Heavenly Eros. We certainly ought to praise all the gods, but we should also attempt to define what is the proper province of each.

It is in general true of any activity that, simply in itself, it is
181 neither good nor bad. Take what we're doing now, for example – that is to say drinking, or singing, or talking. None of these is good or bad in itself, but each becomes so, depending on the way it is done. Well and rightly done, it is good; wrongly done, it is bad. And it's just the same with loving, and Eros. It's not all good, and doesn't all deserve praise. The Eros we should praise is the one which encourages people to love in the right way.

The Eros associated with Common Aphrodite is, in all senses
b of the word, common, and quite haphazard in his operation. This is the love of the man in the street. For a start, he is as likely to fall in love with women as with boys. Secondly, he falls in love with their bodies rather than their minds. Thirdly, he picks the most unintelligent people he can find, since all he's interested in is the sexual act. He doesn't care whether it's done in the right way or not. That is why the effect of this Eros is haphazard – sometimes good, sometimes the reverse. This love derives its existence from the much younger Aphrodite, the one
c composed equally of the female and male elements.

The other Eros springs from Heavenly Aphrodite, and in the first place is composed solely of the male element, with none of the female (so it is the love of boys we are talking about), and in the second place is older, and hence free from lust. In consequence, those inspired by this love turn to the male, attracted by what is naturally stronger and of superior intelligence. And even
d among those who love boys you can tell the ones whose love is purely heavenly. They only fall in love with boys old enough to think for themselves – in other words, with boys who are nearly grown up.

Those who start a love affair with boys of that age are

prepared, I think, to be friends, and live together, for life. The others are deceivers, who take advantage of youthful folly, and then quite cheerfully abandon their victims in search of others. There ought really to be a law against loving young boys, to e stop so much energy being expended on an uncertain end. After all, no one knows how good or bad, in mind and body, young boys will eventually turn out. Good men voluntarily observe this rule, but the common lovers I am talking about should be compelled to do the same, just as we stop them, so far as we can, falling in love with free women. They are actually the people 182 who have brought the thing into disrepute, with the result that some people even go so far as to say that it is wrong to satisfy your lover. It is the common lover they have in mind when they say this, regarding his demands as premature and unfair to the boy. Surely nothing done with restraint and decency could reasonably incur criticism.

What is more, while sexual conventions in other states are clear-cut and easy to understand, here and in Sparta, by b contrast, they are complex. In Elis, for example, or Boeotia, and places where they are not sophisticated in their use of language, it is laid down, quite straightforwardly, that is it right to satisfy your lover. No one, old or young, would say it was wrong, and the reason, I take it, is that they don't want to have all the trouble of trying to persuade them verbally, when they're such poor speakers. On the other hand, in Ionia and many other places under Persian rule, it is regarded as wrong. That is because the Persians' system of government (dictator-ships) makes them distrust it, just as they distrust philosophy c and communal exercise. It doesn't suit the rulers that their subjects should think noble thoughts, nor that they should form the strong friendships or attachments which these activities and in particular love tend to produce. Dictators here in Athens learnt the same lesson, by experience. The relationship between Harmodius and his lover, Aristogeiton, was strong enough to put an end to the dictators' rule.

In short, the convention that satisfying your lover is wrong is a result of the moral weakness of those who observe the d convention – the rulers' desire for power, and their subjects' cowardice. The belief that it is always right can be attributed to mental laziness. Our customs are much better but, as I said, not easy to understand. Think about it – let's take the lover first. Open love is regarded better than secret love, and so is love of the noblest and best people, even if they are not the best-looking. In fact, there is remarkable encouragement of the lover from all sides. He is not regarded as doing anything wrong; it is a good thing if he gets what he wants, and a shame if he doesn't.

e And when it comes to trying to get what he wants, we give the lover permission to do the most extraordinary things, and be applauded for them – things which, if he did them with any

183 other aim or intention, would cover him in reproach. Think of the way lovers behave towards the boys they love – think of the begging and entreating involved in their demands, the oaths they swear, the nights they spend sleeping outside the boys' front doors, the slavery they are prepared to endure (which no slave would put up with). If they behaved like this for money, or position, or influence of any kind, they would be told to stop by friends and enemies alike. Their enemies would call their

b behaviour dependent and servile, while their friends would censure them sharply, and even be embarrassed for them. And yet a lover can do all these things, and be approved of. Custom attaches no blame to his actions, since he is reckoned to be acting in a wholly honourable way. The strangest thing of all is that, in most people's opinion, the lover has a unique dispensation from the gods to swear an oath and then break it. Lovers' vows, apparently, are not binding.

c So far, then, gods and men alike give all kinds of licence to the lover, and an observer of Athenian life might conclude that it was an excellent thing, in this city, both to be a lover and to be friendly to lovers. But when we come to the boy, the position is quite different. Fathers give their sons escorts, when men fall in love with them, and don't allow them to talk to their lovers – and those are the escort's instructions as well. The boy's peers and friends jeer at him if they see anything of the kind going on, and when their elders see them jeering, they don't stop them, or

d tell them off, as they should if the jeers were unjustified. Looking at this side of things, you would come to the opposite conclusion – that this kind of thing is here regarded as highly reprehensible.

The true position, I think, is this. Going back to my original statement, there isn't one single form of love. So love is neither right nor wrong in itself. Done rightly, it is right; done wrongly, it is wrong. It is wrong if you satisfy the wrong person, for the wrong reasons, and right if you satisfy the right person, for the right reasons. The wrong person is the common lover I was talking about – the one who loves the body rather than the mind. His love is not lasting, since *what* he loves is not lasting e either. As soon as the youthful bloom of the body (which is what he loves) starts to fade, he 'spreads his wings and is off', as they say, making a mockery of all his speeches and promises. On the other hand, the man who loves a boy for his good character will stick to him for life, since he has attached himself to what is lasting.

Our customs are intended to test these lovers well and truly, 184 and get the boys to satisfy the good ones, and avoid the bad. That's why we encourage lovers to chase after boys, but tell the boys not to be caught. In this way we set up a trial and a test, to see which category the lover comes in, and which category the boy he loves comes in. This explains a number of things – for instance, why it's thought wrong for a boy to let himself be caught too quickly. It is felt that some time should elapse, since time is a good test of most things. Also why it is wrong to be caught by means of money or political influence – whether it's a case of the boy being threatened, and yielding rather than b holding out, or a case of being offered some financial or political inducement, and not turning it down. No affair of this kind is likely to be stable or secure, quite apart from the fact that it is no basis for true friendship.

There is just one way our customs leave it open for a boy to satisfy his lover, and not be blamed for it. It is permissible, as I have said, for a lover to enter upon any kind of voluntary slavery he may choose, and be the slave of the boy he loves. This is not c regarded as self-seeking, or in any way demeaning. Similarly there is one other kind of voluntary slavery which is not regarded as demeaning. This is the slavery of the boy, in his desire for improvement. It can happen that a boy chooses to serve a man, because he thinks that by association with him he will improve in wisdom in some way, or in some other form of goodness. This kind of voluntary slavery, like the other, is widely held among us not to be wrong, and not to be self-seeking.

So it can only be regarded as right for a boy to satisfy his lover
d if both these conditions are satisfied – both the lover's behaviour, and the boy's desire for wisdom and goodness. Then the lover and the boy have the same aim, and each has the approval of convention – the lover because he is justified in performing any service he chooses for a boy who satisfies him, the boy because he is justified in submitting, in any way he will, to the man who can make him wise and good. So if the lover has
e something to offer in the way of sound judgment and moral goodness, and if the boy is eager to accept this contribution to his education and growing wisdom, then, and only then, this favourable combination makes it right for a boy to satisfy his lover. In no other situation is it right.

Nor, in this situation, is there any disgrace in making a mistake, whereas in all other situations it is equally a disgrace to
185 be mistaken or not. For example, suppose a boy satisfies his lover for money, taking him to be rich. If he gets it wrong, and doesn't get any money, because the lover turns out to be poor, it is still regarded as immoral, because the boy who does this seems to be revealing his true character, and declaring that he would do anything for anyone in return for money. And that is not a good way to behave. Equally, a boy may satisfy a man because he thinks he is a good man, and that he himself will become better through his friendship. If he gets it wrong, and
b his lover turns out to be a bad man, of little moral worth, still there is something creditable about his mistake. He too seems to have revealed his true character – namely, that he is eager to do anything for anyone in return for goodness and self-improvement. And this is the finest of all qualities.

So it is absolutely correct for boys to satisfy their lovers, if it is done in pursuit of goodness. This is the love which comes from the heavenly goddess; it is itself heavenly, and of great value to state and individual alike, since it compels both lover and boy
c to devote a lot of attention to their own moral improvement. All other sorts of love derive from the other goddess, the common one.

Well, Phaedrus, that's the best I can offer, without prepara-
tion, on the subject of Eros.

Pausanias paused (sorry about the pun — sophistic influence).
After that it was Aristophanes' turn to speak. But he had just got
hiccups. I don't know if it was from eating too much, or for
some other reason; anyway he was unable to make his speech.
All he could say, since Eryximachus, the doctor, happened to be d
sitting just below him, was this: 'Eryximachus, you're just the
man. Either get rid of my hiccups, or speak instead of me until
they stop.'

'I'll do both. I'll take your turn to speak, and when you get rid
of your hiccups, you can take mine. While I'm speaking, try
holding your breath for a long time, to see if they stop. Failing
that, gargle with some water. And if they are very severe, tickle
your nose and make yourself sneeze. Do that once or twice, and e
they'll stop, however severe.'

'Will you please speak first, then?' said Aristophanes. 'And I'll
do as you suggest.'

ERYXIMACHUS

Pausanias made an impressive start to his speech, but I do not
think he brought it to a very satisfactory conclusion. So I think
it is important that I should try to complete his account. His 186
analysis of the twofold nature of Eros seems to me to be a
valuable distinction. But I cannot accept his implication that
Eros is found only in human hearts, and is aroused only by
human beauty. I am a doctor by profession, and it has been my
observation, I would say, throughout my professional career,
that Eros is aroused by many other things as well, and that he is
found also in nature — in the physical life of all animals, in plants
that grow in the ground, and in virtually all living organisms.
My conclusion is that he is great and awe-inspiring, this god, b
and that his influence is unbounded, both in the human realm
and in the divine.

I will begin by talking about my medical experience, to show
my respect for my profession. The nature of the human body
shows this twofold Eros, since it is generally agreed that health
and sickness in the body are separate and unalike, and that

unlike is attracted to unlike, and desires it. So there is one force of attraction for the healthy, and another for the sick. Pausanias was talking just now about it being right to satisfy men, if they are good men, but wrong if all they are interested in is physical c pleasure. It is just the same with the body. It is right to satisfy the good and healthy elements in the body, and one should do so. We call this 'medicine'. Conversely it is wrong to satisfy the bad, unhealthy elements, and anyone who is going to be a skilled doctor should deny these elements.

Medical knowledge is thus essentially knowledge of physical impulses or desires for ingestion or evacuation. In this, the man d who can distinguish healthy desires from unhealthy is the best doctor. Moreover he needs the ability to change people's desires, so that they lose one and gain another. There are people who lack desires which they should have. If the doctor can produce these desires, and remove the existing ones, then he is a good doctor. He must, in fact, be able to reconcile and harmonise the most disparate elements in the body. By 'the most disparate' I mean those most opposed to one another – e cold and hot, bitter and sweet, dry and wet, and so forth. It was by knowing how to produce mutual desire and harmony among these that our forerunner Asclepius, as the poets say (and I believe) established this art of ours.

Medicine, then, as I say, is completely governed by this god. 187 Likewise physical training, and farming. Music too is no exception, as must be clear to anyone who gives the matter a moment's thought. Perhaps that is what Heraclitus means, though he does not actually express it very clearly, when he says that 'the One' is 'in conflict and harmony with itself', 'like the stringing of a bow or lyre'. Clearly there is a contradiction in saying that a harmony is in conflict, or is composed of conflicting elements. Perhaps what he meant was that, starting b from initially discordant high and low notes, the harmony is only created when these are brought into agreement by the skill of the musician. Clearly there could be no harmony between high and low, if they were still in conflict. For harmony is a consonance, and consonance is a kind of agreement. Thus it is impossible that there should be a harmony of conflicting elements, in which those elements still conflict, nor can one harmonise what is different, and incapable of agreement. Or take rhythm as another example; it arises out of the conflict of quick and slow, but only when they cease to conflict. Here it is c the art of music which imposes harmony on all the elements, by producing mutual attraction and agreement between them, whereas in the body it is the art of medicine. So music, again, is knowledge of Eros applied to harmony and rhythm.

In the actual formation of harmony and rhythm it is a simple matter to detect the hand of Eros, which at this stage is not the twofold Eros. It is altogether more complicated when we come to apply rhythm and harmony to human activity, either to the making of music, which we call composing, or to the correct d use of melody and tempo in what we call education. This really does demand a high degree of skill. And the same argument again holds good, that one should satisfy the most well-ordered people, in the interests of those as yet less well-ordered; one should pay due regard to their desires, which are in fact the good, heavenly Eros, companion of the heavenly muse, Ourania. Common Eros, by contrast, goes with the common muse, Polymnia. The greatest caution is called for in its employment, e if one is to gain enjoyment from it without encouraging pure self-indulgence. Similarly, in my profession, there is a great art in the correct treatment of people's desire for rich food, so that they can enjoy it without ill effects.

Thus in music and medicine, and in all other spheres of activity, human and divine, we must keep a careful eye, so far as 188 is practicable, on both forms of Eros. For both are present. The seasons of the year likewise fully illustrate their joint operation. When all the things I was talking about just now (such as hot and cold, wet and dry) hit upon the right Eros in their relation to one another, and consequently form the right sort of mixture and harmony, then they bring what is seasonable and healthy, to men and to the rest of the world of animals and plants; and all is as it should be. But when the other Eros, in violence and excess, takes over in the natural seasons of the year, it does all sorts of damage, and upsets the natural order. When that happens the result, generally, is plague and a variety of diseases – for animals b and plants alike. Frost, hail and mildew are the result of this kind

of competition and disorder involving Eros. Knowledge of Eros
in connection with the movements of the stars and the seasons
of the year is called astronomy.

Then again, all sacrifices, and everything which comes under
the direction of the prophetic arts (that is to say, the whole
c relationship of gods and men to one another) have as their sole
concern the observance and correct treatment of Eros. If, in
their behaviour towards their parents, the living and the dead, or
the gods, people stop satisfying the good, well-ordered Eros, if
they stop honouring him and consulting him in every enter-
prise, and start to follow the other Eros, then the result is all
kinds of wickedness. So the prophetic arts have to keep an eye
on, and treat, the two forms of Eros. Their knowledge of Eros
d in human affairs, the Eros who is conducive to piety and correct
observance, makes them the architects of friendship between
gods and men.

So great and widespread – in fact, universal – is the power
possessed, in general by all Eros, but in particular by the Eros
which, in the moral sphere, acts with good sense and justice
both among us and among the gods. And not only does it
possess absolute power; it also brings us complete happiness,
enabling us to be companions and friends both of each other
and of our superiors, the gods.

e   Well, I too may have left a lot out in my praise of Eros, but I
have not done so deliberately. And if I have left anything out, it
is up to you, Aristophanes, to fill the gap. Or if you intend to
praise the god in some other way, go ahead and do that, now
that you have got rid of your hiccups.

189 ARISTOPHANES: Yes, they've stopped, but not without resort to
the sneezing treatment. I wondered if it was the 'well-ordered'
part of my body which demanded all the noise and tickling
involved in sneezing. Certainly the hiccups stopped the moment
I tried sneezing.

ERYXIMACHUS: Careful, my dear friend. You haven't started yet,
and already you're playing the fool. You'll force me to act as
b censor for your speech, if you start fooling around as soon as
you get a chance to speak in peace.

ARISTOPHANES (laughing): Fair enough, Eryximachus. Regard

my remarks so far as unsaid. But don't be too censorious. I'm worried enough already about what I'm going to say – not that it may arouse laughter (after all, there would be some point in that, and it would be appropriate to my profession), but that it may be laughed out of court.

ERYXIMACHUS: Aristophanes, you're trying to eat your cake and have it. Come on, concentrate. You'll have to justify what you say, but perhaps, if I see fit, I will acquit you.   c

ARISTOPHANES

Well, Eryximachus, I do intend to make a rather different kind of speech from the kind you and Pausanias made. It's my opinion that mankind is quite unaware of the power of Eros. If they were aware of it, they would build vast temples and altars to him, and make great offerings to him. As it is, though it is of crucial importance that this observance should be paid to him, none of these things is done.

Of all the gods, Eros is the most friendly towards men. He is our helper, and cures those evils whose cure brings the greatest d happiness to the human race. I'll try to explain his power to you, and then you can go off and spread the word to others.

First of all you need to know about human nature and what has happened to it. Our original nature was not as it is now, but quite different. For one thing there were three sexes, rather than the two (male and female) we have now. The third sex was a e combination of these two. Its name has survived, though the phenomenon itself has disappeared. This single combination, comprising both male and female, was, in form and name alike, hermaphrodite. Now it survives only as a term of abuse.

Secondly, each human being formed a complete whole, spherical, with back and ribs forming a circle. They had four hands, four legs, and two faces, identical in every way, on a circular neck. They had a single head for the two faces, which 190 looked in opposite directions; four ears, two sets of genitals, and everything else as you'd expect from the description so far. They walked upright, as we do, in whichever direction they wanted. And when they started to run fast, they were just like people doing cartwheels. They stuck their legs straight out all round, and went bowling along, supported on their eight limbs, and rolling along at high speed.

The reason for having three sexes, and of this kind, was this:
b the male was originally the offspring of the sun, the female of the earth, and the one which was half-and-half was the offspring of the moon, because the moon likewise is half-sun and half-earth. They were circular, both in themselves and in their motion, because of their similarity to their parents. They were remarkable for their strength and vigour, and their ambition led them to make an assault upon the gods. The story which Homer tells of the giants, Ephialtes and Otus, is told of them – that they
c tried to make a way up to heaven, to attack the gods. Zeus and the other gods wondered what to do about them, and couldn't decide. They couldn't kill them, as they had the giants – striking them with thunderbolts and doing away with the whole race – because the worship and sacrifices they received from men would have been done away with as well. On the other hand, they couldn't go on allowing them to behave so outrageously.

In the end Zeus, after long and painful thought, came up with a suggestion. 'I think I have an idea. Men could go on existing, but behave less disgracefully, if we made them weaker. I'm
d going to cut each of them in two. This will have two advantages: it will make them weaker, and also more useful to us, because of the increase in their numbers. They will walk upright, on two legs. And if it's clear they still can't behave, and they refuse to lead a quiet life, I'll cut them in half again and they can go hopping along on one leg.'

That was his plan. So he started cutting them in two, like
e someone slicing vegetables for pickling, or slicing eggs with a wire. And each time he chopped one up, he told Apollo to turn the face and the half-neck round towards the cut side (so that the man could see where he'd been split, and be better behaved in future), and then to heal the rest of the wound. So Apollo twisted the faces round and gathered up the skin all round to what is now called the stomach, like a purse with strings. He made a single outlet, and tied it all up securely in the middle of
191 the stomach; this we now call the navel. He smoothed out most of the wrinkles, and formed the chest, using a tool such as cobblers use for smoothing out wrinkles in a hide stretched over

a last. He left a few wrinkles, however, those around the stomach itself and the navel, as a reminder of what happened in those far-off days.

When man's natural form was split in two, each half went round looking for its other half. They put their arms round one another, and embraced each other, in their desire to grow together again. They started dying of hunger, and also from b lethargy, because they refused to do anything separately. And whenever one half died, and the other was left, the survivor began to look for another, and twined itself about it, either encountering half of a complete woman (i.e. what we now call a woman) or half a complete man. In this way they kept on dying.

Zeus felt sorry for them, and thought of a second plan. He moved their genitals to the front – up till then they had had them on the outside, and had reproduced, not by copulation, c but by discharge on to the ground, like grasshoppers. So, as I say, he moved their genitals to the front, and made them use them for reproduction by insemination, the male in the female. The idea was that if, in embracing, a man chanced upon a woman, they could produce children, and the race would increase. If man chanced upon man, they could get full satisfaction from one another's company, then separate, get on with their work, and resume the business of life.

That is why we have this innate love of one another. It brings d us back to our original state, trying to reunite us and restore us to our true human form. Each of us is a mere fragment of a man (like half a tally-stick); we've been split in two, like filleted plaice. We're all looking for our 'other half'. Men who are a fragment of the common sex (the one called hermaphrodite), are womanisers, and most adulterers are to be found in this category. Similarly, women of this type are nymphomaniacs and e adulteresses. On the other hand, women who are part of an original woman pay very little attention to men. Their interest is in women; lesbians are found in this class. And those who are part of a male pursue what is male. As boys, because they are slices of the male, they are fond of men, and enjoy going to bed with men and embracing them. These are the best of the boys 192 and young men, since they are by nature the most manly. Some people call them immoral – quite wrongly. It is not immorality, but boldness, courage and manliness, since they take pleasure in what is like themselves. This is proved by the fact that, when they grow up and take part in public life, it's only this kind who prove themselves men. When they come to manhood, they are lovers of boys, and don't naturally show any interest in marriage b or producing children; they have to be forced into it by convention. They're quite happy to live with one another, and not get married.

People like this are clearly inclined to have boyfriends or (as boys) inclined to have lovers, because they always welcome what is akin. When a lover of boys (or any sort of lover) meets the real thing (i.e. his other half), he is completely overwhelmed c by friendship and affection and desire, more or less refusing to be separated for any time at all. These are the people who spend their whole lives together, and yet they cannot find words for what they want from one another. No one imagines that it's simply sexual intercourse, or that sex is the reason why one gets such enormous pleasure out of the other's company. No, it's obvious that the soul of each has some other desire, which it d cannot express. It can only give hints and clues to its wishes.

Imagine that Hephaestus came and stood over them, with his smith's tools, as they lay in bed together. Suppose he asked them, 'What is it you want from one another, mortals?' If they couldn't tell him, he might ask again, 'Do you want to be together as much as possible, and not be separated, day or night? If that's what you want, I'm quite prepared to weld you together, and make you grow into one. You can be united, the e two of you, and live your whole life together, as one. Even down in Hades, when you die, you can be a single dead person, rather than two. Decide whether that's what you want, and whether that would satisfy you.' We can be sure that no one would refuse this offer. Quite clearly, it would be just what they wanted. They'd simply think they'd been offered exactly what they'd always been after, in sexual intercourse, trying to melt into their lovers, and so be united.

So that's the explanation; it's because our original nature was as I have described, and because we were once complete. And the 193 name of this desire and pursuit of completeness is Eros, or love. Formerly, as I say, we were undivided, but now we've been split up by god for our misdeeds – like the Arcadians by the Spartans. And the danger is that, if we don't treat the gods with respect, we may be divided again, and go round looking like figures in a bas-relief, sliced in half down the line of our noses. We'd be like torn-off counterfoils. That's why we should all encourage the utmost piety towards the gods. We're trying to avoid this fate, and achieve the other. So we take Eros as our guide and leader. b Let no one oppose this aim – and incurring divine displeasure *is* opposing this aim – since if we are friends with god, and make our peace with him, we shall find and meet the boys who are part of ourselves, which few people these days succeed in doing.

I hope Eryximachus won't misunderstand me, and make fun of my speech, and say it's about Pausanias and Agathon. Perhaps they do come in this class, and are both males by nature. All I'm c saying is that in general (and this applies to men and women) this is where happiness for the human race lies – in the successful pursuit of love, in finding the love who is part of our original self, and in returning to our former state. This is the ideal, but in an imperfect world we must settle for the nearest to this we can get, and this is finding a boyfriend who is mentally congenial. And if we want to praise the god who brings this about, then we should praise Eros, who in this predicament is d our great benefactor, attracting us to what is part of ourselves, and gives us great hope for the future that he will reward respect for the gods by returning us to our original condition, healing us, and making us blessed and perfectly happy.

There you are then, Eryximachus. There is my speech about Eros. A bit different from yours, I'm afraid. So please, again, don't laugh at it, and let's hear what all the others have to say – or rather, both the others, since only Agathon and Socrates are left. e

ERYXIMACHUS: All right, I won't laugh. In any case, I thought it was a most enjoyable speech. In fact, if I did not know Socrates and Agathon to be experts on love, I would be very worried that they might have nothing to say, so abundant and varied have been the speeches so far. But knowing them as I do, I have no such anxiety.

SOCRATES: It's fine for you, Eryximachus. You've already made 194 an excellent speech. If you were in my shoes – or rather, perhaps, the shoes I will be in when Agathon has made a good speech as well — then you might well be alarmed, and be in precisely the state that I am in now.

AGATHON: Ah! Trying a little black magic, are you, Socrates? Are you hoping it'll make me nervous if I think the audience is expecting a great speech from me?

b SOCRATES: Agathon, I've seen your nerve and courage in going up on the platform with the actors, to present your plays, before the eyes of that vast audience. You were quite unperturbed by that, so it'd be pretty stupid of me to imagine that you'd be nervous in front of the few people here.

AGATHON: I may be stage-struck, Socrates, but I'm still aware that, to anyone with any sense, a small critical audience is far more daunting than a large uncritical one.

c SOCRATES: It would be quite wrong for me, of all people, to suggest that you are lacking in taste or judgement. I'm well aware that in all your contacts with those you consider discriminating, you value their opinion more highly than that of the public. But don't put us in that category — after all, we were there, we were part of 'the public'. Anyway, let's pursue this: if you came across truly discriminating people (not us), you would perhaps be daunted by them, if you thought you were producing something second-rate. Is that right?

AGATHON: It is.

SOCRATES: Whereas offering the public something second-rate would not worry you, would it?

d PHAEDRUS: Agathon, if you answer Socrates, he won't give a thought to the rest of us, so long as he has someone to talk to, particularly someone good-looking. For myself, I love hearing Socrates talk, but it's my job to supervise the progress of the speeches in praise of Eros, and get a speech out of each of you. When you've both paid your tribute to the god, then the two of you can get on with your discussion.

e AGATHON: Quite right, Phaedrus. There's no reason why I shouldn't make my speech. I shall have plenty of other opportunities to talk to Socrates.

AGATHON

I want first to talk about *how* I should talk, and then talk. All the speakers so far have given me the impression that they were not so much praising the god as congratulating mankind on the good things the god provides. No one has told us what the giver of these benefits is really like, in himself. And yet, in any speech 195 of praise on any subject, the only correct procedure is to work systematically through the subject under discussion, saying what its nature is, and what benefits it gives. That is how we too should by rights be praising Eros, describing first his nature, then his gifts.

I claim, then, that though all the gods are blessed, Eros, if I may say this without offending the other gods, is the most blessed, since he is the most beautiful and the best. The most beautiful? Well, for a start, Phaedrus, he is the youngest of the b gods. He proves this himself by running away at top speed from old age. Yet old age is swift enough, and swifter than most of us would like. It is Eros' nature to hate old age, and steer well clear of it. He lives and exists always with the young. 'Birds of a feather', and all that. So, though there was much in Phaedrus' speech with which I agreed, I didn't agree with his claim that Eros was older than Cronus or Iapetus. I would say he's the youngest of the gods – eternally young, in fact. The earliest c troubles among the gods, which Hesiod and Parmenides write about, were, if those writers are correct, the work of Necessity, not of Eros. If Eros had been there, there would have been none of this cutting, or tying, each other up, or any of the other acts of violence. There would have been friendship and peace, as there has been since Eros became king of the gods.

So, he is young. And not only young, but delicate. You need a poet like Homer to show how delicate. Homer describes Ate d as a god and as delicate (or at any rate, with delicate feet): 'delicate are her feet; she walks not upon the ground, but goes upon the heads of men.' Presumably he's giving an example here to show how delicate – she goes not on what is hard, but on what is soft. We too can use a similar argument to show how delicate Eros is. He does not walk upon the ground, nor yet on e men's heads (which aren't that soft anyway); he lives and moves among the softest of all things, making his home in the hearts and minds of gods and men. And not in all hearts equally. He avoids any hard hearts he comes across, and settles among the tender-hearted. He must therefore be extremely delicate, since he only ever touches (either with his feet or in any other way) the softest of the soft.

196   Very young, then, and very delicate. Another thing about him is that he's very supple. He can't be rigid and unyielding, because he wouldn't be able to insinuate himself anywhere he likes, entering and leaving men's hearts undetected. Eros' outstanding beauty is universally agreed, and this again suggests that he is well-proportioned and supple. Ugliness and Eros are ever at odds with one another. Finally, the beauty of his skin is attested by his love of flowers. He will not settle in a man's
b body, or heart, or anywhere else, if it is past the first flower and bloom of youth. But he does settle down, and remain, in any flowery and fragrant place.

So much for the god's beauty, though I've left out more than I've said. Now I must say something about his goodness. The main thing about Eros is that no one, god or man, wrongs him or is wronged by him. Nothing is done to him, when it is done, by force. Force cannot touch Eros. When he acts, he acts
c without force, since everyone serves Eros quite willingly, and it's agreed by 'our masters, the laws' that where there is mutual consent and agreement, there is justice. Moreover, he is a paragon of virtue as well as well as justice. After all, virtue is agreed to be control of pleasures and desires, and no pleasure is stronger than love. But if they are weaker than love, then he has control over them, and if he has control over pleasures and desires, he must be highly virtuous.

And what about courage? 'Ares himself cannot hold his
d ground' against Eros. Ares does not take Eros prisoner; it is Eros – the love of Aphrodite, so the story goes – who takes Ares prisoner, and the captor is stronger than the captive. He who overcomes the bravest is himself the bravest of all.

So much for the god's justice, virtue and courage. Now for his wisdom. I must try as hard as I can not to leave anything out, and so I too, in my turn, will start with a tribute to my own profession, following Eryximachus' example. Eros is an

accomplished poet, so accomplished that he can turn others into e
poets. Everyone turns to poetry, 'however philistine he may have
been before', when moved by Eros. We should take this as an
indication that, in general, Eros is master of all forms of literary or
artistic creation. After all, no one can impart, or teach, a skill
which he does not himself possess or know. And who will deny
that the creation of all living things is the work of Eros' wisdom, 197
which makes all living things come into being and grow?

   It's the same with any skilled activity. It is common knowledge
that those who have this god for their teacher win fame and
reputation; those he passes by remain in obscurity. For example,
Apollo's discoveries (archery, medicine and prophecy) were all
guided by desire and love, so he too can be called a disciple of b
Eros. Likewise with the Muses and the arts, Hephaestus and
metalworking, Athene and weaving, and Zeus and 'the
governance of gods and men'. And if we ask why the quarrels of
the gods were settled as soon as Eros appeared, without doubt
the reason was love of beauty (there being no love of ugliness).
In earlier times, as I said originally, there were many violent
quarrels among the gods – or so we are told – because they were
in the grip of Necessity. But since Eros' birth, all manner of
good has resulted, for gods and men, from the love of beauty.

   Such, Phaedrus, is my view of Eros. He stands out as beautiful c
and excellent in himself; and secondly, he is the origin of similar
qualities in others. I am tempted to speak in verse, and say he
brings

        Sweet peace to men, and calm o'er all the deep,
        Rest to the winds, to those who sorrow, sleep.

He gives us the feeling, not of longing, but of belonging, since d
he is the moving spirit behind all those occasions when we meet
and gather together. Festivals, dances, sacrifices – in these he is
the moving spirit. Implanter of gentleness, supplanter of fierce-
ness; generous with his kindness, ungenerous with unkindness;
gracious, gentle; an example to the wise, a delight to the gods;
craved by those without him, saved by those who have him; of
luxury, delicacy, elegance, charm, yearning and desire he is the
father; heedful of the good, heedless of the bad; in hardship and

in fear, in need and in argument, he is the best possible
e helmsman, comrade, ally, and saviour; the glory of gods and
men; the best and finest guide, whom every man should follow,
singing glorious praises to him, and sharing in the song which
he sings to enchant the minds of gods and men.

That is my speech, Phaedrus, in part fun, in part (as far as I
could make it) fairly serious. Let it be an offering to the god.

198 When Agathon finished speaking, we all burst into applause.
We thought the young man had done full justice both to
himself and to the god.

SOCRATES (to Eryximachus): Well, son of Acumenus, do you
still think my earlier fear unfounded? Wasn't I right when I
predicted Agathon would make a brilliant speech, and there
would be nothing left for me to say?

ERYXIMACHUS: Your prediction was half-true. Agathon did make
a good speech. But I don't think you will find nothing to say.

b SOCRATES: My dear fellow, what is there left for me or anyone
else to say, after such a fine and varied speech? Maybe it wasn't
all equally brilliant, but that bit at the end was enough to silence
anyone with the beauty of its language and phraseology. When I
realised I wasn't going to be able to make anything like such a
c good speech, I nearly ran away and disappeared, in embarrass-
ment, only there was nowhere to go. The speech reminded me
of Gorgias, and put me in exactly the position described by
Homer. I was afraid, at the end of his speech there, that
Agathon was going to brandish the head of Gorgias, the great
speaker, at my speech, turning me to stone and silencing me. I
realised then how fatuous it was to have agreed to take my turn
d with you in praising Eros, and to have claimed to be an expert
on love. It turns out now that I know nothing at all about
making speeches of praise. I was naive enough to suppose that
one should speak the truth about whatever it was that was being
praised, and that from this raw material one should select the
most telling points, and arrange them as pleasingly as possible. I
was pretty confident I would make a good speech, because I
thought I knew about speeches of praise. However, it now
seems that praising things well isn't like that; it seems to be a

question of hyperbole and rhetoric, regardless of truth or e
falsehood. And if it's false, that's immaterial. So our original
agreement, as it now seems, was that each of us should pretend
to praise Eros, rather than really praise him.

   That, I imagine, is why you credit Eros with all the good points
you have dug out in his favour. You say his nature is this, and the
blessings he produces are these; your object is to make him
appear as noble and fine as possible (in the eyes of the ignorant, 199
presumably, since those who know about Eros clearly aren't
going to believe you). Certainly your praise of him looks very
fine and impressive, but I didn't realise this was what was called
for; if I had known I wouldn't have agreed to take my turn in
praising him. 'My tongue promised, not my heart.' Anyway, it
can't be helped, but I don't propose to go on praising him like
that – I wouldn't know how to. What I am prepared to do, if you
like, is tell the truth, in my own way, and not in competition b
with your speeches. I don't want to make a complete fool of
myself. What do you think, Phaedrus? Do you want a speech of
that sort? Do you want to hear the truth told about Eros? And
may I use whatever language and forms of speech come naturally?

Phaedrus and the others told him to make his speech, in what
ever way he thought best.

SOCRATES: One other point before I start, Phaedrus. Will you let
me ask Agathon a few brief questions? I'd like to get his
agreement before I begin.

PHAEDRUS: Yes, I'll let you. Ask away.   c

So Socrates began his speech, something like this.

SOCRATES

Well, my dear Agathon, I liked the beginning of your speech.
You said the first thing to do was to reveal the nature of Eros;
after that his achievements. I think that was an excellent starting
point. And since you've explained everything else about the
nature of Eros so impressively and so well, can you tell me one
more thing? Is Eros' nature such that he is love produced by d
something, or by nothing? I don't mean, is he the son of a father

or a mother – it would be an absurd question, to ask whether Eros is son of a father or mother. But suppose I asked you, about this thing 'father', whether a father is father of something or not? If you wanted to give an accurate answer, you would say, presumably, that a father is father of a son or a daughter, wouldn't you?

AGATHON: Yes, I would.

SOCRATES: And the same with a mother?

AGATHON: Yes, the same.

e SOCRATES: Let's take a few more questions, so you can be quite clear what I mean. Suppose I ask, 'What about a brother, simply as a brother? Is he someone's brother, or not?'

AGATHON: Yes, he is.

SOCRATES: His brother's or sister's, I take it?

AGATHON: Yes.

SOCRATES: Try, then, to answer my question about Eros. Is Eros love of nothing, or of something?

AGATHON: Of something, certainly.

SOCRATES: Good. Hold on to that answer. Keep it in mind, and
200 make a mental note what it is that Eros is love of. But first tell me this, this thing which Eros is love of, does he desire it, or not?

AGATHON: Certainly.

SOCRATES: And does he possess that which he desires and loves, or not?

AGATHON: Probably not.

SOCRATES: I'm not interested in probability, but in certainty. Consider this proposition: anything which desires something desires what it does not have, and it only desires when it is
b lacking something. This proposition, Agathon, seems to me to be absolutely certain. How does it strike you?

AGATHON: Yes, it seems certain to me too.

SOCRATES: Quite right. So would a big man want to be big, or a strong man want to be strong?

AGATHON: No, that's impossible, given what we have agreed so far.

SOCRATES: Because if he possesses these qualities, he cannot also lack them.

AGATHON: True.

SOCRATES: So if a strong man wanted to be strong, or a fast runner to be fast, or a healthy man to be healthy – but perhaps I'd better explain what I'm on about. I'm a bit worried that you may think that people like this, people having these qualities, can also want the qualities which they possess. So I'm trying to remove this misapprehension. If you think about it, Agathon, people cannot avoid possession of whichever of these qualities they do possess, whether they like it or not. So obviously there's no point in desiring to do so. When anyone says, 'I'm in good health, and I also desire to be in good health', or 'I am rich and also desire to be rich', i.e. 'I desire those things which I already have', then we should answer him: 'What you want is to go on possessing, in the future, the wealth, health, or strength you possess now, since you have them now, like it or not. So when you say you desire what you've already got, are you sure you don't just mean you want to continue to possess in the future what you possess now?' Would he deny this?

AGATHON: No, he would agree.

SOCRATES: But isn't this a question of desiring what he doesn't already have in his possession – i.e. the desire that what he does have should be safely and permanently available to him in the future?

AGATHON: Yes, it is.

SOCRATES: So in this, or any other, situation, the man who desires something desires what is not available to him, and what he doesn't already have in his possession. And what he neither has nor himself is – that which he lacks – this is what he wants and desires.

AGATHON: Absolutely.

SOCRATES: Right then, let's agree on the argument so far. Eros has an existence of his own; he is in the first place love of something, and secondly, he is love of that which he is without.

201 AGATHON: Yes.

SOCRATES: Keeping that in mind, just recall what you said were the objects of Eros, in your speech. I'll remind you, if you like. I think what you said amounted to this: trouble among the gods was ended by their love of beauty, since there could be no love of what is ugly. Isn't that roughly what you said?

AGATHON: Yes, it is.

SOCRATES: And a very reasonable statement too, my friend. And this being so, Eros must have an existence as love of beauty, and not love of ugliness, mustn't he?

AGATHON: Yes.

b SOCRATES: But wasn't it agreed that he loves what he lacks, and does not possess?

AGATHON: Yes, it was.

SOCRATES: So Eros lacks, and does not possess, beauty.

AGATHON: That is the inevitable conclusion.

SOCRATES: Well then, do you describe as beautiful that which lacks beauty and has never acquired beauty?

AGATHON: No.

SOCRATES: If that is so, do you still maintain that Eros is beautiful?

AGATHON: I rather suspect, Socrates, that I didn't know what I was talking about.

c SOCRATES: It sounded marvellous, for all that, Agathon. Just one other small point. Would you agree that what is good is also beautiful?

AGATHON: Yes, I would.

SOCRATES: So if Eros lacks beauty, and if what is good is beautiful, then Eros would lack what is good also.

AGATHON: I can't argue with you, Socrates. Let's take it that it is as you say.

SOCRATES: What you mean, Agathon, my very good friend, is that you can't argue with the truth. Any fool can argue with Socrates. Anyway, I'll let you off for now, because I want to d pass on to you the account of Eros which I once heard given by a woman called Diotima, from Mantinea. She was an expert on this subject, as on many others. In the days before the plague she came to the help of the Athenians in their sacrifices, and managed to gain them a ten-years' reprieve from the disease. She also taught me about love.

I'll start from the position on which Agathon and I reached agreement, and I'll give her account, as best I can, in my own words. So first I must explain, as you rightly laid down, e Agathon, what Eros is and what he is like; then I must describe what he does. I think it'll be easiest for me to explain things as she explained them when she was questioning me, since I gave her pretty much the same answers Agathon has just been giving me. I said Eros was a great god, and a lover of beauty. Diotima proved to me, using the same argument by which I have just proved it to Agathon, that, according to my own argument, Eros was neither beautiful nor good.

'What do you mean, Diotima,' I said, 'Is Eros then ugly or bad?'

'Careful what you say. Do you think what is not beautiful must necessarily be ugly?'

'Obviously.'

202

'And that what is not wise is ignorant? Don't you realise there is an intermediate state, between wisdom and ignorance?'

'And what is that?'

'Think of someone who has a correct opinion, but can give no rational explanation of it. You wouldn't call this knowledge (how can something irrational be knowledge?), yet it isn't ignorance either, since an opinion which accords with reality cannot be ignorance. So correct opinion is the kind of thing we are looking for, between understanding and ignorance.'

'That's true.'

'So don't insist that what is not beautiful must necessarily be b ugly, nor that what is not good must be bad. The same thing is equally true of Eros; just because, as you yourself admit, he is not good or beautiful, you need not regard him as ugly and bad, but as something between these extremes.'

'Yet he is universally agreed to be a great god.'

'By those who don't know what they are talking about, do you mean? Or those who do?'

'I mean by absolutely everyone.'

Diotima laughed. 'How can Eros be agreed to be a great god
c by people who don't even admit that he's a god at all?'

'What people?'

'Well, you, for one. And me, for another.'

'What do you mean?'

'Quite simple. The gods are all happy and beautiful, aren't they? You wouldn't go so far as to claim that any of the gods is not happy and beautiful?'

'Good Lord, no.'

'And you agree that "happy" means "possessing what is good and beautiful"?'

'Certainly.'

d 'But you have already admitted that Eros lacks what is good and beautiful, and that he desires them because he lacks them.'

'Yes, I have.'

'How can he be a god, then, if he is without beauty and goodness?'

'He can't, apparently.'

'You see, even you don't regard Eros as a god.'

'What can Eros be, then? A mortal?'

'Far from it.'

'What, then?'

'As in the other examples, something between a mortal and an immortal.'

'And what is that, Diotima?'

'A great spirit, Socrates. Spirits are midway between what is
e divine and what is human.'

'What power does such a spirit possess?'

'He acts as an interpreter and means of communication between gods and men. He takes requests and offerings to the gods, and brings back instructions and benefits in return. Occupying this middle position he plays a vital role in holding the world together. He is the medium of all prophecy and religion, whether it concerns sacrifice, forms of worship, incantations, or any kind of divination or sorcery. There is no 203 direct contact between god and man. All association and communication between them, waking or sleeping, takes place through Eros. This kind of knowledge is knowledge of the spirit; any other knowledge (occupational or artistic, for example) is purely utilitarian. Such spirits are many and varied, and Eros is one of them.'

'Who are his parents?'

'That is not quite so simple, but I'll tell you, all the same. b When Aphrodite was born, the gods held a banquet, at which one of the guests was Resource, the son of Ingenuity. When they finished eating, Poverty came begging, as you would expect (there being plenty of food), and hung around the doorway. Resource was drunk (on nectar, since wine hadn't been invented), so he went into Zeus' garden, and was overcome by sleep. Poverty, seeing here the solution to her own lack of resources, decided to have a child by him. So she lay with him, and conceived Eros. That's why Eros is a follower c and servant of Aphrodite, because he was conceived at her birthday party – and also because he is naturally attracted to what is beautiful, and Aphrodite is beautiful.

So Eros' attributes are what you would expect of a child of Resource and Poverty. For a start, he's always poor, and so far from being soft and beautiful (which is most people's view of him), he is hard, unkempt, barefoot, homeless. He sleeps on the d ground, without a bed, lying in doorways or in the open street. He has his mother's nature, and need is his constant companion. On the other hand, from his father he has inherited an eye for beauty and the good. He is brave, enterprising and determined – a marvellous huntsman, always intriguing. He is intellectual, resourceful, a lover of wisdom his whole life through, a subtle magician, sorcerer and thinker.

His nature is neither that of an immortal nor that of a mortal. e In one and the same day he can be alive and flourishing (when things go well), then at death's door, later still reviving as his father's character asserts itself again. But his resources are always running out, so that Eros is never either totally destitute or affluent. Similarly he is midway between wisdom and folly, as I

204   will show you. None of the gods searches for wisdom, or tries
to become wise – they are wise already. Nor does anyone else
wise search for wisdom. On the other hand, the foolish do not
search for wisdom or try to become wise either, since folly is
precisely the failing which consists in not being fine and good,
or intelligent – and yet being quite satisfied with the way one is.
You cannot desire what you do not realise you lack.'

'Who then are the lovers of wisdom, Diotima, if they are
neither the wise nor the foolish?'

b   'That should by now be obvious, even to a child. They must
be the intermediate class, among them Eros. We would classify
wisdom as very beautiful, and Eros is love of what is beautiful,
so it necessarily follows that Eros is a lover of wisdom (lovers of
wisdom being the intermediate class between the wise and the
foolish). The reason for this, too, is to be found in his parentage.
His father is wise and resourceful, while his mother is foolish
and resourceless.

'Such is the nature of this spirit, Socrates. Your views on Eros
c   revealed a quite common mistake. You thought (or so I infer
from your comments) that Eros was what was loved, rather than
the lover. That is why you thought Eros was beautiful. After all,
what we love really *is* beautiful and delicate, perfect and
delightful, whereas the lover has the quite different character I
have outlined.'

'Fair enough, my foreign friend, I think you're right. But if
that's what Eros is like, what use is he to men?'

d   'That's the next point I want to explain to you, Socrates. I've
told you what Eros is like, and what his parentage is; he is also
love of what is beautiful, as you say. Now let's imagine someone
asking us, "Why is Eros love of the beautiful, Socrates and
Diotima?" Let me put it more clearly: what is it that the lover of
beauty desires?'

'To possess it.'

'That prompts the further question, what good does it do
someone to possess beauty?'

'I don't quite know how to give a quick answer to that
question.'

e   'Well, try a different question, about goodness rather than
beauty: Socrates, what does the lover of goodness want?'

'To possess it.'

'What good will it do him to possess it?'

'That's easier. It will make him happy.'

'Yes, because those who are happy are happy because they 205
possess what is good. The enquiry seems to have reached a
conclusion, and there is no need to ask the further question, "If
someone wants to be happy, why does he want to be happy?" '

'True.'

'Do you think this wish and this desire are common to all
mankind, and that everyone wants always to possess what is
good? Or what do you think?'

'I think it is common to all men.'

'In that case, Socrates, why do we not describe all men as
lovers, if everyone always loves the same thing? Why do we
describe some people as lovers, but not others?'   b

'I don't know. I agree with you, it is surprising.'

'Not really. We abstract a part of love, and call it by the name
of the whole – love – and then for the other parts we use
different names.'

'What names? Give me an example.'

'What about this? Take a concept like creation, or composition. Composition means putting things together, and covers a
wide range of activities. Any activity which brings anything at all
into existence is an example of creation. Hence the exercise of c
any skill is composition, and those who practise it are composers.'

'True.'

'All the same, they aren't all called composers. They all have
different names, and it's only one subdivision of the whole class
(that which deals with music and rhythm) which is called by the
general name. Only this kind of creation is called composing,
and its practitioners composers.'

'True.'

'Well, it's the same with love. In general, for anyone, any d
desire for goodness and happiness is love – and it is a powerful
and unpredictable force. But there are various ways of pursuing
this desire – through money-making, through physical fitness,
through philosophy – which do not entitle their devotees to call
themselves lovers, or describe their activity as loving. Those
who pursue one particular mode of loving, and make that their

concern, have taken over the name of the whole (love, loving and lovers).'

'You may well be right.'

e 'There is a theory that lovers are people in search of their other half. But according to my theory, love is not love of a half, nor of a whole, unless it is good. After all, men are prepared to have their own feet and hands cut off, if they think there's something wrong with them. They're not particularly attached to what is their own, except in so far as they regard the good as their own property, and evil as alien to them. And that's 206 because the good is the only object of human love, as I think you will agree.'

'Yes, I certainly do agree.'

'Can we say, then, quite simply, that men love the good?'

'Yes.'

'And presumably we should add that they want to possess the good?'

'Yes, we should.'

'And not merely to possess it, but to possess it for ever.'

'That also.'

'In short, then, love is the desire for permanent possession of the good.'

'Precisely.'

b 'If this is always the object of our desire, what is the particular manner of pursuit, and the particular sphere of activity, in which enthusiasm and effort qualify for the title "love"? What is this activity? Do you know?'

'No, I don't. That's why I find your knowledge so impressive. In fact, I've kept coming to see you, because I want an answer to just that question.'

'Very well, I'll tell you. The activity we're talking about is the use of what is beautiful for the purpose of reproduction, whether physical or mental.'

'I'm no good at riddles. I don't understand what you mean.'

c 'I'll try to make myself clearer. Reproduction, Socrates, both physical and mental, is a universal human activity. At a certain age our nature desires to give birth. To do so, it cannot employ an ugly medium, but insists on what is beautiful. Sexual intercourse between man and woman is this reproduction. So there is the divine element, this germ of immortality, in mortal creatures – i.e. conception and begetting. These cannot take place in an uncongenial medium, and ugliness is uncongenial to everything divine, while beauty is congenial. Therefore pro- d creation has Beauty as its midwife and its destiny, which is why the urge to reproduce becomes gentle and happy when it comes near beauty: then conception and begetting become possible. By contrast, when it comes near ugliness it becomes sullen and offended, it contracts, withdraws, and shrinks away and does not beget. It stifles the reproductive urge, and is frustrated. So in anyone who is keen (one might almost say bursting) to reproduce, beauty arouses violent emotion, because beauty can release its possessor from the agony of reproduction. Your e opinion, Socrates, that love is desire for beauty, is mistaken.'

'What is the correct view, then?'

'It is the desire to use beauty to beget and bear offspring.'

'Perhaps.'

'Certainly! And why to beget? Because begetting is, by human standards, something eternal and undying. So if we were right in 207 describing love as the desire always to possess the good, then the inevitable conclusion is that we desire immortality as well as goodness. On this argument, love must be desire for immortality as much as for beauty.'

Those were her teachings, when she talked to me about love. And one day she asked me, 'What do you think is the reason for this love and this desire? You know how strangely animals behave when they want to mate. Animals and birds, they're just the same. Their health suffers, and they get all worked up, first over sexual intercourse, and then over raising the young. For b these ends they will fight, to the death, against far stronger opponents. They will go to any lengths, even starve themselves, to bring up their offspring. We can easily imagine human beings behaving like this from rational motives, but what can be the cause of such altruistic behaviour in animals? Do you know?'

'No, I don't.'   c

'Do you think you can become an expert on love without knowing?'

'Look, Diotima, I know I have a lot to learn. I've just admitted that. That's why I've come to you. So please tell me the cause of these phenomena, and anything else I should know about love.'

'Well, if you believe that the natural object of love is what we have often agreed it to be, then the answer is not surprising, d since the same reasoning still holds good. What is mortal tries, to the best of its ability, to be everlasting and immortal. It does this in the only way it can, by always leaving a successor to replace what decays. Think of what we call the life-span and identity of an individual creature. For example, a man is said to be the same individual from childhood until old age. The cells in his body are always changing, yet he is still called the same person, despite being perpetually reconstituted as parts of him decay – hair, flesh, e bones, blood, his whole body, in fact. And not just his body, either. Precisely the same happens with mental attributes. Habits, dispositions, beliefs, opinions, desires, pleasures, pains and fears 208 are all varying all the time for everyone. Some disappear, others take their place. And when we come to knowledge, the situation is even odder. It is not just a question of one piece of knowledge disappearing and being replaced by another, so that we are never the same people, as far as knowledge goes: the same thing happens with each individual piece of knowledge. What we call studying presupposes that knowledge is transient. Forgetting is loss of knowledge, and studying preserves knowledge by creating memory afresh in us, to replace what is lost. Hence we have the illusion of continuing knowledge.

'All continuous mortal existence is of this kind. It is not the case that creatures remain always, in every detail, precisely the same – only the divine does that. It is rather that what is lost, b and what decays, always leaves behind a fresh copy of itself. This, Socrates, is the mechanism by which mortal creatures can taste immortality – both physical immortality, and other sorts. (For immortals, of course, it's different.) So it's not surprising that everything naturally values its own offspring. They all feel this concern, and this love, because of their desire for immortality.'

I found these ideas totally novel, and I said, 'Well, Diotima, c that's a very clever explanation. Is it really all true?' And she, in her best lecturer's manner, replied, 'There can be no question of it. Take another human characteristic, ambition. It seems absurdly irrational until you remember my explanation. Think of the extraordinary behaviour of those who, prompted by Eros, are eager to become famous, and "amass undying fame for the whole of time to come." For this they will expose themselves to danger even more than they will for their children. They will spend money, endure any hardship, even die for it. Think of d Alcestis' willingness to die for Admetus, or Achilles' determination to follow Patroclus in death, or your Athenian king Codrus and his readiness to give up his life for his children's right to rule. Would they have done these things if they hadn't thought they were leaving behind them an undying memory which we still possess – of their courage? Of course not. The desire for undying nobility, and the good reputation which goes with it, is a universal human motive. The nobler people are, the more e strongly they feel it. They desire immortality.

'Those whose creative urge is physical tend to turn to women, and pursue Eros by this route. The production of children gains them, as they imagine, immortality and a name and happiness for themselves, for all time. In others the impulse is mental or 209 spiritual – people who are creative mentally, much more than physically. They produce what you would expect the mind to conceive and produce. And what is that? Thought, and all other human excellence. All poets are creators of this kind, and so are those artists who are generally regarded as inventive. However, under the general heading "thought", by far the finest and most important item is the art of political and domestic economy, what we call good judgement, and justice.

'Someone who, right from his youth, is mentally creative in these areas, when he is ready, and the time comes, feels a strong b urge to give birth, or beget. So he goes around, like everyone else, searching, as I see it, for a medium of beauty in which he can create. He will never create in an ugly medium. So in his desire to create he is attracted to what is physically beautiful rather than ugly. But if he comes across a beautiful, noble, well-formed mind, then he finds the combination particularly attractive. He'll drop everything and embark on long conversations about goodness, with such a companion, trying to teach him about the nature and behaviour of the good man. Now that he's made c contact with someone beautiful, and made friends with him, he can produce and bring to birth what he long ago conceived. Present or absent, he keeps it in mind, and joins with his friends

in bringing his conception to maturity. In consequence such
people have a far stronger bond between them than there is
between the parents of children; and they form much firmer
friendships, because they are jointly responsible for finer, and
more lasting, offspring.

'We would all choose children of this kind for ourselves,
d rather than human children. We look with envy at Homer and
Hesiod, and the other great poets, and the marvellous progeny
they left behind, which have brought them undying fame and
memory: or, if you like, at children of the kind which Lycurgus
left in Sparta, the salvation of Sparta and practically all Greece.
In your city, Solon is highly thought of, as the father of your
e laws, as are many other men in other states, both Greek and
foreign. They have published to the world a variety of noble
achievements, and created goodness of every kind. There are
shrines to such people in honour of their offspring, but none to
the producers of ordinary children.

'You, too, Socrates, could probably be initiated this far into
210 knowledge of Eros. But all this, rightly pursued, is a mere
preliminary to the full rites, and final revelation, which might
well be beyond you. Still, I'll tell you about it, so that if I fail, it
won't be for want of trying. Try to follow if you can.

'The true follower of this subject must begin, as a young man,
with the pursuit of physical beauty. In the first place, if his
mentor advises him properly, he should be attracted, physically,
to one individual; at this stage his offspring are beautiful
discussions and conversations. Next he should realise that the
b physical beauty of one body is akin to that of any other body,
and that if he's going to pursue beauty of appearance, it's the
height of folly not to regard the beauty which is in all bodies as
one and the same. This insight will convert him into a lover of
all physical beauty, and he will become less obsessive in his
pursuit of his one former passion, as he realises its unimportance.

'The next stage is to put a higher value on mental than on
physical beauty. The right qualities of mind, even in the
absence of any great physical beauty, will be enough to awaken
c his love and affection. He will generate the kind of discussions
which are improving to the young. The aim is that, as the next
step, he should be compelled to contemplate the beauty of

customs and institutions, to see that all beauty of this sort is related, and consequently to regard physical beauty as trivial.

'From human institutions his teacher should direct him to knowledge, so that he may, in turn, see the beauty of different types of knowledge. Whereas before, in servile and contemptible fashion, he was dominated by the individual case, loving the d beauty of a boy, or a man, or a single human activity, now he directs his eyes to what is beautiful in general, as he turns to gaze upon the limitless ocean of beauty. Now he produces many fine and inspiring thoughts and arguments, as he gives his undivided attention to philosophy. Here he gains in strength and stature until his attention is caught by that one special knowledge – the knowledge of a beauty which I will now try to describe to you. So pay the closest possible attention.   e

'When a man has reached this point in his education in love, studying the different types of beauty in correct order, he will come to the final end and goal of this education. Then suddenly he will see a beauty of a breathtaking nature, Socrates, the beauty which is the justification of all his efforts so far. It is 211 eternal, neither coming to be nor passing away, neither increasing nor decreasing. Moreover it is not beautiful in part, and ugly in part, nor is it beautiful at one time, and not at another; nor beautiful in some respects, but not in others; nor beautiful here and ugly there, as if beautiful in some people's eyes, but not in others. It will not appear to him as the beauty of a face, or hands, or anything physical – nor as an idea or branch of knowledge, nor as existing in any determinate place, such as a living creature, or the earth, or heaven, or anywhere like that. It exists for all time, by itself and with itself, unique. All other b forms of beauty derive from it, but in such a way that their creation or destruction does not strengthen or weaken it, or affect it in any way at all. If a man progresses (as he will do, if he goes about his love affairs in the right way) from the lesser beauties, and begins to catch sight of this beauty, then he is within reach of the final revelation. Such is the experience of the man who approaches, or is guided towards, love in the right way, beginning with the particular examples of beauty, but c always returning from them to the search for that one beauty. He uses them like a ladder, climbing from the love of one person to love of two; from two to love of all physical beauty; from physical beauty to beauty in human behaviour; thence to beauty in subjects of study; from them he arrives finally at that branch of knowledge which studies nothing but ultimate beauty. Then at last he understands what true beauty is.

d   'That, if ever, is the moment, my dear Socrates, when a man's life is worth living, as he contemplates beauty itself. Once seen, it will not seem to you to be a good such as gold, or fashionable clothes, or the boys and young men who have such an effect on you now when you see them. You, and any number of people like you, when you see your boyfriends and spend all your time with them, are quite prepared (or would be, if it were possible) to go without food and drink, just looking at them and being with them. But suppose it were granted to someone to see beauty itself

e   quite clearly, in its pure, undiluted form – not clogged up with human flesh and colouring, and a whole lot of other worthless and corruptible matter. No, imagine he were able to see the divine beauty itself in its unique essence. Don't you think he

212 would find it a wonderful way to live, looking at it, contemplating it as it should be contemplated, and spending his time in its company? It cannot fail to strike you that only then will it be possible for him, seeing beauty as it should be seen, to produce, not likenesses of goodness (since it is no likeness he has before him), but the real thing (since he has the real thing before him); and that this producing, and caring for, real goodness earns him the friendship of the gods and makes him, if anyone, immortal.'

b   There you are, then, Phaedrus and the rest of you. That's what Diotima said to me, and I, for one, find it convincing. And it's because I'm convinced that I now try to persuade other people as well that man, in his search for this goal, could hardly hope to find a better ally than Eros. That's why I say that everyone should honour Eros, and why I myself honour him, and make the pursuit of Eros my chief concern, and encourage others to do the same. Now, and for all time, I praise the power and vigour of Eros, to the limits of my ability.

c   That's my speech, Phaedrus. You can take it, if you like, as a formal eulogy of Eros. Or you can call it by any other name you please.

This speech was greeted with applause, and Aristophanes started saying something about Socrates' reference to his speech, when suddenly there was a tremendous sound of hammering at the front door – people going home from a party, by the sound of it. You could hear the voice of a flute-girl.

AGATHON (to his slaves): Could you see who that is? If it's one of my friends, ask him in. Otherwise, say we've stopped drinking d and are just going to bed.

Almost at once we heard Alcibiades' voice from the courtyard. He was very drunk, and shouting at the top of his voice, asking 'where Agathon was', and demanding 'to be taken to Agathon'. So in he came, supported by the girl, and some of his followers. He stood there in the doorway, wearing a luxuriant garland of ivy and violets, with his head covered in ribbons.   e

ALCIBIADES: Greetings, gentlemen. Will you allow me to join your gathering completely drunk? Or shall we just crown Agathon (which is what we've come for) and go away? I couldn't come yesterday, but now here I am, with ribbons in my hair, so that I can take a garland from my own head, and crown the man whom I hereby proclaim the cleverest and handsomest man in Athens. Are you going to laugh at me for being drunk? Well, you may laugh, but I'm sure I'm right, all the same. Anyway, those are my terms. So tell me right away: 213 should I come in? Will you drink with me, or not?

Then everyone started talking at once, telling him to come in and sit down. And Agathon called him over. So over he came, assisted by his companions. He was taking off his ribbons, getting ready to put the garland on Agathon, and with the ribbons in front of his eyes he didn't see Socrates. So he sat down next to Agathon, between him and Socrates, Socrates b moving aside, when he saw him, to make room. As he sat down he greeted Agathon, and put the garland on his head.

AGATHON (to his slaves): Take Alcibiades' shoes off. He can make a third at this table.

ALCIBIADES: Excellent, but who is the other person drinking at our table? (Turning and seeing Socrates, and leaping to his feet) My God, what's this? Socrates here? You've been lying in wait

here for me, just as you used to do. You were always turning up
c unexpectedly, wherever I least expected you. What are you
doing here this time? And come to that, how've you managed
to get yourself a place next to the most attractive person in the
room? You ought to be next to someone like Aristophanes; he
sets out to make himself ridiculous, and succeeds. Shouldn't you
be with him?

SOCRATES: I'm going to need your protection, Agathon. I've
d found the love of this man a bit of a nightmare. From the day I
took a fancy to him, I haven't been allowed to look at, or talk
to, anyone attractive at all. If I do he gets envious and jealous,
and starts behaving outrageously. He insults me, and can barely
keep his hands off me. So you make sure he doesn't do anything
now. You reconcile us, or defend me if he resorts to violence.
His insane sexuality scares me stiff.

ALCIBIADES: There can be no reconciliation between you and
me. However, I'll get my revenge another time. For the
e moment, give me some of those ribbons, Agathon, so I can
make a garland for this remarkable head of his as well. I don't
want him complaining that I crowned you, and not him,
though he is the international grandmaster of words – and not
just the day before yesterday, like you, but all the time. (As he
said this he took some of the ribbons, made a garland for
Socrates, and sat down.) Well, gentlemen, you seem to me to be
pretty sober. We can't have that. You'll have to drink. After all,
that's what we agreed. So I'm going to choose a Master of
Ceremonies, to see you all get enough to drink. I choose myself.
Agathon, let them bring a large cup, if you've got one. No,
wait! (Suddenly catching sight of an ice-bucket holding upwards
of half a gallon.) No need for that. Boy, bring me that ice-
bucket. (He filled it, and started off by draining it himself. Then
214 he told the slave to fill it up again for Socrates.) A useless ploy
against Socrates, gentlemen. It doesn't matter how much you
give him to drink, he'll drink it and be none the worse for wear.
(So the slave filled the bucket for Socrates, who drank it.)

ERYXIMACHUS: What's the plan, Alcibiades? Are we just going to
sit here and drink as if we were dying of thirst? Aren't we going
b to talk, or sing, at all while we drink?

ALCIBIADES: Ah, Eryximachus. Most excellent scion of a most excellent and sensible father. Good evening.

ERYXIMACHUS: Good evening to you too. But what *do* you want us to do?

ALCIBIADES: Whatever you recommend. We must do as you say. After all, 'a doctor is worth a dozen ordinary men'. So you tell us your prescription.

ERYXIMACHUS: Very well, listen. We had decided, before you came, that going round anticlockwise, each of us in turn should c make the best speech he could about Eros, in praise of him. We've all made our speeches. You've drunk but you haven't spoken. So it's only fair that you should speak now; after that you can give any instructions you like to Socrates, and he can do the same to the man on his right, and so on all the way round.

ALCIBIADES: That's a good idea, Eryximachus. But it's grossly unfair to ask me, drunk, to compete with you sober. Also, my dear friend, I hope you didn't pay any attention to Socrates' remarks just now. Presumably you realise the situation is the d exact opposite of what he said. He's the one who will resort to violence, if I praise anyone else, god or man, in his presence.

SOCRATES: Can't you hold your tongue?

ALCIBIADES: Don't worry, I wouldn't dream of praising anyone else if you're here.

ERYXIMACHUS: Well, that'll do, if you like. Praise Socrates.

ALCIBIADES: Really? You think I should, Eryximachus? Shall I set e about him, and get my own back on him, here in front of you all?

SOCRATES: Hey! What are you up to? Are you trying to make a fool of me by praising me? Or what?

ALCIBIADES: I'm going to tell the truth. Do you mind that?

SOCRATES: Of course not. In fact, I'm all in favour of it.

ALCIBIADES: I can't wait to start. And here's what you can do. If I say anything that's not true, you can interrupt me, if you like, 215 and tell me I'm wrong. I shan't get anything wrong on purpose, but don't be surprised if my recollection of things is a bit higgledy-piggledy. It's not easy, when you're as drunk as I am, to give a clear and orderly account of someone as strange as you.

ALCIBIADES

Gentlemen, I'm going to try and praise Socrates using similes. He may think I'm trying to make a fool of him, but the point of the simile is its accuracy, not its absurdity. I think he's very like
b one of those Silenus-figures sculptors have on their shelves. They're made with flutes or pipes. You can open them up, and when you do you find little figures of the gods inside. I also think Socrates is like the satyr Marsyas. As far as your appearance goes, Socrates, even you can't claim these are poor comparisons; but I'll tell you how the likeness holds good in other ways: just listen. You're a troublemaker, aren't you? Don't deny it, I can
c bring witnesses. You may not play the pipes, like Marsyas, but what you do is much more amazing. He had only to open his mouth to delight men, but he needed a musical instrument to do it. The same goes for anyone nowadays who plays his music – I count what Olympus played as really Marsyas', since he learnt from him. His is the only music which carries people away, and reveals those who have a desire for the gods and their rites. Such is its divine power, and it makes no difference whether it's played by an expert, or by a mere flute-girl.

You have the same effect on people. The only difference is that you do it with words alone, without the aid of any
d instrument. We can all listen to anyone else talking, and it has virtually no effect on us, no matter what he's talking about, or how good a speaker he is. But when we listen to you, or to someone else using your arguments, even if he's a hopeless speaker, we're overwhelmed and carried away. This is true of men, women and children alike.

For my own part, gentlemen, I would like to tell you on my honour (only you would certainly think I was drunk) the effect
e what he says has had on me in the past – and still does have, to this day. When I hear him, it's like the worst kind of religious hysteria. My heart pounds, and I find myself in floods of tears, such is the effect of his words. And I can tell lots of other people feel the same. I used to listen to Pericles and other powerful speakers, and I thought they spoke well. But they never had the

effect on me of turning all my beliefs upside down, with the
disturbing realisation that my whole life is that of a slave. 216
Whereas this Marsyas here has often made me feel that, and
decide that the kind of life I lead is just not worth living. You
can't deny it, Socrates.

Even now I know in my heart of hearts that if I were to listen
to him, I couldn't resist him. The same thing would happen
again. He forces me to admit that with all my faults I do nothing
to improve myself, but continue in public life just the same. So I b
tear myself away, as if stopping my ears against the Sirens;
otherwise I would spend my whole life there sitting at his feet.
He's the only man who can appeal to my better nature (not that
most people would reckon I *had* a better nature), because I'm
only too aware I have no answer to his arguments. I know I
should do as he tells me, but when I leave him I have no
defence against my own ambition and desire for recognition. So
I run for my life, and avoid him, and when I see him, I'm
embarrassed, when I remember conclusions we've reached in c
the past. I would often cheerfully have seen him dead, and yet I
know that if that did happen, I should be even more upset. So I
just can't cope with the man.

I'm by no means the only person to be affected like this by his
satyr's music, but that isn't all I have to say about his similarity
to those figures I likened him to, and about his remarkable
powers. Believe me, none of you really knows the man. So I'll
enlighten you, now that I've begun.   d

Your view of Socrates is of someone who fancies attractive
men, spends all his time with them, finds them irresistible – and
you know how hopelessly ignorant and uncertain he is. And yet
this pose is extremely Silenus-like. It's the outward mask he
wears, like the carved Silenus. Open him up, and he's a model
of restraint – you wouldn't believe it, my dear fellow-drinkers.
Take my word for it, it makes no difference at all how attractive
you are, he has an astonishing contempt for that kind of thing.
Similarly with riches, or any of the other so-called advantages e
we possess. He regards all possessions as worthless, and us
humans as insignificant. No, I mean it – he treats his whole life
in human society as a game or puzzle.

But when he's serious, when he opens up and you see the real

Socrates – I don't know if any of you has ever seen the figure inside. I saw it once, and it struck me as utterly godlike and golden and beautiful and wonderful. In fact, I thought I must simply do anything he told me. And since I thought he was

217 serious about my good looks, I congratulated myself on a fantastic stroke of luck, which had given me the chance to satisfy Socrates, and be the recipient, in return, of all his knowledge. I had, I may say, an extremely high opinion of my own looks.

That was my plan, so I did what I had never done up to then – I sent away my attendant, and took to seeing him on my own.

b You see, I'm going to tell you the whole truth, so listen carefully, and you tell them, Socrates, if I get anything wrong. Well, gentlemen, I started seeing him – just the two of us – and I thought he would start talking to me as lovers do to their boyfriends when they're alone together. I was very excited. But nothing like that happened at all. He spent the day talking to me

c as usual, and then left. I invited him to the gymnasium with me, and exercised with him there, thinking I might make some progress that way. So he exercised and wrestled with me, often completely on our own, and (needless to say) it got me nowhere at all. When that turned out to be no good, I thought I'd better make a pretty determined assault on the man, and not give up, now that I'd started. I wanted to find out what the trouble was. So I asked him to dinner, just like a lover with designs on his boyfriend.

d He took some time to agree even to this, but finally I did get him to come. The first time he came, he had dinner, and then got up to go. I lost my nerve, that time, and let him go. But I decided to try again. He came to dinner, and I kept him talking late into the night. When he tried to go home, I made him stay, saying it was too late to go. So he stayed the night on the couch next to mine. There was no one else sleeping in the room.

e What I've told you so far I'd be quite happy to repeat to anyone. The next part I'm only telling you because (a) I'm drunk – 'in vino veritas', and all that – and (b) since I've started praising Socrates, it seems wrong to leave out an example of his superior behaviour. Besides, I'm like someone who's been bitten by an adder. They say that a man who's had this happen to him will only say what it was like to others

who've been bitten; they're the only people who will under- 218
stand, and make allowances for, his willingness to say or do
anything, such is the pain. Well, I've been bitten by something
worse than an adder, and in the worst possible place. I've been
stung, or bitten, in my heart or soul (whatever you care to call
it) by a method of philosophical argument, whose bite, when it
gets a grip on a young and intelligent mind, is sharper than any
adder's. It makes one willing to say or do anything. I can see all
these Phaedruses and Agathons, Eryximachuses, Pausaniases, b
Aristodemuses and Aristophaneses here, not to mention Socrates himself and the rest of you. You've all had a taste of this
wild passion for philosophy, so you'll understand me, and
forgive what I did then, and what I'm telling you now. As for
the servants, and anyone else who's easily shocked, or doesn't
know what I'm talking about, they'll just have to put something over their ears.

There we were, then, gentlemen. The lamp had gone out, the
slaves had gone to bed. I decided it was time to abandon c
subtlety, and say plainly what I was after. So I nudged him.
'Socrates, are you asleep?' 'No.' 'Do you know what I've
decided?' 'What?' 'I think you're the ideal person to be my
lover, but you seem to be a bit shy about suggesting it. So I'll
tell you how I feel about it. I think I'd be crazy not to satisfy
you in this way, just as I'd do anything else for you if it was in
my power – or in my friends' power. Nothing matters more to
me than my own improvement, and I can't imagine a better d
helper than you. Anyone with any sense would think worse of
me for not giving a man like you what he wants than most
ignorant people would if I did give you what you want.'

Socrates listened to this. Then, with characteristic irony, he
replied. 'My dear Alcibiades, you're certainly nobody's fool, if
you're right in what you say about me, and I do have some e
power to improve you. It must be remarkable beauty you see in
me, far superior to your own physical beauty. If that's the aim of
your deal with me, to exchange beauty for beauty, then you're
trying to get much the better of the bargain. You want to get
real beauty in exchange for what is commonly mistaken for it,
like Diomedes getting gold armour in return for his bronze.
Better think again, however. You might be wrong about me. 219

Judgment begins when eyesight starts to fail, and you're still a long way from that.'

I listened, then said: 'Well, as far as I am concerned, that's how things stand. I've told you my real feelings. You must
b decide what you think best for yourself and for me.' 'That's good advice. We must think about it some time, and act as seems best to us, in this matter as in others.'

After this exchange, thinking my direct assault had made some impact, I got up, before he could say anything more, wrapped my cloak around him (it was winter), and lay down with him under his rough cloak. I put my arms round him. I spent the
c whole night with him, remarkable, superhuman being that he is — still telling the truth, Socrates, you can't deny it — but he was more than equal to my advances. He rejected them, laughed at my good looks, and treated them with contempt; and I must admit that, as far as looks went, I thought I was quite something, members of the jury. (I call you that, since I'm accusing Socrates of contempt.) In short, I promise you faithfully, I fell asleep, and when I woke up in the morning I'd slept with Socrates all night, but absolutely nothing had happened. It was just like sleeping
d with one's father or elder brother.

Imagine how I felt after that. I was humiliated and yet full of admiration for Socrates' character — his restraint and strength of mind. I'd met a man whose equal, in intelligence and control, I didn't think I should ever meet again. I couldn't have a row
e with him; that would just lose me his friendship. Nor could I see any way of attracting him. I knew money would make as little impression on him as Trojan weapons on Ajax, and he'd already escaped my one sure means of ensnaring him. I didn't know what to do, and I went around infatuated with the man. No one's ever been so infatuated.

That was the background to our military service together in Potidaea, where we were messmates. In the first place there was his toughness — not only greater than mine, but greater than anyone else's. Sometimes we were cut off and had to go without
220 food, as happens on campaign. No one could match him for endurance. On the other hand, he was the one who really made the most of it when there was plenty. He wouldn't drink for choice, but if he had to, he drank us all under the table.

Surprising as it may seem, no man has ever seen Socrates drunk. I've no doubt you'll see confirmation of that this evening. As for the weather (they have pretty savage winters up there), his indifference to it was always astonishing, but one occasion stands out in particular. There was an incredibly severe frost. No one b went outside, or if they did, they went muffled up to the eyeballs, with their feet wrapped up in wool or sheepskin. In these conditions Socrates went out in the same cloak he always wore, and walked barefoot over the ice with less fuss than the rest of us who had our feet wrapped up. The men didn't like it at all; they thought he was getting at them. c

So much for that. But there's another exploit of this 'conquering hero' during that campaign, which I ought to tell you about. He was studying a problem one morning, and he stood there thinking about it, not making any progress, but not giving up either – just standing there, trying to find the answer. By midday people were beginning to take notice, and remark to one another in some surprise that Socrates had been standing there thinking since dawn. Finally, in the evening after supper, some of the Ionians brought out their mattresses (this was in summer), and slept in the open, keeping an eye on him to see if he'd stand d there all night. And sure enough he did stand there, until dawn broke and the sun rose. Then he said a prayer to the sun and left.

Should I say something about his conduct in action? Yes, I think he's earned it. In the battle in which the generals gave me a decoration, my own life was saved by none other than Socrates. e He refused to leave me when I was wounded, and saved both me and my weapons. So I recommended that the generals should give you the decoration. Isn't that true, Socrates? You can't object to that, or say I'm lying, can you? In fact the generals were inclined to favour me, because of my social position, and wanted to give it to me, but you were keener than they were that I should get it, rather than you.

And you should have seen him, gentlemen, on the retreat from Delium. I was with him, but I was on horseback, and he 221 was on foot. He was retreating, amid the general rout, with Laches. I came upon them, and when I saw them I told them not to panic, and said I'd stick by them. This time I got a better view of Socrates than I had at Potidaea, since I was on

horseback, and less worried about my own safety. For a start, he
b was much more composed than Laches. And then I thought
your description of him, Aristophanes, was as accurate there as it
is here in Athens, 'marching along with his head in the air,
staring at all around him', calmly contemplating friend and foe
alike. It was perfectly clear, even from a distance, that any
attempt to lay a finger on him would arouse vigorous resistance.
So he and his companion escaped unhurt. On the whole, in
c battle, you don't meddle with people like that. You go after the
ones in headlong flight.

I could go on praising Socrates all night, and tell you some
surprising things. Many of his qualities can be found in other
people, and yet it's remarkable how unlike he is to anyone in the
past or present. You can compare Brasidas, or someone like that,
d with Achilles; Pericles with Nestor or Antenor (for example);
and make other similar comparisons. But you could go a long
way and not find a match, dead or living, for Socrates. So
unusual are the man himself and his arguments. You have to go
back to my original comparison of the man and his arguments, to
Silenuses and satyrs. I didn't say this at the beginning, but his
arguments, when you really look at them, are also just like
e Silenus-figures. If you decided to listen to one, it would strike
you at first as ludicrous. On the face of it, it's just a collection of
irrelevant words and phrases; but those are just the outer skin of
this trouble-making satyr. It's all donkeys and bronzesmiths,
shoemakers and tanners. He always seems to be repeating
himself, and people who haven't heard him before, and aren't
222 too quick on the uptake, laugh at what he says. But look beneath
the surface, and get inside them, and you'll find two things. In
the first place, they're the only arguments which really make any
sense; on top of that they are supremely inspiring, because they
contain countless models of excellence and pointers towards it.
In fact, they deal with everything you should be concerned
about, if you want to lead a good and noble life.

That's my speech, gentlemen, in praise of Socrates – though
I've included a bit of blame as well for his outrageous treatment
b of me. And I'm not the only sufferer. There's Charmides, the
son of Glaucon, and Euthydemus, the son of Diocles, and lots of

others. He seduces them, like a lover seducing his boyfriend, and then it turns out he's not their lover at all; in fact, they're his lovers. So take my advice, Agathon, and don't be seduced. Learn from our experience, rather than at first hand, like Homer's 'fool who learnt too late'. Don't trust him an inch.

Alcibiades' candour aroused some amusement. He seemed to be c still in love with Socrates.

SOCRATES: Not so drunk after all, Alcibiades; or you wouldn't have avoided, so elegantly and so deviously, revealing the real object of your speech, just slipping it in at the end, as if it were an afterthought. What you're really trying to do is turn Agathon and me against one another. You think that I should be your d lover, and no one else's; and that you, and no one else, should be Agathon's. Well, it hasn't worked. All that stuff about satyrs and Silenuses is quite transparent. You mustn't let him get away with it, my dear Agathon; you must make sure no one turns us against each other.

AGATHON: You may be right, Socrates. His sitting between us, to keep us apart, bears that out. But it won't work. I'll come round and sit next to you.   e

SOCRATES: Good idea. Sit here, round this side.

ALCIBIADES: Ye gods. What I have to put up with from the man. He has to keep scoring off me. Look, at least let Agathon sit in the middle.

SOCRATES: Out of the question. You've just praised me, and now I must praise the person on my right. If Agathon sits next to you, he can't be expected to make *another* speech in praise of me. I'd better make one in praise of him instead. No, you'll have to admit defeat, my good friend, and put up with me 223 praising the boy. I look forward to it.

AGATHON: What a bit of luck. I'm certainly not staying here, Alcibiades. I'd much rather move, and get myself praised by Socrates.

ALCIBIADES: That's it, the same old story. Whenever Socrates is around, no one else can get near anyone good-looking. Like now, for example. Look how easily he finds plausible reasons why Agathon should sit next to him.

b Agathon got up to come and sit by Socrates. Suddenly a whole crowd of people on their way home from a party turned up at the door, and finding it open (someone was just leaving), they came straight in, and sat down to join us. Things became incredibly noisy and disorderly, and we couldn't avoid having far too much to drink. Eryximachus and Phaedrus and some others went home. I fell asleep, and slept for some time, the
c nights being long at that time of year. When I woke up it was almost light, and the cocks were crowing. I could see that everyone had gone home or to sleep, apart from Agathon, Aristophanes, and Socrates. They were still awake and drinking (passing a large bowl round anticlockwise). Socrates was holding
d the floor. I've forgotten most of what he was saying, since I missed the beginning of it, and was still half-asleep anyway. The gist of it was that he was forcing them to admit that the same man could be capable of writing comedy and tragedy, and hence that a successful tragedian must also be able to write comedy. As they were being driven to this conclusion, though not really following the argument, they dropped off. Aristophanes went to sleep first, and then, as it was getting light, Agathon. Socrates made them both comfortable, and got up to leave himself. I followed him, as usual. He went to the Lyceum, had a bath, spent the rest of the day as he normally would, and then, towards evening, went home to bed.

EUTHYPHRO

EUTHYPHRO: What on earth can have happened, Socrates, to ² make you leave your usual haunts in the Lyceum, and come and spend time here in the king's colonnade? I don't suppose you too have some private lawsuit to plead before the king magistrate, as I have.

SOCRATES: No. At least, the Athenians don't call it a lawsuit, Euthyphro. They call it a prosecution in the public interest.

EUTHYPHRO: Really? Someone has brought a prosecution against b you, I assume. I can't believe it of you, that you would bring one against someone else.

SOCRATES: No, I haven't.

EUTHYPHRO: So someone has brought a case against you?

SOCRATES: Exactly.

EUTHYPHRO: Who is he?

SOCRATES: I really don't know the man myself, Euthyphro. Some youngster, I think. Nobody in particular. His name is Meletus, I believe. He's from the deme Pitthus, if you know a Meletus from the deme Pitthus, with straight hair, not much by way of a beard, and a hooked nose.

EUTHYPHRO: No, I don't know him, Socrates. What charge has he brought against you?   c

SOCRATES: What charge? One which does him credit, I think. It is no small thing for a young man to possess the knowledge he possesses. He knows, so he claims, what has a harmful effect on the young, and who has this effect. I think he must be someone very clever, who has seen my ignorance and my bad influence on his contemporaries. So he comes running to the city, as if he were running to his mother, to accuse me. I think he's unique among politicians in beginning his career in the right way. The d right way is to concern yourself first with making the young as good as possible – just as you'd expect a good farmer to concern himself first with his young plants, and only after that with the others. The same with Meletus. Maybe the first thing he's doing

3 is to weed out those of us he says are damaging the young – his new shoots. After that he'll obviously start taking an interest in those who are older. He's going to be a great benefactor to the city – as you'd expect from someone starting off in this way.

EUTHYPHRO: I'd like to think so, Socrates. But I'm rather afraid it will be just the opposite. He's striking at the very heart of the city, I think, if he's trying to do you an injury. Tell me, what does he say you do which has a harmful effect on the young?

b SOCRATES: Something rather strange, my friend, at first hearing. He says I'm a maker of gods. I make new gods, and don't recognise the old ones. And this is why he has brought a charge against me, he says.

EUTHYPHRO: I see, Socrates. It's because of the supernatural sign which you say appears to you. He thinks you're a revolutionary in religious matters, so he has brought this charge and is coming to court to discredit you. He knows it's easy to create a wrong impression with this kind of accusation. I have the same trouble.

c When I speak about religious matters in the assembly, telling them what's going to happen in the future, they laugh at me as if I'm mad. None of my predictions has proved false, but still they always resent people like us. We mustn't take them seriously. We must stand up to them.

SOCRATES: My dear Euthyphro, being laughed at is no very serious matter, perhaps. I don't think the Athenians mind all that much if they think someone is clever, so long as he doesn't teach his wisdom. But they do get angry – either from envy, as

d you suggest, or for some other reason – with anyone who makes other people like himself.

EUTHYPHRO: Well, what their view of me is in that regard is something I have absolutely no desire to find out.

SOCRATES: Perhaps they regard you as making yourself unavailable, and refusing to teach your wisdom. Whereas in my case, I'm afraid my generosity may make them think I impart whatever I possess freely to everyone. And not just free of charge. I'd even *pay* a fee to anyone prepared to listen to me. So as I said a moment ago, if they were just going to laugh at me, as you say they laugh at you, we could have a nice enough time in court, e laughing and joking. But if they're going to be serious about it, then the outcome is clear only to you soothsayers.

EUTHYPHRO: It may all come to nothing, Socrates. Your case may go as you would like, as I think mine will go as I would like.

SOCRATES: What *is* your case, Euthyphro? Are you defending or prosecuting?

EUTHYPHRO: Prosecuting.

SOCRATES: Whom?

EUTHYPHRO: Someone I must seem mad to be prosecuting.   4

SOCRATES: Really? Is it some sort of wild goose chase, your prosecution?

EUTHYPHRO: By no means a wild goose chase. In fact, it's a very old man.

SOCRATES: Who is he?

EUTHYPHRO: My father.

SOCRATES: Your *father*?

EUTHYPHRO: Absolutely.

SOCRATES: What is the charge? What is the case about?

EUTHYPHRO: Murder, Socrates.

SOCRATES: Heracles! I wouldn't have thought most people had any idea what was the right course of action there. It's not absolutely anyone, if you ask me, who would act in this way. b Only someone far advanced in wisdom, I should imagine.

EUTHYPHRO: Far advanced indeed, Socrates.

SOCRATES: Was he a member of your family, the man killed by your father? Yes, obviously. I don't suppose you'd be prosecuting him for the murder of a stranger.

EUTHYPHRO: What an absurd suggestion, Socrates! As if it made any difference whether the man who was killed was a stranger or a member of my family. The only thing we should take any notice of is whether or not he that slew, slew justly. If justly, we should allow it; if unjustly, we should prosecute, even if he that

c slew shares your hearth and shares your table. After all, your pollution is the same if you knowingly keep the company of such a man, and do not purify yourself and him by prosecuting. The man who was killed was in fact a casual labourer of mine. We used to farm on Naxos, and he was a tenant on our estate there. In a fit of drunken violence he lost his temper with one of the slaves, and cut his throat. So my father bound him hand and foot, and threw him into a ditch. Then he sent a man here to

d ask the Interpreter what he should do. In the meantime he paid little attention to the man he had bound, neglecting him on the grounds that he was a murderer, and it didn't too much matter if he died. Which is what in fact happened. He died of hunger and cold and his bonds before the messenger sent to the Interpreter returned.

That's why my father and the rest of my family are actually quite annoyed with me, because I'm prosecuting my father for murder on behalf of a murderer. As they see it, my father did not kill him, and even if he did, there was no need to worry about someone like that, because he was a murderer. They said

e it was unholy for a son to prosecute his father for murder. They have very little idea, Socrates, of the gods' attitude to the holy and the unholy.

SOCRATES: And what about you, for heaven's sake, Euthyphro? Do you regard yourself as such an authority on religion – on things holy and things unholy – that after events such as you describe you can take your father to court with no fear that you in your turn may in fact be doing something unholy?

EUTHYPHRO: I wouldn't be much use, Socrates – nor would

5 Euthyphro be very different from everyone else – if I weren't an authority on all these kinds of things.

SOCRATES: I've had a marvellous idea, Euthyphro! Why don't I become your pupil? Then I can challenge Meletus, before the case, on precisely this point. I can say I've always in the past set great store by knowing about religion, and now especially, since he says I make things up as I go along and am a religious revolutionary, I have become a pupil of yours. 'Look, Meletus,' I can say, 'if you agree that Euthyphro is an expert on the subject, then you can take it that I have the right attitude too, b and you needn't go on with your lawsuit. Or else take him, my teacher, to court rather than me, for being a bad influence on the older generation – on me by his teaching, and on his father by his criticism and punishment.' If he won't listen to me, and won't drop his prosecution or prosecute you instead, then when it comes to court I can quote the exact words of my challenge to him.

EUTHYPHRO: Heavens, yes, Socrates. I'm sure I'd soon find a chink in his armour if he tried to prosecute me. And when we c got to court, we'd very soon find ourselves enquiring into his behaviour rather than mine.

SOCRATES: I'm well aware of that, my dear friend. That's why I want to be a pupil of yours. I'm sure anyone – particularly this Meletus – is going to pretend he can't see you. But he's seen me all right – clearly and easily enough to bring a charge of impiety against me. So tell me, in heaven's name – since you claimed to be quite confident about it a moment ago – what kind of thing do you say piety is – and impiety – both where murder is concerned and in other situations? Or rather, isn't what is holy d unvarying in every activity, while what is unholy is the opposite of everything holy, and also unvarying – so that anything at all which is going to be unholy possesses a single form in respect of its unholiness?

EUTHYPHRO: That's absolutely right, Socrates.

SOCRATES: Tell me then, what do you say the holy is? And what do you say the unholy is?

EUTHYPHRO: I say the holy is what I am doing now, prosecuting the person who is guilty of an offence such as murder, or stealing from temples, or some other crime of that sort – be he father, mother, or anyone at all. And not prosecuting him is e unholy. And see what a compelling argument I can give you, Socrates, that the law is as I say. I have pointed it out before, to other people, to show that the kind of thing I am doing is right, and that we shouldn't let the person who acts impiously get away with it, whoever he is. But the same people who regard Zeus as the best and most just of the gods – though they admit

6 he bound his own father for swallowing his children unjustly, and that he in his turn had castrated *his* father before him for the same kind of reasons – still get annoyed with me for prosecuting my father when he does wrong. So they contradict themselves in what they say about the gods and about me.

SOCRATES: Is *that* the reason, Euthyphro, why I am having a charge brought against me – because I can't bring myself to accept it when people tell stories like that about the gods? That could be the reason why people will say I'm at fault. If it now turns out that you accept these stories – you who are an expert

b on the subject – then the rest of us have no alternative, apparently, but to go along with them as well. What are we going to say, those of us who freely admit that we know nothing about the subject? Tell me honestly, do you really believe those things happened?

EUTHYPHRO: Yes, and things stranger than those, Socrates. Things most people know nothing of.

SOCRATES: And is there really war against one another among the gods, do you think? And terrible quarrels and battles, and all those stories we hear about from the poets? Our temples in

c general are decorated with them – the work of great sculptors – and in particular, at the Great Panathenaea, the goddess's cloak which is taken as an offering to the Acropolis is full of pictures of this sort. Are we to say these stories are true, Euthyphro?

EUTHYPHRO: Yes. And not just these stories, Socrates. As I was just saying, I can tell you any number of stories to do with gods, if you like – stories which I have no doubt will astonish you when you hear them.

SOCRATES: I'm sure you can. And please do tell me them – some other time, when we're not busy. For the moment, though, try

and give a clearer answer to the question I asked you. I asked d
you what exactly the holy was, and your first answer did not
completely enlighten me. You told me the holy was in fact
doing what you're doing now, prosecuting your father for
murder.

EUTHYPHRO: I did. And I was right, Socrates.

SOCRATES: I dare say. But you agree, Euthyphro, that there are
lots of other things which are holy as well.

EUTHYPHRO: Yes, there are.

SOCRATES: Do you remember my question, then? I didn't ask
you to tell me just one or two of the many holy things, but to
tell me the actual form as a result of which all holy things *are*
holy. You did say, didn't you, that unholy things were unholy,
and holy things holy, as a result of a single form? Or don't you e
remember that?

EUTHYPHRO: No, I do remember it.

SOCRATES: That's what I want you to tell me about – what the
form itself is. I want to be able to refer to it and use it as an
example. Then of the actions which you or anyone else
perform, I can call holy the ones – performed by you or anyone
else – which resemble it, but not the ones which don't
resemble it.

EUTHYPHRO: If that is what you want, Socrates, that is what I
shall tell you.

SOCRATES: I certainly wish you would.

EUTHYPHRO: Very well. What is dear to the gods is holy. What is
not dear to them is unholy.   7

SOCRATES: Excellent, Euthyphro. This time you've given me
exactly the kind of answer I was asking you to give me. I don't
yet know whether it's *true*, but obviously you're going to prove
that it is.

EUTHYPHRO: I certainly am.

SOCRATES: Come on, then. Let's examine what we are saying.
What is loved by the gods, and the man who is loved by the

gods, is holy. What is hated by the gods, and the man who is hated, is unholy. The holy is not the same as the unholy, but its exact opposite. Isn't that it?

EUTHYPHRO: Yes, it is.

SOCRATES: Do you think that definition is right?

b EUTHYPHRO: Yes, Socrates, I do.

SOCRATES: And that there is civil war among the gods, Euthyphro – that they disagree with one another, that there is hostility among them towards one another – has this been said as well?

EUTHYPHRO: Yes, it has.

SOCRATES: This hostility and these quarrels, my good sir – what kind of disagreement are they the result of? Let's look at it like this. If you and I disagreed about number – which of two quantities was the larger – would our disagreement about this make us enemies, make us lose our tempers with one another? Or would we find a quick way out of that kind of thing by
c having resort to calculation?

EUTHYPHRO: That's exactly what we should do.

SOCRATES: And if we disagreed about larger or smaller size, we could put a quick end to our disagreement by resort to measuring?

EUTHYPHRO: That is so.

SOCRATES: And questions of heavier and lighter, I imagine, by resort to weighing.

EUTHYPHRO: Of course.

SOCRATES: So what sort of disagreement, and inability to come to a decision, would arouse hostility between us and make us lose our tempers with one another? And if you can't answer that straight away, let me make a suggestion, and you can think
d about that. Isn't it the just and the unjust, the beautiful and the ugly, the good and the bad? Isn't it when we disagree about those, without being able to come to a satisfactory decision, that we become enemies – when we do become enemies? That goes for you, me and everyone.

EUTHYPHRO: Yes, it is this disagreement, Socrates – and about these things.

SOCRATES: What about the gods, Euthyphro? If they disagree at all, wouldn't these be just the things they would disagree about?

EUTHYPHRO: They're bound to be.

SOCRATES: In which case, my noble Euthyphro, the gods have conflicting opinions about what things are just, according to your account of the matter. The same with beautiful and ugly, and good and bad. If they didn't disagree on these subjects, presumably they wouldn't quarrel with one another, would they?

EUTHYPHRO: That's right.

SOCRATES: What one group of gods regards as beautiful, good and just – is that what is dear to them? And are their opposites hateful to them?

EUTHYPHRO: Precisely.

SOCRATES: And the same things, according to you, are regarded as just by one group and unjust by another. This is what they disagree about when they quarrel and fight against one another. Isn't that right?

EUTHYPHRO: It is.

SOCRATES: So the same things are apparently both hated by the gods and loved by them. And the same things would be both hateful to the gods and dear to the gods.

EUTHYPHRO: Apparently.

SOCRATES: In which case, Euthyphro, on this argument, would the same things be both holy and unholy?

EUTHYPHRO: It looks like it.

SOCRATES: Then you haven't answered my question! I didn't ask you for one single thing which was in fact both holy and unholy. But now it appears that what is dear to the gods is also hateful to them. Take what you are doing in punishing your father. It wouldn't be at all surprising if in acting like this you are doing what pleases Zeus, but offends Cronus and Uranus – what is pleasing to Hephaestus, but offensive to Hera. And if any of the other gods disagree with one another about it, what you are doing will strike them in the same way.

EUTHYPHRO: There is at any rate one point, Socrates, on which I don't think any of the gods would disagree with one another – that the man who kills someone unjustly should pay the penalty.

SOCRATES: And what about the world of men, Euthyphro? Have you never heard anyone there arguing that the man who has
c killed someone unjustly, or acted unjustly in some other way, should not pay the penalty?

EUTHYPHRO: They never *stop* arguing about it – particularly in the lawcourts. They do all kinds of wrong, and then do and say anything to avoid punishment.

SOCRATES: Do they actually admit to doing wrong, Euthyphro? And then claim, despite this admission, that they should not pay the penalty?

EUTHYPHRO: No, that's not what they say.

SOCRATES: In which case, they don't say and do absolutely anything. I don't think they have the nerve to say or argue that
d if they *are* doing wrong they should not pay the penalty. What they say, I think, is that they're not doing wrong. Isn't that it?

EUTHYPHRO: True.

SOCRATES: In which case, they're not arguing that the wrong-doer should not pay the penalty. What they're arguing about, perhaps, is who is doing wrong, what he is doing, and when.

EUTHYPHRO: True.

SOCRATES: Isn't it just the same with the gods, if they quarrel about justice and injustice – as you say they do? Each party says the other is in the wrong, while the others deny it. You're not going to tell me that anyone – god or man – has the nerve to
e claim that a wrongdoer should not pay the penalty.

EUTHYPHRO: Yes, on this point you are right, Socrates. In general, at least.

SOCRATES: But when people argue, Euthyphro, they argue about a particular action, I think. Both men and gods, if the gods *do* argue. There is some activity they disagree about, and some say it was done justly, while others say it was done unjustly. Isn't that so?

EUTHYPHRO: It certainly is.

SOCRATES: Come on, then, my dear Euthyphro, tell me too. 9 Enlighten me. What proof have you that all the gods believe the dead man was wrongly killed? He was your tenant, and a murderer. He was bound by the master of the man he killed. And he died of his bonds before the man who bound him could find out from the Interpreters what he ought to do with him? What proof have you that it is right for a son to prosecute and denounce his father on behalf of a man of that sort? Come on. Try in this case to give me a clear demonstration that all the b gods are utterly convinced that this action is correct. If you can give me a satisfactory demonstration, I shall never stop praising you for your wisdom.

EUTHYPHRO: It might be no small task, Socrates, though I certainly *could* give you a clear demonstration.

SOCRATES: I see. You think I'm stupider than the jurymen, since you're obviously going to demonstrate to *them* that your father's actions were wrong, and that all the gods hate actions of that sort.

EUTHYPHRO: I am. And very clearly too, if they listen to what I have to say.

SOCRATES: They will listen – if they think what you say is right. c But one thing struck me while you were speaking. I ask myself this question: 'Even if Euthyphro made it completely clear to me that all the gods believe that sort of killing to be unjust, in what way has Euthyphro made me any the wiser about what exactly the holy and the unholy are? This deed would be hated by the gods, it seems. But that wouldn't help, since what is holy and what is not were shown, a few moments ago, not to be defined in this way. What was hated by the gods was clearly also loved by the gods.' So I'll let you off that, Euthyphro. Let's assume, if you like, that all the gods believe it was unjust, and that they all hate it. But what about this new version of our d definition? What all the gods hate is unholy, and what they all love is holy. What some of them love, and others hate, is neither or both. Are you content that this should now be our definition of the holy and the unholy?

EUTHYPHRO: Why not, Socrates?

SOCRATES: No reason, Euthyphro. Not as far as I'm concerned. And you? Ask yourself whether, on this definition, you will find it just as easy to teach me what you promised.

e EUTHYPHRO: Yes. Speaking for myself, I would say the holy is what all the gods love, and its opposite, the unholy, is what all the gods hate.

SOCRATES: In that case, ought we to have a look at this definition in its turn, Euthyphro, to see if it is a good one? Or should we let it go, and take it on trust – take our own or other people's word for it? So long as someone merely asserts that something is the case, should we just agree that that is how it is? Or should we ask what he means by what he says?

EUTHYPHRO: We should ask. Personally, however, I think we've now got an excellent definition.

10 SOCRATES: We shall soon know for sure, my friend. Now, here's a question for you. Is the holy loved by the gods because it is holy? Or is it holy because it is loved?

EUTHYPHRO: I don't know what you mean, Socrates.

SOCRATES: I'll try and make it clearer. Do we talk about being carried and carrying? Being led and leading? Being seen and seeing? In all these examples, are you aware that the two are different from one another – and what the difference is?

EUTHYPHRO: I *think* I am.

SOCRATES: Is there a thing loved and – different from it – a thing which loves?

EUTHYPHRO: Yes, of course.

b SOCRATES: Tell me this. The thing carried – is it a thing carried because it is being carried, or for some other reason?

EUTHYPHRO: No, for this reason.

SOCRATES: And the thing led because it is led, and the thing seen because it is seen?

EUTHYPHRO: Precisely.

SOCRATES: So the reason for its being seen isn't because it is a thing seen. It's the other way round. It's a thing seen because it *is* seen. Nor is anything led because it's a thing led; it's a thing led because it *is* led. And it's not carried because it is a thing carried; it's a thing carried because it *is* carried. Is my meaning clear, Euthyphro? What I mean is this: if something is done, or c has something done to it, it isn't done because it's a thing which is done; it's a thing which is done because it *is* done. Nor does it have something done to it because it's a thing which has something done to it; it's a thing which has something done to it because it *does* have something done to it. Don't you agree?

EUTHYPHRO: I do.

SOCRATES: And is the thing loved either a thing which is done or a thing which has something done to it by someone?

EUTHYPHRO: It certainly is.

SOCRATES: Is this example, then, the same as the earlier ones? It's not because it's a thing loved that it is loved by those who do love it. It's a thing loved because it *is* loved.

EUTHYPHRO: It must be.

SOCRATES: What then do we say about the holy, Euthyphro? d Isn't it just loved by all the gods, according to your definition?

EUTHYPHRO: Yes.

SOCRATES: Is the reason for this the fact that it is holy? Or is there some other reason?

EUTHYPHRO: No, this is the reason.

SOCRATES: So it is loved because it is holy, and not holy because it is loved?

EUTHYPHRO: Apparently.

SOCRATES: But it's because it is loved that it is a thing loved by the gods, and dear to the gods?

EUTHYPHRO: Of course.

SOCRATES: In which case, what is dear to the gods is not holy, nor is the holy dear to the gods, as you claim. They are two different things.

e EUTHYPHRO: Why is that, Socrates?

SOCRATES: Because we agree that the holy is loved because it is holy, and not holy because it is loved. Or don't we?

EUTHYPHRO: No, we do.

SOCRATES: And that what is dear to the gods is dear to the gods because it is loved by the gods — by this very fact of being loved by the gods. It is not loved because it is what is dear to the gods.

EUTHYPHRO: You are right.

SOCRATES: If what is dear to the gods and the holy were the same thing, Euthyphro, then if the holy was loved because it 11 was holy, and what is dear to the gods was loved because it was dear to the gods, and if what is dear to the gods was dear to the gods because it was loved by the gods, *then* the holy would be holy because it was loved. But as it is, you can see that the two terms are applied in opposite ways, because they are completely different from one another. One is lovable because it is loved; the other is loved because it is lovable. My guess is, Euthyphro, that when you were asked what exactly the holy is, you didn't want to reveal its essential being to me. So you told me one of its properties. You said the holy has the property of being loved b by all the gods. What it is, you haven't yet told me. So please, if you've no objection, don't keep me in the dark. Tell me again, starting at the beginning, what exactly the holy is that *makes* it loved by the gods, or gives it any of its properties. We're not going to disagree over those, after all. So tell me, without reservation, what the holy is and what the unholy is.

EUTHYPHRO: I can't explain to you what I mean, Socrates. Whatever definition we put forward seems to keep going round us in circles somehow. It won't stay in the place where we put it.

SOCRATES: The things you say are like the creations of my c ancestor Daedalus, Euthyphro. If I were the one saying them,

and putting them forward, you'd probably be laughing at me
because my verbal creations were running away from me – as
you'd expect, given my descent from him – and refusing to stay
where they were put. But as it is, the definitions are yours, so
you'll have to find some other reason for laughing at me. It's
your definitions which won't stay put, as you yourself admit.

EUTHYPHRO: Yes, it seems to me the things that are being said
are open to being laughed at in very much that kind of way,
Socrates. They *are* going round in circles, and they *won't* stay in
the same place. But I'm not the one responsible. I think you are
the Daedalus in this. If I had anything to do with it, they would d
stay where they were put.

SOCRATES: In that case, my friend, perhaps this is one way in
which I am more skilled in my art than he was in his. For him,
the only things which didn't stay put were his own creations.
For me it's not just my own works, apparently, but other
people's as well. And the thing about this skill of mine is that I
am clever despite myself. I'd give the wisdom of Daedalus *and*
the wealth of Tantalus, if only the argument would keep still e
and settle down in one place. Well, enough of that. You strike
me as being a bit lazy, so I'm going to do my best to help you
teach me about what is holy. Don't give up yet. See whether
you think that everything holy must necessarily be just.

EUTHYPHRO: Yes, I do.

SOCRATES: In which case, is everything which is just, holy? Or is
everything which is holy just, whereas the just is not all holy – 12
part of it being holy and part of it something else?

EUTHYPHRO: I can't keep up with the argument, Socrates.

SOCRATES: And yet you're younger than I am – and wiser! But as
I say, wealth – of wisdom – has made you lazy. Come on, apply
yourself! It's not difficult to understand what I mean. I mean the
opposite of what the poet said, when he wrote:

> With the creator Zeus,
> Who caused all things to grow, he will not fight.
> Where fear is, there will reverence be found.   b

I disagree with the poet. Shall I tell you in what way?

EUTHYPHRO: Please do.

SOCRATES: I don't think it's a question of 'Where fear is, there will reverence be found.' I think a lot of people fear illness, poverty, and any number of things like that. They fear them. They don't feel any reverence for the things they fear. Don't you agree?

EUTHYPHRO: Absolutely.

SOCRATES: But I *do* think that where there is reverence, there also is fear. Doesn't anyone who feels reverence and awe about
c something feel fear as well? Isn't he afraid of getting a reputation for wickedness?

EUTHYPHRO: Yes, he is.

SOCRATES: So it isn't right to say 'Where fear is, there will reverence be found.' It should be 'Where there is reverence, there also is fear', not 'Wherever there is fear there is always reverence.' Fear is more widespread than reverence, I think. Reverence is a subset of fear, in the way that odd is a subset of number. You don't say 'Where number is, there will odd be found', but you do say 'Where odd is, there will number be found.' You must follow now, surely?

EUTHYPHRO: I certainly do.

SOCRATES: Well, my question a few moments ago was the same
d kind of thing. Is it: 'Where justice is, there will holiness be found'? Or is it: 'Where holiness is, there justice will be found, but where justice is, there holiness will not always be found'? Is the holy a subset of the just? Are we going to say that, or something different, do you think?

EUTHYPHRO: That. You seem to me to have got it right.

SOCRATES: See what follows, then. If the holy is part of the just, it looks as if we need to find out what *kind* of part of the just the holy is. Now, if you were asking me about one of the things we've just been talking about – what part of number the even is, for example, and what an even number in fact is – I would say it's a number which is not scalene, but isosceles. Don't you agree?

EUTHYPHRO: I do.

SOCRATES: Now it's your turn. Try and instruct me in the same e
way. Tell me what part of the just the holy is, so that I can tell
Meletus to stop treating me unjustly and prosecuting me for
impiety, since I have now received a satisfactory education from
you in piety and holiness and their opposites.

EUTHYPHRO: Very well, Socrates. In my opinion, that part of the
just which has to do with looking after the gods is pious and
holy. The part which looks after men forms the remaining part
of justice.

SOCRATES: That sounds to me like a good answer, Euthyphro.
But there's still one small detail I need from you. This 'looking 13
after' you mention — I don't at the moment understand that.
Presumably you don't mean that looking after the gods is like
looking after other things. After all, we do *use* the word like
that. Take horses, for example. We say not everyone can look
after them — only a horseman. Or don't we say that?

EUTHYPHRO: No, we certainly do.

SOCRATES: Horsemanship consists, I take it, in looking after
horses.

EUTHYPHRO: Yes.

SOCRATES: Nor does everybody know how to look after dogs —
only a master of hounds.

EUTHYPHRO: That is so.

SOCRATES: His art consists in looking after dogs, I imagine.

EUTHYPHRO: Yes.   b

SOCRATES: And the herdsman's in looking after cattle.

EUTHYPHRO: Exactly.

SOCRATES: And holiness and piety in looking after the gods,
Euthyphro? Is that what you're saying?

EUTHYPHRO: It is.

SOCRATES: In which case, does all looking after have the same
effect? The kind of thing I mean is this. Looking after is in some

way for the good or benefit of the thing looked after. When horses are looked after by the art of horsemanship, for example, you can see that it does them some good. They become better, don't you think?

EUTHYPHRO: I do.

SOCRATES: The same, I take it, with dogs and the art of the
c master of hounds. Or cows and the herdsman's art. Or anything else. Or do you think that looking after is harmful to the thing looked after?

EUTHYPHRO: Good heavens, no!

SOCRATES: Beneficial, then?

EUTHYPHRO: Of course.

SOCRATES: In that case, is holiness too, since it looks after the gods, a question of helping the gods and making the gods better? And you yourself – would you agree that when you do something holy, the effect is to make one of the gods better?

EUTHYPHRO: Good heavens, no!

SOCRATES: No, I don't for a moment imagine that's what you're saying, Euthyphro. Far from it. That's why I asked you what
d exactly you meant by 'looking after' the gods, since I didn't think *this* was the kind of looking after you meant.

EUTHYPHRO: Quite right, Socrates. It's not the kind I mean.

SOCRATES: Well, then. What kind of looking after the gods would holiness be, in that case?

EUTHYPHRO: The kind practised by slaves, Socrates, when they look after their masters.

SOCRATES: Some sort of service to the gods, by the sound of it.

EUTHYPHRO: Exactly.

SOCRATES: Very well. Take the art which is a service to doctors. In the achievement of what end is it in fact of service? Don't you think it's health?

EUTHYPHRO: Yes, I do.

SOCRATES: What about the art which serves the shipbuilder? In e the achievement of what end is that of service?

EUTHYPHRO: That's obvious, Socrates. In the building of a ship.

SOCRATES: And the art which serves the builder? In the building of a house, presumably?

EUTHYPHRO: Yes.

SOCRATES: Pray, tell me, then. This art which is of service to the gods – in the achievement of what end would it be of service? You obviously know, since you claim to be an authority on religious matters.

EUTHYPHRO: And rightly, Socrates.

SOCRATES: Then tell me, in heaven's name, what exactly *is* this wonderful result which is achieved by the gods, using us as their servants?

EUTHYPHRO: They bring about all sorts of good results, Socrates.

SOCRATES: So do generals, my friend. But you'd find it easy 14 enough to summarise their achievement, for all that. You'd say generals achieve victory in war, wouldn't you?

EUTHYPHRO: Of course.

SOCRATES: Farmers too, I think, bring about all sorts of good results. But the summary of their achievement is that it is food from the earth.

EUTHYPHRO: It certainly is.

SOCRATES: What about all those good results the gods bring about? What is the summary of *their* achievement?

EUTHYPHRO: I told you, Socrates, a short while back, that a detailed understanding of the way all these things are was rather b a large undertaking. I *can* tell you in general, however, that if you know how to say and do what is pleasing to the gods in your prayers and sacrifices, then that is holiness. This is the kind of behaviour which keeps private households and whole states safe. The opposite of what pleases them is impiety, which overturns and destroys everything.

SOCRATES: You *could* give me the summary I asked for if you

chose, Euthyphro, without being nearly so long-winded. The
c trouble is, you don't want to tell me. That's obvious. It was on
the tip of your tongue just now, but you turned your back on it.
If you'd given me that answer, I would by now have learnt from
you, to my complete satisfaction, what holiness is. As it is, since
the lover has no choice but to follow his beloved wherever he
leads, let me ask you again. What is your definition of the holy
and holiness? Aren't you saying it is some sort of knowledge of
sacrifice and prayer?

EUTHYPHRO: Yes, I am.

SOCRATES: And is sacrifice a gift to the gods, and prayer a request
for something from the gods?

EUTHYPHRO: Precisely, Socrates.

d SOCRATES: On this definition, then, the holy would be a
knowledge of asking the gods for things and giving things to
them.

EUTHYPHRO: Excellent, Socrates. You have grasped what I
meant.

SOCRATES: I'm an admirer of your wisdom, my friend. I keep
my eyes fixed firmly on it, so that nothing you say will be lost
on me. Now, tell me about this service to the gods. You say it's
asking them for things and giving them things?

EUTHYPHRO: I do.

SOCRATES: Well, wouldn't the best way of asking be to ask them
for what we want from them?

EUTHYPHRO: Of course.

e SOCRATES: Equally, wouldn't the best way of giving be to offer
them in return a gift of what they do in fact want from us? It
wouldn't be much of an art, presumably, for the donor to
present the recipient with something he had no need of.

EUTHYPHRO: True, Socrates.

SOCRATES: Some sort of trader's art, then, holiness – for gods and
men, Euthyphro, in their dealings with one another.

EUTHYPHRO: Yes, a trader's art, if that's what you prefer to call it.

SOCRATES: I only prefer it if in fact it is true. Tell me, though, what is the actual benefit to the gods of the presents they get from us? What they give is plain to anyone. Every good thing 15 we possess is their gift to us. But the things they get from us, what use are they to them? Or are we so greedy in our trading with them that we receive every good thing from them, while they receive nothing from us?

EUTHYPHRO: Are you suggesting the gods get some benefit from the offerings they receive from us, Socrates?

SOCRATES: Well, if they don't, what *would* these gifts of ours to the gods be, Euthyphro?

EUTHYPHRO: What you'd expect. Respect, honour, and as I said a little while ago, what gives them pleasure.

SOCRATES: So the holy is what gives pleasure to the gods, b Euthyphro, not what is useful to them or loved by them.

EUTHYPHRO: No, I think it is above all loved by them.

SOCRATES: In which case, apparently, the holy turns out once again to be what is loved by the gods.

EUTHYPHRO: Precisely.

SOCRATES: How can you say that, and still sound surprised when your definitions clearly won't keep still, but start moving around? Do you blame me, and call me Daedalus for making them move, when you yourself are far more cunning than Daedalus in getting things to go round in circles? Don't you realise our definition has gone round in a circle and come back to where we started? Presumably you remember it being clear to c us earlier on that the holy and what is dear to the gods were not the same. They were different from one another. Or don't you remember?

EUTHYPHRO: No. I do remember.

SOCRATES: And don't you realise you are now saying that what is loved by the gods is the holy? But this is just the same as what is dear to the gods, isn't it?

EUTHYPHRO: It certainly is.

SOCRATES: So either our agreement then was wrong, or if that was right, then our present definition is wrong.

EUTHYPHRO: It looks like it.

SOCRATES: We must go back to the beginning, in that case, and ask again what the holy is. I'm not prepared to give in without
d finding out. So don't turn me down. Apply your mind in all seriousness, and tell me the truth. You know the answer, if anyone on earth does, but you're like Proteus, and I must not let go of you until you answer. If you didn't have a clear idea of the holy and the unholy, you couldn't possibly have set about prosecuting your father, who is an old man, on a charge of murder, on behalf of a mere tenant. Your fear of the gods would have kept you from taking the chance that you might turn out to be acting incorrectly. And you'd have been worried about public opinion. But as it is, you think you know perfectly well
e what the holy and the unholy are, I'm sure of it. So tell me, most excellent Euthyphro. Don't hide your thoughts on the subject from me.

EUTHYPHRO: Some other time, Socrates. I'm due somewhere else, and I have to go.

SOCRATES: Are you leaving, my friend? How can you? Are you going to disappoint the great hopes I had? I thought I could learn about the holy and the unholy from you, and in that way escape from Meletus' accusation, when I proved to him that on
16 matters of religion I had learnt wisdom from Euthyphro – that I no longer made things up as I went along or held revolutionary views on the subject, and that indeed I was going to be a better person for the rest of my life.

APOLOGY

I don't know what effect my accusers have had on you,
Athenians. As far as I'm concerned, they made me all but forget
the position I am in, they spoke so plausibly. And yet to all
intents and purposes there wasn't a word of truth in what they
said. Of their many lies, one in particular filled me with
astonishment. They said you should be careful to avoid being
led astray by my skill in speaking. They weren't in the least b
embarrassed at the prospect of being immediately proved wrong
by my actual performance, when it becomes clear that I'm not
in the least skilled in speaking. That was what I found the most
shameless thing about their behaviour – unless of course by
'skilled in speaking' they mean someone who speaks the truth. If
that's what they mean, then I would agree that I'm in a different
class from them as an orator.

Anyway, these people, as I say, have told you little or nothing
that was true, whereas from me you will hear the whole truth –
certainly not a piece of polished rhetoric like theirs, Athenians,
with its words and phrases so cleverly arranged. No, the speech c
you're going to hear from me will use everyday language
arranged in a straightforward way – after all, I have confidence
in the justice of what I have to say – so I hope no one is
expecting anything different. And I shall tell the truth, because it
wouldn't be appropriate to appear before you at my age making
up stories like a schoolboy.

However, there's one important request and concession I am
going to ask of you, Athenians. If you hear me making my
defence in the same language I generally use in the city, among
people doing business – where many of you have heard me –
and elsewhere, do not be surprised on that account, or start d
interrupting. The reason for it is this. This is the first time I have
ever appeared in court, though I am now seventy years of age.
The kind of speaking practised here is, quite simply, foreign to
me. Imagine I really were a foreigner. You wouldn't hold it

against me, presumably, if I spoke in the dialect and manner in
18 which I had been brought up. In the same way now, I make this
request – justified, in my view – that you pay no attention to
the manner in which I speak, be it inferior or superior. Please
consider one point only, and focus your attention on that. Is
there any justice in what I have to say, or not? That, after all, is
the juryman's job. The speaker's is to tell the truth.

First of all, then, Athenians, I am entitled to defend myself
against the earliest false accusations made against me, and against
my earliest accusers. Only then can I defend myself against the
more recent falsehoods and my present accusers. That's because
b there have been many people, over the years, making accusations about me to you – and speaking not a word of truth. I fear
them more than I fear Anytus and his supporters, dangerous
though they are as well. But the earlier ones are more
dangerous, gentlemen. They took you in hand from childhood,
for the most part, and tried to win you over, making accusations
every bit as false as these today. They told you there was this
man Socrates, an intellectual, a thinker about the heavens, an
expert on everything under the earth, a man who could turn the
c weaker argument into the stronger. These people, Athenians,
the ones who have saddled me with this reputation, are my most
dangerous accusers. And the reason for that is that those who
listen to them think that students of these subjects do not
recognise the gods. There are also a great many of these
accusers, and they've been accusing me for a long time now.
And thirdly, they were speaking to you at the age when you
were most likely to believe them, when many of you were
children or adolescents. Quite simply, they were prosecuting in
an uncontested case, since there was no one there to answer
their charges.

What is particularly unfair is that I cannot even know, or tell
d you, their names – unless maybe one of them is a writer of
comedies. But all those who tried to influence you out of spite
and malice, together with those who were trying to influence
others because they were genuinely convinced themselves – all
these accusers are very hard to deal with. It's not possible to call
any of them as a witness here, or cross-examine them. I just
have to make my defence like someone shadow-boxing, and

conduct my cross-examination with no one there to answer. So I hope you will accept my claim that I have two sets of accusers – the ones who have just now brought this case against me, and the ones from way back, the ones I have been telling you about. Please believe also that I must make my defence against this *e* second set first. After all, you heard their accusations at an earlier age, and on many more occasions, than you heard the later ones.

Very well. I must make my defence, Athenians, and try to remove from your minds, in the very brief time available, the 19 prejudice which you have so long held. I hope that is how things will turn out, provided it really *is* the best outcome for you and for me, and that I shall achieve something by my defence. But I think it is difficult, and I am well aware of the magnitude of the task. Anyway, let it turn out as god wills, I must obey the law, and make my defence.

Let us go back to the beginning, then, and see what the accusation is which has created this prejudice against me – the *b* prejudice Meletus was counting on, presumably, when he brought this case against me. What exactly did its originators say? We ought really to read out a sworn statement from them, just like the prosecution's. 'Socrates is guilty of being a busybody. He enquires into things under the earth and in the heavens, and turns the weaker argument into the stronger, and he teaches these same things to other people.' That's roughly *c* how it goes. You saw it for yourselves in Aristophanes' comedy. You saw a Socrates there, swinging round and round, claiming he was walking on air, and spouting a whole lot of other drivel on subjects about which I make not the slightest claim to knowledge. Not that I have anything against knowledge of this kind, if anyone is an expert on such subjects. I hope Meletus will never bring enough cases against me to reduce me to that. No, it's just that I myself have no share in such knowledge. Once again, I can call most of you as witnesses. I'm sure you can *d* explain, and make the position clear to one another, those of you who have ever heard me talking – and a lot of you come in that category. Tell one another then if any of you has ever heard me breathe so much as a word on such topics. That will help you to see that the rest of what is generally said about me has as little foundation.

No, there's no truth in these stories. And if anyone has told you I undertake to educate people, or that I make money out of it, there's equally little truth in that either. Mind you, if anyone *can* educate people – as Gorgias from Leontini can, or Prodicus from Ceos, or Hippias from Elis – then that seems to me to be a fine thing. Any of these men, gentlemen, can go to any city and persuade the young men – who are at liberty to spend their time, free of charge, with whichever of their fellow-citizens they choose – to abandon the company of those fellow-citizens and spend time with him instead – *and* pay money to do so, and be grateful into the bargain. Come to that, there's even one of them here in Athens, a wise man from Paros. I found out he was staying here when I ran into Callias, the son of Hipponicus, the man who has paid more money to sophists than everyone else put together. So I asked him – you know he has two sons – 'Callias,' I said, 'if your sons were colts or calves, we'd be able to find and employ someone to look after them, someone who would turn them into outstanding examples of their particular species. And this person would be a trainer or farmer of some kind. But as it is, they aren't colts or calves. They are men. Whom do you propose to find to look after them? Who is expert in this kind of excellence – the excellence of a human being and a citizen? I imagine, since you have sons, you must have thought about this question. Is there someone,' I asked him, 'or not?' 'There certainly is,' he said. 'Who is he?' I asked. 'Where does he come from? What does he charge?' 'Evenus,' he said. 'He's from Paros, Socrates, and he charges 500 drachmas.' I took my hat off to Evenus, if he really did have this ability, and yet taught for so reasonable a fee. *I* wouldn't. I'd start giving myself airs and become extremely choosy, if I had this kind of knowledge. But I don't have it, Athenians.

I can imagine one of you interrupting me and saying, 'That's all very well, Socrates; but what *do* you do? Where have all these prejudices against you come from? I take it all this gossip and rumour about you is not the result of your behaving just like anyone else. You must be doing *something* out of the ordinary. Tell us what it is, so we can avoid jumping to conclusions about you.' This seems to me to be a fair question, so I'll try and explain to you what it is that has given me my reputation and created the prejudice against me. Give me a hearing. It may seem to some of you that I am not being serious, but I promise you, every word I say will be the truth. I have gained this reputation, Athenians, as a direct result of a kind of wisdom. What sort of wisdom? The sort we might perhaps call human wisdom. In fact, if we're talking about this kind of wisdom, I probably *am* wise. The men I mentioned just now may well be wise with some more–than–human wisdom; I don't know how else to describe it. It's not a wisdom *I* know anything about. Anyone who says I do is lying, in an attempt to increase the prejudice against me.

Please don't interrupt me, Athenians, even if you find what I say a bit boastful. The claim I am about to make is not *my* claim. I shall appeal to a reliable authority. I shall call the god at Delphi to give evidence to you about my wisdom. He can tell you if I really do possess any, and what it is like. You remember Chaerephon, I expect. He was a friend of mine from an early age, and a friend of most of you. He shared your recent exile, and returned from exile with you. You know what Chaerephon was like, how impetuous he was when he set about something. And sure enough, he went to Delphi one day, and went so far as to put this question to the oracle – I repeat, gentlemen, please don't interrupt. He asked if there was anyone wiser than me. And the priestess of Apollo replied that there was no one wiser. His brother here will give evidence to you about this, since Chaerephon himself is dead.

Let me remind you of my reason for telling you this. I'm trying to show you the origin of the prejudice against me. When I heard the priestess's reply, my reaction was this: 'What on earth is the god saying? What is his hidden meaning? I'm well aware that I have no wisdom, great or small. So what can he mean by saying I'm so wise? He can't be lying; he's not allowed to.' I spent a long time wondering what he could mean. And finally, with great reluctance, I decided to verify his claim. What I did was this: I approached one of those who seemed to be wise, thinking that there, if anywhere, I could prove the reply wrong, and say quite clearly to the oracle, 'This man is wiser than I am, whereas you said that I was the wisest.' So I examined this man – there's no need for me to mention his name, let's just say he was a politician – and the result of my examination, Athenians, and of my conversations with him, was this. I decided that although the man seemed to many people, and above all to himself, to be wise, in reality he was not. I tried to demonstrate to him that he thought he was wise, but actually

d was not, and as a result I made an enemy of him, and of many of those present. To myself, as I left him, I reflected: 'Here is one man less wise than I. In all probability neither of us knows anything worth knowing. But he thinks he knows when he doesn't, whereas I, given that I don't in fact know, am at least aware that I don't know. Apparently, therefore, I am wiser than him in just this one small detail, that when I don't know something, I don't think I know it either.' From him I went to another man, one of those who seemed wiser than the first. I

e came to exactly the same conclusion, and made an enemy of him and many others besides.

After that I began approaching people in a systematic way. I could see, with alarm and regret, that I was making enemies, yet I thought it was essential to take the god seriously. So on I had to go, in my enquiry into the meaning of the oracle, to

22 everyone who seemed to have any knowledge. And I swear to you, Athenians – after all, I am bound to tell you the truth – what I found was this. Those with the highest reputations seemed to me to be pretty nearly the most useless, if I was trying to find out the meaning of what the god had said, whereas others, who appeared of less account, were a much better bet when it came to thinking sensibly. I can best give an account of my quest by likening it to a set of labours. And all, as it turned out, to satisfy myself of the accuracy of the oracle.

After the politicians I went to the writers – writers of plays

b and songs, and the rest of them. That would be an open-and-shut case, I thought. I should easily show myself up as less wise than them. So I took to reading their works, the ones which struck me as showing the greatest skill in composition, and asking them what they meant. I hoped to learn from them. Well, I'm embarrassed to tell you the truth, gentlemen, but I must tell you. Practically anyone present could have given a better account than they did of the works they had themselves written. As a result, I quickly came to a decision about the

writers too, in their turn. I realised that their achievements are
not the result of wisdom, but of natural talent and inspiration. c
Like fortune-tellers and clairvoyants, who also say many striking
things, but have no idea at all of the meaning of what they say.
Writers, I felt, were clearly in the same position. Moreover, I
could see that their works encouraged them to think they were
the wisest of men in other areas where they were not wise. So I
left them too feeling that I had got the better of them in the
same way as I had got the better of the politicians.

Finally I went to the craftsmen. I was well aware that I knew
virtually nothing, and confident that I would find much fine d
knowledge in them. Nor was I disappointed. They *did* know
things which I didn't know; in this respect they *were* wiser than I
was. However, our good friends the skilled workmen seemed
also to me, Athenians, to have the same failing as the writers.
Each one, because of his skill in practising his trade, thought
himself extremely wise in other matters of importance as well.
And this presumptuousness of theirs seemed to me to obscure
the wisdom they did have. So I asked myself, on behalf of the e
oracle, whether I should accept being the way I was – without
any of their wisdom or any of their foolishness – or whether I
ought to possess both the qualities they possessed. The answer I
gave myself and the oracle was that it was best for me to remain
as I was.

This survey, Athenians, has aroused much hostility against me,
of the most damaging and serious kind. The result has been a 23
great deal of prejudice, and in particular this description of me as
being wise. That's because the people who were present on
such occasions think I'm an expert myself on those subjects in
which I demolish the claims of others. The reality, gentlemen, is
that in all probability god is wise, and what he means by his
reply to Chaerephon is that human wisdom is of little or no
value. When he refers to the man here before you – to
Socrates – and goes out of his way to use my name, he is using
me as an example, as if he were saying: 'That man is the wisest b
among you, mortals, who realises, as Socrates does, that he
doesn't really amount to much when it comes to wisdom.' That
is why, to this day, I go round investigating and enquiring, as
the god would have me do, if I think anyone – Athenian or

foreigner – is wise. And when I find he is not, then I support
the god by demonstrating that he is not wise. My preoccupation
with this task has left me no time worth speaking of to take any
part in public life or family life. Instead I live in extreme
c poverty, as a result of my service to the god.

Another problem is that young people follow me of their own
free will. Those with most time at their disposal, the sons of the
rich. They love listening to people being cross-examined. They
often imitate me themselves, and set about cross-examining
others. Nor do I imagine they have any difficulty in finding
people who think they know something when in fact they
know little or nothing. The result is that the victims of their
cross-examination are angry with me, rather than themselves.
d They say Socrates is some sort of criminal, and that he has a bad
influence on the young. When you ask them what I do and
what I teach that makes me a criminal, they can't answer. They
don't know. But since they don't want to lose face, they come
out with the standard accusations made against all philosophers,
the stuff about 'things in heaven and things under the earth', and
'not recognising the gods' and 'turning the weaker argument
into the stronger'.

The truth, I think, they would refuse to admit, which is that
they have been shown up as pretenders to knowledge who
really know nothing. Since they are ambitious, energetic and
e numerous, and since they speak forcibly and persuasively about
me, they have been filling your ears for some time now, and
most vigorously, with their attacks on me. That's what Meletus
relied on when he brought this charge against me, with Anytus
and Lycon – Meletus taking offence as a representative of the
poets, Anytus representing the craftsmen and politicians, and
24 Lycon the orators. The result, as I said at the beginning, is that it
would surprise me if I were able to remove from your minds, in
so short a time, a prejudice which has grown so strong. This is
the truth, Athenians, I assure you. I speak with absolutely no
concealment or reservation. I'm pretty sure it is this way of
speaking which makes me unpopular. My unpopularity is the
proof that I am speaking the truth, that this *is* the prejudice
b against me, and these *are* the reasons for it. You can enquire into
these matters – now or later – and you will find them to be so.

So much for the accusations made by my first group of accusers. I hope you will find what I've said a satisfactory defence against them. Now let me try and defend myself against Meletus, that excellent patriot (as he claims), and my more recent accusers. Let's treat them as a separate prosecution, and consider in its turn the charge brought by them. It runs something like this. It says Socrates is guilty of being a bad influence on the young, and not recognising the gods whom the state recognises, but practising a new religion of the supernatural. c That's what the charge consists of. So let's examine this charge point by point.

He says I am guilty of having a bad influence on the young. But *I* claim, Athenians, that Meletus is guilty of playing games with what is deadly serious. He is too quick to bring people to trial, pretending to be serious and care about things to which he has never given a moment's thought. That this is the truth, I will try to prove to you as well. Come now, Meletus, tell me this. I take it you regard the well-being of the young as of the d utmost importance?

I do.

In that case, please tell these people who it is who is a good influence on the young. Obviously you must know, since you're so concerned about it. You've tracked down the man you say is a bad influence – me – and you're bringing me here before these people and accusing me. So come on, tell them who is a good influence. Point out to them who it is. You see, Meletus? You are silent. You have nothing to say. Don't you think that's a disgrace, and a sufficient proof of what I am saying – that you haven't given it any thought? Come on, my friend, tell us. Who is a good influence?

The laws.

Brilliant! But that's not what I'm asking. The question is what e man – who will of course start off with just this knowledge, the laws.

These men, Socrates, the members of the jury.

Really, Meletus? These men are capable of educating the young and being a good influence on them?

They certainly are.

All of them? Or are some capable, and others not?

All of them.

How remarkably fortunate! No shortage of benefactors there, then. How about the spectators in court? Do they have a good
25 influence, or not?

Yes, they do too.

What about the members of the council?

Yes, the members of the council as well.

But surely, Meletus, the people in the assembly – the citizens meeting *as* the assembly – surely they don't have a bad influence on the young? Don't they too, all of them, have a good influence?

Yes, they do too.

In which case, it looks as if the entire population of Athens – myself excepted – makes the young into upright citizens. I alone am a bad influence. Is that what you mean?

Yes, that's exactly what I mean.

That's certainly a great failing to charge me with. Answer me this, though. Do you think the situation is the same with horses
b as well? Do the people who are good for them make up the entire population, and is there just one person who has a harmful effect on them? Isn't it the exact opposite? Isn't there just one person, or very few people – trainers of horses – capable of doing them any good? Don't most people, if they spend time with horses, or have anything to do with them, have a harmful effect on them? Isn't that the situation, Meletus, both with horses and with all other living creatures? Well, it certainly is, whether you and Anytus deny it or admit it. After all, it would be a piece of great good fortune for the young if only one person has a bad influence on them, and everyone else has a
c good influence. No, Meletus. You show quite clearly that you have never cared in the slightest for the young. You reveal your own lack of interest quite plainly, since you've never given a moment's thought to the things you're prosecuting me for.

Another point. Tell us honestly, Meletus, is it better to live with good fellow-citizens or with bad? Answer, can't you? It's not a difficult question. Isn't it true that bad citizens do some harm to those who are their neighbours at any particular time, while good citizens do some good?

Yes, of course.

That being so, does anyone choose to be harmed by those d close to him rather than helped by them? Answer, there's a good fellow. Besides, the law requires you to answer. Is there anyone who chooses to be harmed?

No, of course not.

Well, then. You bring me to court for being a bad influence on the young and making them worse people. Are you saying I do this intentionally or unintentionally?

Intentionally, I'm sure of it.

Really, Meletus? How odd. Are you at your age so much wiser than me at mine? Are you aware that bad people generally have a harmful effect on those they come into contact with, and that good people have a good effect? And have I reached such a e height of stupidity as not even to realise that if I make one of my neighbours a worse man, I am likely to come to some harm at his hands? And is the result that I intentionally do such great damage as you describe? On this point I don't believe you, Meletus. And neither does anyone else, I suspect.

No, either I am not a bad influence on the young, or if I do have a bad influence, I do so unintentionally. Either way you are wrong. And if I have a bad influence unintentionally, it is 26 not our custom to bring people here to court for errors of this sort, but to take them on one side and instruct them privately, pointing out their mistakes. Obviously, if I am taught, I shall stop doing this thing I don't realise I *am* doing. But you avoided spending time with me and instructing me. You refused to do it. Instead you bring me here to court, where it is our custom to bring those who need punishment, not those who need to learn.

I needn't go on, Athenians. It must now be clear, as I've said, that Meletus has never given the slightest thought to these b matters. All the same, Meletus, tell us this: *in what way* do you claim I'm a bad influence on the young? Isn't it obvious I do it in the way described in the charge you've brought against me — by teaching them not to recognise the gods the city recognises, but to practise this new religion of the supernatural instead? Isn't that your claim, that it's by teaching them these things that I have a bad influence?

Yes, that certainly is exactly what I claim.

Well then, Meletus, in the name of these gods we are now

talking about, make yourself a little clearer, both to me and to
c these gentlemen here, since *I* at least cannot understand you. Do
you mean I teach them to accept that there are *some* gods – not
the gods the state accepts, but other gods? In that case I myself
must also accept that there are gods, so I am not a complete
atheist, and am not guilty on that count. Is this what you charge
me with, accepting other gods? Or are you saying that I don't
myself recognise any gods at all, and that I teach these beliefs to
others?

Yes, that is what I am saying. You don't recognise any gods
at all.

d Meletus, you're beyond belief. What can possess you to say
that? Don't I accept that the sun and moon are gods, in the same
way everyone else does?

Heavens, no. He says the sun is a stone, gentlemen of the jury,
and that the moon is made of earth.

Is it Anaxagoras you think you're accusing, my dear Meletus?
Do you have such contempt for these men here? Do you think
them so illiterate as to be unaware that the works of Anaxagoras
of Clazomenae are stuffed full of speculations of that sort? And
do the young really learn these things from me, when as often as
not there are books on sale, for a drachma at the very most, in
e the Orchestra, in the Agora? They can laugh at Socrates if he
claims these views as his own – especially such eccentric views.
However, as god is your witness, is that your view of me? Do I
not accept the existence of any god at all?

As god is my witness, none.

What you say is unbelievable, Meletus. Even, I think, to
yourself. This man here strikes me as an arrogant lout, Athenians. His prosecution of me is prompted entirely by arrogance,
27 loutishness and youth. It's as if he were setting a trick question
to test me: 'Will Socrates the wise realise I am playing with
words and contradicting myself, or will I deceive him and the
others who hear what I say?' He certainly seems to me to be
contradicting himself in his accusation. He might as well say
'Socrates is guilty of not recognising the gods, but recognising
the gods instead.' And that is not a serious proposition.

Please join me, gentlemen, in examining the reasons why I
think this is what his accusation amounts to. You, Meletus,

answer us. And all of you, as I asked you at the beginning, remember not to interrupt me if I construct my argument in my b usual way.

Is there anyone in the world, Meletus, who accepts the existence of human activity, but not of human beings? He must answer, gentlemen. Don't allow him to keep making all these interruptions. Is there anyone who denies horses, but accepts equine activity? Or denies the existence of players of the pipes, but accepts pipe-playing? No, my very good friend, there isn't. If you refuse to answer, then I'll say it – to you and everyone else present here. But do answer my next question: is there anyone who accepts the activity of the supernatural, but denies c supernatural beings?

No, there isn't.

How kind of you. Forced to answer, against your will, by these people here. Very well, then. You claim that I practise and teach a religion of the supernatural – whether of a new or conventional kind – so I do at least, on your own admission, accept the existence of the supernatural. You even swore to it, on oath, in your indictment. But if I accept the supernatural, it must necessarily follow that I accept the existence of super-natural beings as well. Isn't that right? Yes, it is. I take your silence for agreement. And don't we regard supernatural beings d as either gods or the children of gods? Yes or no?

We certainly do.

In that case, if I accept supernatural beings – as you admit – and if supernatural beings are gods of some sort, then you can see what I mean when I say you're setting trick questions and playing with words, claiming first that I *don't* believe in gods, and then again that I *do* believe in gods, since I do believe in supernatural beings. Or again, if supernatural beings are some form of illegitimate children of gods – born of nymphs or of some of the other mothers they are said to be born from – who on earth could believe that there are children of gods, but no gods? It would be as absurd as saying you believed there were e such things as mules, the offspring of horses and donkeys, but didn't believe there were horses and donkeys. No, Meletus, the only possible explanation for your bringing this accusation against me is that you wanted to test us – and that you didn't have any genuine offence to charge me with. There's no conceivable way you could persuade anyone in the world with a grain of intelligence that the person who believes in the supernatural does not also believe in the divine, or that the same

28 person again does not believe in supernatural beings, divine beings and heroes.

Well, enough of this, Athenians. I don't think it takes much of a defence to show that in the terms of Meletus' indictment I am not guilty. What I have said so far should be enough. There remains what I said in the earlier part of my speech, which is that there is strong and widespread hostility towards me. Be in no doubt that this is true. It is this which will convict me – if it *does* convict me. Not Meletus, not Anytus, but the prejudice and malice of the many. What has convicted many good men

b before me will, I think, convict again. There's no danger of its stopping at me.

That being so, you might ask: 'Well, Socrates, aren't you ashamed of living a life which has resulted in your now being on trial for your life?' I would answer you, quite justifiably, 'You are wrong, sir, if you think that a man who is worth anything at all should take into account the chances of life and death. No, the only thing he should think about, when he acts, is whether he is acting rightly or wrongly, and whether this is the behaviour of a good man or a bad man. If we accept your

c argument, then those of the demigods who died at Troy would have been sorry creatures – and none more so than Achilles, the son of Thetis. He regarded danger as of no importance at all, compared with the threat of dishonour. When he was eager to kill Hector, his mother, who was a goddess, said something like this to him, I imagine: "My son, if you avenge the death of your friend Patroclus and kill Hector, you will yourself be killed, since death awaits you immediately after Hector." When Achilles heard this, he gave no thought to death or danger.

d What he feared much more was living as a coward, and not avenging his friends. "Let me die immediately," he said, "after making the wrongdoer pay the penalty, rather than remain here by the curved ships, a laughing-stock, like a clod of earth." You don't imagine *he* gave any thought to death or danger.'

That's the way of things, Athenians, it really is. Where a man takes up his position, in the belief that it is the best position – or where he is told to take up a position by his commanding officer – there he should stay, in my view, regardless of danger. He should not take death into account, or anything else apart from dishonour. As for me, when the commanders whom you e chose to command me told me to take up position at Potidaea and Amphipolis and Delium, on those occasions I stayed where they posted me, like anyone else, and risked death. Would it not have been very illogical of me, when *god* deployed me, as I thought and believed, to live my life as a philosopher, examining myself and others, then to be afraid of death – or anything else at all – and abandon my post? It would indeed be illogical, and in 29 that case you certainly *would* be fully justified in bringing me to court for not accepting the existence of the gods, since I disobey their oracle, and am afraid of death, and think I am wise when I am not. After all, gentlemen, that's just what the fear of death is – thinking we are wise when we are not – since it's a claim to know what we don't know.

For all anyone knows, death may in fact be the best thing in the world that can happen to a man. Yet men fear it as if they had certain knowledge that it is the greatest of all evils. This is b without doubt the most reprehensible folly – the folly of thinking we know what we don't know. As for me, gentlemen, perhaps here too – in this one particular – I *am* different from most people. And if I did claim to be in any way wiser than anyone else, it would be in this, that lacking any certain knowledge of what happens after death, I am also aware that I have no knowledge. But that it is evil and shameful to do wrong, and disobey one's superiors, divine or human – that I *do* know. Compared therefore with the evils which I know to be evils, I shall never fear, or try to avoid, what for all I know may turn out to be good.

Suppose you now acquit me, rejecting Anytus' argument that c either this case should not have been brought in the first place or, since it had been brought, that it was out of the question not to put me to death. He told you that if I got away with it, your sons would all start practising the teachings of Socrates, and be totally overwhelmed by my bad influence. Suppose your response to this was to say to me: 'Socrates, on this occasion we will not

do what Anytus wants. We acquit you – on this condition, however, that you give up spending your time in this enquiry, and give up the search for wisdom. If you are caught doing it
d again, you will be put to death.' Even if, then, to repeat, you were to acquit me on these conditions, I would say to you: 'I have the highest regard and affection for you, Athenians, but I will obey god rather than you. While I have breath and strength, I will not give up the search for wisdom. I will carry on nagging at you, and pointing out your errors to those of you I meet from day to day. I shall say, in my usual way, "My very good sir, you are a citizen of Athens, that great city, renowned for its wisdom and power. Are you not ashamed to care about money and how to make as much of it as possible, and about
e reputation and public recognition, while for wisdom and truth, and making your soul as good as it can possibly be, you do not care, and give no thought to these things at all?" And if any of you objects, and says he does care, I shall not just let him go, or walk away and leave him. No, I shall question him, cross-examine him, try to prove him wrong. And if I find he has not achieved a state of excellence, but still claims he has, then I shall
30 accuse him of undervaluing what is most important, and paying too much attention to what is less important.

'That is what I shall do for anyone I meet – young or old, foreigner or citizen – but especially for my fellow-citizens, since you are more closely related to me. That is what god tells me to do, I promise you, and I believe this service of mine to god is the most valuable asset you in this city have ever yet possessed. I spend my whole time going round trying to persuade both young and old among you not to spend your time or energy in
b caring about your bodies or about money, but rather in making your souls as good as possible. I tell you, "Money can not create a good soul, but a good soul can turn money – and everything else in private life and public life – into a good thing for men." If saying things like this is a bad influence on the young, then things like this must be harmful. But if anyone claims I say anything different from this, he is lying. With that in mind, Athenians,' I would say, 'either do what Anytus wants, or don't do it. Either acquit me or don't, knowing that even if I am to be
c put to death a thousand times over, I will not behave differently.'

Don't interrupt, Athenians. Please stick to what I asked you to do, which was not to interrupt what I say, but to give me a hearing. It will be in your interest to hear me, I think. Now, I have some more things to say which might cause an outcry among you, but please don't make a disturbance. I have just described the kind of man I am. If you put me to death, take my word for it, you will harm yourselves more than you will harm me. As for me, no harm can come to me from Meletus – or Anytus. He *cannot* injure me, since I don't think god allows a better man ever to be injured by a worse. Oh, I know he might d put me to death, possibly, or send me into exile, or deprive me of citizen rights. And perhaps *he* regards these as great evils – as I suppose others may too. However, *I* do not. I regard it as a much greater evil to do as he is doing now, attempting to put a man to death unjustly.

It follows, Athenians, that what I am doing here today is not what you might imagine. So far from defending myself, I am actually defending you. I don't want you to fail to recognise god's gift to you, and find me guilty. If you put me to death, e you won't easily find another like me. I have, almost literally, settled on the city at god's command. It's as if the city, to use a slightly absurd simile, were a horse – a large horse, high-mettled, but somewhat sluggish on account of its size and needing to be stung into action by some kind of horsefly. I think god has caused me to settle on the city as this horsefly, the sort that never stops, all day long, coming to rest on every part of you, stinging each one of you into action, persuading and 31 criticising each one of you. Another like me will not easily come your way, gentlemen, so if you take my advice you will spare me. You may very likely get annoyed with me, as people do when they are dozing and somebody wakes them up. And you might then swat me, as Anytus wants you to, and kill me quite easily. Then you could spend the rest of your lives asleep, unless god cared enough for you to send you someone else.

To convince yourselves that someone like me really is a gift from god to the city, look at things this way. Behaviour like b mine does not seem to be natural. I have completely neglected my own affairs, and allowed my family to be neglected, all these years, while I devoted myself to looking after your interests. I have approached each one of you individually, like a father or elder brother, and tried to persuade you to consider the good of your soul. If I made anything out of it, and charged a fee for this advice, there would be some sense in my doing it. But as it is, you can see for yourselves that although the prosecution accused me, in their unscrupulous way, of everything under the sun, there was one point on which they were not so unscrupulous as

c to produce any evidence. They didn't claim that I ever made any money, or asked for any. I can produce convincing evidence, I think, that I am telling the truth – namely my poverty.

It may perhaps seem odd that in my private life I go round interfering and giving people advice like this, without having the courage to come forward in public life before you, the people, and give advice on matters of public interest. The reason for this is what you have often heard me talking about, in all sorts of places – the kind of divine or supernatural sign that

d comes to me. Perhaps this was what Meletus was making fun of when he wrote out the charge against me. It started when I was a child, a kind of voice which comes to me, and when it comes, always stops me doing what I am just about to do. It never tells me what I *should* do. It is this which opposes my taking part in politics – and rightly opposes it, in my opinion. You can be sure, Athenians, that if I had tried in the past to go into politics, I would have been dead long ago, and been no use at all either

e to you or myself. Please don't be annoyed with me for speaking the truth. There's no one in the world who can get away with deliberately opposing you – or any other popular assembly – or trying to put a stop to all the unjust and unlawful things which

32 are done in politics. It is essential that the true fighter for justice, if he is to survive for even a short time, should remain a private individual and not go into public life.

I shall give you compelling evidence for this. Not words, but what you value, actions. Listen to things which have actually happened to me, and you will realise that I would never obey anyone if it was wrong to do so, simply through fear of dying. No, I would refuse to obey, even if it meant my death. What I am going to say now is the kind of boasting you often hear in the lawcourts, but it is true, for all that. I have never held any

public office in the city, Athenians, apart from being a member b
of the Council. It turned out that our tribe, Antiochis, formed
the standing committee when you decided, by a resolution of
the Council, to put on trial collectively the ten generals who
failed to pick up the survivors from the sea battle. This was
unconstitutional, as you afterwards all decided. On that occasion
I was the only member of the standing committee to argue
against you. I told you not to act unconstitutionally, and voted
against you. The politicians were all set to bring an immediate
action against me and have me arrested on the spot, and you
were encouraging them to do so, and shouting your approval,
but still I thought I ought to take my chance on the side of law c
and justice, rather than side with you, through fear of imprisonment or death, when you were proposing to act unjustly.

That was when the city was still a democracy. When the
oligarchy came to power, the Thirty in their turn sent for me,
with four others, and gave me the task of bringing Leon of
Salamis from his home in Salamis to the Council chamber, so
that he could be put to death. They often gave orders of this
kind, to all sorts of people, because they wanted to implicate as
many people as possible in their crimes. Again I demonstrated –
by what I did this time, rather than what I said – that my fear of d
death was, if you don't mind my saying so, negligible. What I
was concerned about, more than anything, was acting without
regard for justice or religion. I was not intimidated by the
Thirty's power – great though it was – into acting unjustly.
When we left the Council chamber, the other four went off to
Salamis and fetched Leon. I left and went home. I might perhaps
have been put to death for that, if their power had not been
brought to an end soon after. Of these events any number of
people will give evidence to you.   e

Do you think I would have survived all these years if I had
taken part in public life, and played the part a good man should
play, supporting what was just and attaching the highest
importance to it, as is right? Don't you believe it, Athenians.
Nor would anyone else in the world have survived. As for me, it
will be clear that throughout my life, if I have done anything at 33
all in public life, my character is as I have described – and in
private life the same. I was never at any time prepared to

tolerate injustice in anyone at all – certainly not in any of the
people my critics say were my pupils. I have never been
anyone's teacher, but equally I never said no to anyone, young
or old, who wanted to listen to me talking and pursuing my
quest. Nor do I talk if I'm paid, and not talk if I'm not paid. I
b make myself available to rich and poor alike, so they can
question me and listen, if anyone feels like it, to what I say in
reply. And if any of these people turn out well or badly, I
cannot legitimately be held responsible. I never promised any of
them any knowledge, nor did I teach them. If anyone claims he
ever learnt or heard anything from me privately, beyond what
anyone else learnt or heard, I can assure you he is lying.

Why then do some people like spending so much of their
c time with me? You have heard the answer to that, Athenians. I
have told you the whole truth. They like hearing the cross-
examination of those who think they are wise when they are
not. After all, it *is* quite entertaining. For me, as I say, this is a
task imposed by god, through prophecies and dreams and in
every way in which divine destiny has ever imposed any task on
a man. All this is the truth, Athenians, and easily tested. If I
d really am a bad influence on some of the young, and have been
a bad influence on others in the past, and if some of them, as
they have grown older, have realised that I gave them bad
advice at some point when they were young, they ought to
come forward now, I'd have thought, to accuse me and punish
me. And if they weren't prepared to do so themselves, some of
the members of their families – fathers, brothers or other close
relatives – ought now to remember, and want to punish me, if
those close to them came to some harm at my hands.

Certainly I can see plenty of them here today. Crito there, for
a start, my contemporary and fellow-demesman, the father of
e Critobulus, who is here too. Then there's Lysanias from the
deme of Sphettos, the father of Aeschines here. Or indeed
Antiphon over there, from Cephisia, the father of Epigenes.
And then there are the ones whose brothers have spent their
time in my company: Nicostratus the son of Theozotides, the
brother of Theodotus. Theodotus of course is dead, so he
couldn't have put any pressure on his brother. And I can see
Paralius, the son of Demodocus, whose brother was Theages.

Then there's Adeimantus I can see, the son of Ariston. And *his* 34
brother is Plato here. Or Aiantodorus, whose brother Apollodorus
is present also. There are plenty more I could name for you.
Ideally, Meletus would have called some of them himself to give
evidence during his speech. However, in case he forgot at the
time, let him call them now — I give up my place to him. Let
him say if he has any evidence of that kind.

It's the exact opposite, gentlemen. You'll find they're all on
my side — even though I'm a bad influence, even though I harm
their relatives, as Meletus and Anytus claim. I can see why the
actual victims of my influence might have some reason to be on   b
my side. But those who have not been influenced — the older
generation, their relatives — what reason do they have for being
on my side, other than the correct and valid reason, which is
that they know Meletus is lying and I am telling the truth?

Well, there we are, gentlemen. That, and perhaps a bit more
along the same lines, is roughly what I might have to say in my
defence. There may possibly be those among you who find it   c
irritating, when you remember your own experience. You may,
in a less important trial than this one, have begged and pleaded
with the jury, with many tears, bringing your own children up
here, and many others among your family and friends, in an
attempt to arouse as much sympathy as possible, whereas I refuse
to do any of these things — even though I am, as it probably
seems to you, in the greatest danger of all. Thoughts like this
could make some of you feel a little antagonistic towards me.
For just this reason, you might get angry, and let anger influence
your vote. If any of you does feel like this — I'm sure you don't, d
but if you did — I think I might fairly say to you: 'Of course I
too have a family, my good friend. I do not come, in Homer's
famous words, "from oak or rock". No, I was born of men,
Athenians, and I do have a family and sons — three of them. One
is not quite grown-up, the other two still boys. All the same, I
am not going to bring any of them up here and beg you to
acquit me.' Why won't I do any of these things? Not out of
obstinacy, Athenians, or disrespect for you. And whether or not e
I'm untroubled by the thought of death is beside the point. No,
it's a question of what is fitting — for me, for you, and for the
whole city. I don't think it's right for me to do any of these

things, at my age and with the reputation I have. Justified or
unjustified, there's a prevailing belief that Socrates is in some
35 way different from other people.

If those of you who seem to be outstanding in wisdom,
courage or any other quality were to behave like this, it would
be deplorable. Yet this is just how I *have* seen men behaving
when they are brought to trial. They may seem to be men of
some distinction, but still they act in the most extraordinary
way. They seem to think it will be a terrible disaster for them if
they are put to death – as if they'd be immortal if you *didn't* put
them to death. I think they bring disgrace on the city. A visitor
to our country might imagine that in Athens people of
b outstanding character – those whom the Athenians themselves
single out from among themselves for positions of office and
other distinctions – that these men are no better than women.
Such behaviour, Athenians, is not right for those of you with
any kind of reputation at all. And if we who are on trial behave
like that, you should not let us get away with it. You should
make one thing absolutely clear, which is that you are much
more ready to convict a defendant who stages one of these
hysterical scenes, and makes our city an object of ridicule, than a
defendant who behaves with decorum.

And quite apart from the city's reputation, gentlemen, I think
c there's no justice, either, in begging favours from the jury or
being acquitted by begging. Justice requires instruction and
persuasion. The juryman does not sit there for the purpose of
handing out justice as a favour. He sits there to decide what
justice is. He has not taken an oath to do a favour to anyone he
takes a fancy to, but rather to reach a verdict in accordance with
the laws. So *we* should not encourage in you the habit of
breaking your oath, nor should *you* allow the habit to develop.
If we did, we should neither of us be showing respect for the
gods. So don't ask me, Athenians, to conduct myself towards
you in a way which I regard as contrary to right, justice and
d religion – least of all, surely, when I'm being accused of impiety
by Meletus here. After all, if I did persuade you and coerce you
by my begging, despite your oath, then clearly I *would* be
teaching you to deny the existence of the gods. My whole
defence would simply amount to accusing myself of not

recognising the gods. And that is far from being the case. I do recognise them, Athenians, as none of my accusers does. And I entrust to you and to god the task of reaching a verdict in my case in whatever way will be best both for me and for you.

[*By 280 votes to 220, the jury finds Socrates guilty*]

If I am not upset, Athenians, at what has just happened – at your finding me guilty – there are a number of reasons. In particular, the result was not unexpected. In fact, I am surprised by the final number of votes on either side. Personally, I was expecting a large margin, not a narrow one. As it is, if only thirty votes had gone the other way, apparently I would have been acquitted. Indeed, on Meletus' charge, as I see it, I *have* been acquitted, even as things are. And not just acquitted. It's clear to anyone that if Anytus had not come forward, with Lycon, to accuse me, Meletus would have incurred a fine of a thousand drachmas for not receiving one fifth of the votes.

So the man proposes the death penalty for me. Very well, what counter-proposal am I to make to you, Athenians? What I deserve, obviously. And what is that? What do I deserve to suffer or pay, for . . . for what? For not keeping quiet all through my life? For neglecting the things most people devote their lives to – business, family life, being general or leader of the assembly or holding some other office, the alliances and factions which occur in political life? Quite honestly, I thought my sense of right and wrong would not allow me to survive in politics. So I did not pursue a course in which I should have been no use either to you or to myself, but rather one in which I could give help to each one of you privately – the greatest help possible, as I claim. That was the direction I took. I tried to persuade each one of you not to give any thought at all to his own affairs until he had first given some thought to himself and tried to make himself as good and wise as possible; not to give any thought to the affairs of the city without first giving some thought to the city itself; and to observe the same priorities in other areas as well.

What then do I deserve for behaving like this? Something good, Athenians, if I really am supposed to make a proposal in accordance with what I deserve. And what is more, a good of a

kind which is some use to me. What then *is* of use to a poor
man, your benefactor, who needs free time in which to advise
you? There can't be anything more useful to a man of this sort,
Athenians, than to be given free meals at the public expense.
This is much more use to him than it is to any Olympic victor
among you, if one of you wins the horse race, or the two-horse
or four-horse chariot race. The Olympic victor makes you *seem*
to be happy; I make you really happy. He doesn't need the
e food; I do need it. So if I must propose a penalty based on
justice, on what I deserve, then that's what I propose: free meals
37 at the public expense.

Here again, I suppose, in the same sort of way as when I was
talking about appeals to pity and pleas for mercy, you may think
I speak as I do out of sheer obstinacy. But it's not obstinacy,
Athenians. It's like this. I myself am convinced that I don't
knowingly do wrong to anyone in the world, but I can't
persuade you of that. We haven't had enough time to talk to
one another. Mind you, if it were the custom here, as it is in
other places, to decide cases involving the death penalty over
several days rather than in one day, I believe you would have
b been persuaded. As it is, it was not easy in a short time to
overcome the strong prejudice against me. But if I am convinced
that I don't do wrong to anyone else, I am certainly not going
to do wrong to myself, or speak against myself – saying I deserve
something bad, and proposing some such penalty for myself.
Why should I? Through fear of undergoing the penalty Meletus
proposes, when I claim not to know whether it is good or bad?
Should I, in preference to that, choose one of the things I know
perfectly well to be bad, and propose that as a penalty?
c Imprisonment? What is the point of living in prison and being
the slave of those in the prison service at any particular time? A
fine? And be imprisoned until I pay? That's the same as the first
suggestion, since I haven't any money to pay a fine. Should I
propose exile? I suppose you might accept that. But I'd have to
be very devoted to life, Athenians, to lose the power of rational
thought so completely, and not be able to work out what would
happen. If you, my fellow-citizens, couldn't stand my discourses
d and conversations, if you found them too boring and irritating,
which is why you now want to be rid of them, will people in

some other country find it any easier to put up with them?
Don't you believe it, Athenians. A fine life I should lead in
exile – a man of my age moving and being driven from city to
city. Wherever I go, I've no doubt the young will listen to me,
the way they do here. If I tell them to go away, they'll send me
into exile of their own accord, bringing pressure to bear on their
elders. If I don't tell them to go away, their fathers and relatives e
will exile me, out of concern for them.

I can imagine someone saying, 'Yes, but how about keeping
your mouth shut, Socrates, and leading a quiet life? Can't you
please go into exile, and live like that?' Of all things, this is the
hardest point on which to convince some of you. If I say it is
disobeying god, and that for this reason I can't lead a quiet life,
you won't believe me. You'll think I'm using that as an excuse. If 38
on the other hand I say that really the greatest good in a man's life
is this, to be each day discussing virtue and the other subjects you
hear me talking about as I examine myself and other people – and
that the unexamined life is not worth living – if I say this, you'll
believe me even less. But it is as I say, gentlemen – hard though it
is to convince you. And on my own account, I can't get used to
the idea that I deserve anything bad. If I had any money, I'd
propose as large a fine as I could afford. That wouldn't do me any b
harm. As it is, I have no money, unless you're willing to have me
propose an amount I *could* afford. I suppose I could pay you
something like a hundred drachmas of silver, if you like. So that's
the amount I propose.

Plato here, Athenians, and Crito, Critobulus and Apollodorus,
tell me to propose a penalty of three thousand drachmas. They
say they guarantee it. I propose that amount, therefore, and they
will offer you full security for the money.

[*The jury votes for the death penalty*]

For just a small gain in time, Athenians, you will now have the c
reputation and responsibility, among those who want to criticise
the city, of having put to death Socrates, that wise man. They
will say I am wise, the people who want to blame you, even
though I am not. If you'd waited a little, you could have had
what you wanted without lifting a finger. You can see what age
I am. Far advanced in years, and close to death. I say that not to

d all of you, but to those who voted for the death penalty. And I
have something else to say to the same people.

You may think, Athenians, that I have lost my case through
inability to make the kind of speech I *could* have used to
persuade you, had I thought it right to do and say absolutely
anything to secure my acquittal. Far from it. I have lost my case,
not for want of a speech, but for want of effrontery and
shamelessness. I refused to make you the kind of speech you
most enjoy listening to. You'd like to have heard me lamenting

e and bewailing, and doing all sorts of other things which are
beneath my dignity, in my opinion – the kind of things you've
grown used to hearing from other people. However, I didn't
think it right, when I was speaking, to demean myself through
fear of danger, nor do I now regret conducting my defence in
the way I did. I'd much rather defend myself like this and be put
to death, than behave in the way I've described and go on
living. Neither in the courts nor in time of war is it right –

39 either for me or for anyone else – to devote one's efforts simply
to avoiding death at all costs. In battle it is often clear that death
can be escaped if you throw away your weapons and appeal to
the mercy of your pursuers. And in any kind of danger there are
all sorts of other devices for avoiding death, if you can bring
yourself not to mind what you do or say. There's no difficulty in
that, gentlemen – in escaping death. What is much harder is
avoiding wickedness, since wickedness runs faster than death. So

b now, not surprisingly, I who am old and slow have been
overtaken by the slower of the two. My accusers, being swift
and keen, have been overtaken by the faster, by wickedness. I
am now departing, to pay the penalty of death inflicted by you.
But they have already incurred the penalty, inflicted by truth,
for wickedness and injustice. I accept my sentence, as they do
theirs. I suppose that's probably how it was bound to turn out –
and I have no complaints.

c   Having dealt with that, I now wish to make you a prophecy,
those of you who voted for my condemnation. I am at the point
where people are most inclined to make prophecies – when
they are just about to die. To you gentlemen who have put me
to death, I say that retribution will come to you directly after
my death – retribution far worse, god knows, than the death

penalty which you have inflicted on me. You have acted as you
have today in the belief that you will avoid having to submit
your lives to examination, but you will find the outcome is just
the opposite. That is my prediction. There will be more people
now to examine you – the ones I have so far been keeping in d
check without your realising it. They will be harder to deal
with, being so much younger, and you will be more troubled by
them. If you think that by putting men to death you can stop
people criticising you for not living your lives in the right way,
you are making a big mistake. As a way of escape, it is neither
effective nor creditable. The best and simplest way lies not in
weeding out other people, but in making yourselves as good as
possible. That is my prophecy to you who voted for my
condemnation, and now I am prepared to let you go.

   To those who voted for my acquittal I'd like to make a few e
remarks about what has just happened, while the magistrates get
on with the formalities, and it is not yet time for me to go
where I must go to die. Please keep me company, gentlemen,
for this little time. There's no reason why we shouldn't talk to
one another while it is permitted. I regard you as my friends,
and so I'm prepared to explain the significance of today's 40
outcome to you.

   Gentlemen of the jury – since you I properly *can* call jurymen – a remarkable thing has happened to me. The prophetic
voice I have got so used to, my supernatural voice, has always
in the past been at my elbow, opposing me even in matters of
little importance, if I was about to take a false step. Now, you
can see for yourselves the situation I am in today. You might
think it was the ultimate misfortune – as indeed it is generally
regarded. Yet the sign from god did not oppose my leaving b
home this morning, nor my appearance here in court, nor was
there any point in my speech when it stopped me saying what I
was about to say. Often in the past, when I've been talking, the
sign has stopped me in full flow. This time it has not opposed
me at any stage in the whole proceedings – either in what I
have done or in what I have said. What do I take to be the
reason for this? I'll tell you. The chances are that what has
happened to me here is a good thing, and that it's impossible
for those of us who think death is an evil to understand it

c properly. I have strong evidence for this. The sign I know so
well would unquestionably have opposed me if things had not
been going to turn out all right for me.

And there's another reason for being confident that death is a
good thing. Look at it like this. Death is one of two things:
either it's like the dead person being nothing at all, and having
no consciousness of anything at all, or — so we are told — it's
actually some sort of change, a journey of the soul from this
place to somewhere different. Suppose it's a total absence of
d consciousness. Like sleep, when the sleeper isn't even dreaming.
Then death would be a tremendous benefit. At least, *I* certainly
think that if a man chose the night on which he slept so soundly
that he didn't even dream, and if he had to compare all the
other nights and days of his life with that night — if he had to
think carefully about it, and then say how many days and nights
he had spent in his life that were better and more enjoyable than
that night — I think that not just a private individual, but even
the great king of Persia could count these dreamless nights on
e the fingers of one hand compared with the other days and
nights. If death is something like that, I call it a benefit. Seen in
this way, the whole of time seems no longer than a single night.

On the other hand, if death is a kind of journey from here to
somewhere different, and if what we're told about all the dead
being there is true, what greater good could there be than that,
gentlemen of the jury? Imagine arriving in the other world,
41 getting away from the people here who claim to be judges, and
finding real judges, the ones who are said to decide cases there —
Minos, Rhadamanthus, Aeacus, Triptolemus, and others of the
demigods who acted with justice in their own lives. Wouldn't
that be a worthwhile journey? Or again, what would any of you
give to join Orpheus and Musaeus, Hesiod and Homer?
Personally, I'm quite prepared to die many times over, if these
b stories are true. For me at least, time spent there would be
wonderful. I'd keep meeting people like Palamedes, or Ajax the
son of Telamon, or any other of the ancients who died as a
result of an unjust verdict. I could compare my own experience
with theirs. That would be entertaining, I imagine.

Best of all, I could spend my time questioning and examining
people there, just as I do people here, to find out which of them

is wise, and which thinks he is wise but isn't. What would you give, gentlemen of the jury, to interview the man who led the great expedition to Troy? Or Odysseus, or Sisyphus? Or c thousands of others one could mention – men and women? It would be an unimaginable pleasure to talk to them there, to enjoy their company and question them. They certainly can't put you to death there for asking questions. They are better off than us in many ways – and not least because they are now immune to death for the rest of time, if what we are told is true.

And *you* must not be apprehensive about death either, gentlemen of the jury. You must regard one thing at least as certain – that no harm can come to a good man either in his life d or after his death. What happens to him is not a matter of indifference to the gods. Nor has my present situation arisen purely by chance. It is clear to me that it was better for me to die now and be released from my task. That's why my sign didn't at any point dissuade me, and why I am not in the least angry with those who voted against me, or with my accusers. Admittedly that wasn't their reason for voting against me and accusing me. They thought they *were* doing me some harm, and that's something we *can* blame them for. I do have one request e to make, however. It concerns my sons. If you think, gentlemen, when they grow up, that they are more interested in money – or anything else – than in goodness, you must get your own back on them, and make their lives a misery in exactly the same way I made yours a misery. If they think they are something when they are nothing, then reproach them as I reproached you. Tell them they are giving no thought to the things that matter, and that they think they are something when they are worth nothing. If you do this, I shall have been fairly 42 treated by you myself, and so will my sons.

I must stop. It is time for us to go. Me to my death, you to your lives. Which of us goes to the better fate, only god knows.

CRITO

SOCRATES: What are you doing here at this time, Crito? Isn't it still early?

CRITO: Yes, it is.

SOCRATES: How early, exactly?

CRITO: It hasn't started to get light yet.

SOCRATES: I'm surprised the warder didn't refuse to answer your knock.

CRITO: He's become something of a friend of mine, Socrates, what with my coming here so often. Besides, he's slightly in my debt.

SOCRATES: Have you just arrived? Or have you been here some time?

CRITO: A little while.

SOCRATES: Why didn't you wake me up straight away? What are b you doing just sitting there beside me in silence?

CRITO: I wouldn't have dreamt of it, Socrates. For my part, I wouldn't choose to be in this state of sleeplessness and misery, and I've been astonished for some time now to see how soundly you sleep. I deliberately didn't wake you because I wanted you to enjoy your rest. It's often struck me in the past – all through my life in fact – how lucky you are in your temperament. And it strikes me much more forcibly in your present misfortune. You bear it so easily and calmly.

SOCRATES: Yes, Crito, I do. It wouldn't make much sense for a man my age to get upset at the prospect of dying.

CRITO: Other people your age find themselves in similar c predicaments, Socrates. Their age doesn't stop them getting upset at their misfortune.

SOCRATES: True. Anyway, why have you come so early?

CRITO: To bring news, Socrates. Bad news. Not bad for you, as far as I can see, but for me and all your friends it is bad and hard to bear. And I think I shall find it as hard to bear as anybody.

SOCRATES: What sort of news? Has the boat from Delos
d arrived – the one my being put to death has been waiting for?

CRITO: It hasn't actually arrived, but I think it will today, to judge by the reports of some people who've just come from Sunium. It was there when they left. It's clear from what they said that it will arrive today, and so tomorrow, Socrates, you will be forced to end your life.

SOCRATES: Well, Crito, I hope it will all turn out for the best, if that is how the gods want it. All the same, I don't think it will come today.

44 CRITO: What is that belief based on?

SOCRATES: I'll tell you. I am to die, as I understand it, on the day after the ship arrives.

CRITO: Yes. At least, that's what the people in charge of these things say.

SOCRATES: Then I think it will come tomorrow, not today. I base that belief on a dream I had last night, just before I woke up. Perhaps it was lucky you didn't wake me.

CRITO: What was the dream?

SOCRATES: I saw a woman, fair and beautiful, in a white cloak.
b She came up to me and called my name. 'Socrates,' she said, ' "Three days will bear you home to Phthia's shore." '

CRITO: A strange dream, Socrates.

SOCRATES: Clear enough, though, I think, Crito.

CRITO: Only too clear, I'm afraid. Now listen, Socrates, it's not too late, even now, to do as I say and escape. If you are put to death, then for me it is a twofold disaster. Quite apart from my losing a friend such as I shall never find again, there will also be a lot of people – those who don't know you or me at all well –
c who will think I had the chance to save you if I'd been prepared

to spend some money, but that I wasn't interested in doing so. Can you imagine people thinking anything worse about you than that? That you put a higher value on money than on your friends? Most people will never believe it was *you* who refused to leave here, and we who strongly encouraged you to do so.

SOCRATES: Honestly, Crito! Why should we care so much about what 'most people' believe? The best people, who are the ones we have to worry about, will realise that things were done in the way they actually were done.

CRITO: But don't you see, Socrates? We have no choice *but* to **d** care about what most people think as well. The present situation is a clear example of how the many can injure us in ways which are not trivial, but just about as great as can be, if they're given the wrong impression about someone.

SOCRATES: If only they could, Crito! If the many could do us the greatest injuries, that would mean they were capable of doing us the greatest good as well, which would be excellent. As it is, they're incapable of doing either. They have no power to make a man either wise or foolish, nor do they care what effect they have.

CRITO: I dare say you're right. But tell me something, Socrates. **e** Are you worried about me and the rest of your friends? Do you think that if you leave here, we shall get into trouble with the people who make a living out of bringing private prosecutions, for smuggling you out of here? Do you think we shall be forced to forfeit all our property, or pay a very large fine, and maybe undergo some further penalty in addition? If something like that is what you're afraid of, don't give it another thought. We're in **45** duty bound to run this risk to save you – that goes without saying – and even greater risks, if need be. So listen to me. Don't say 'no'.

SOCRATES: That is something I worry about, Crito. That, and many other things besides.

CRITO: Well then, don't be afraid on that score. There are people prepared, for not a very large sum of money, to save you and get you out of here. And apart from them, can't you see how easily bought they are, the men who make their living out

of prosecutions? It wouldn't need a lot of money to take care of
b them. You have my resources at your disposal. That should be
plenty, I imagine. And if you're worried about me, and feel you
shouldn't spend my money, look at the people we've got here
who are not Athenians, who are ready to spend theirs. One of
them, Simmias the Theban, has actually brought enough money
for just this purpose. Cebes too is fully prepared, and so are
many others. So as I say, you shouldn't let these fears stop you
saving yourself. And don't let it be an objection, as you claimed
in court, that you wouldn't know what to do with yourself if
c you went into exile. There are lots of places you can go where
they'll be glad to see you. If you'd like to go to Thessaly, for
example, my family has friends there who'll be delighted to see
you. They'll give you sanctuary. Nobody in Thessaly will give
you any trouble.

And apart from that, Socrates, it is actually wrong, in my
opinion, to sacrifice yourself, as you are proposing to do, when
you could escape. You seem to be voluntarily choosing for
yourself the kind of fate your enemies would have chosen for
you – and *did* choose for you when they were trying to destroy
you. Worse still, I think, is the betrayal of your own sons, when
d there's nothing to stop you bringing them up and educating
them – and yet you're going to go away and leave them, and for
all you care they can turn out how they will. The chances are
they'll have the kind of life orphans generally do have without
their parents. No, either you shouldn't have children, or you
should play your part, and go through with the labour of raising
and educating them. You seem to me to be taking the easy way
out. What you should do is choose what a decent and courageous man would choose – you who have spent your whole life
claiming to be concerned with virtue. Personally, I'm ashamed,
e both for you and for those of us who are your friends. I think
this whole business of yours will be thought to be the result of
some lack of resolution on our part. There was the bringing of
the case, for a start – the fact that it came to court when it
needn't have done. Then there was the actual conduct of the
case *in* court. And now this, the final absurdity of the whole
affair, that we shall be thought to have missed the opportunity –
through our own cowardice and lack of resolution, since we

didn't save you, nor did you save yourself, though it was possible 46
and within your power with even a modest amount of help from
us. Don't let all this be a humiliation, Socrates – both for you
and for us – in addition to being an evil. Think it over. Or
rather, the time for thinking it over is past. You should by now
have thought it over – there is only one course of action. The
whole thing must be done this coming night. If we wait any
longer, it will be impossible. The opportunity will be gone. I
cannot urge you too strongly, Socrates. Listen to me. Do as I say.

SOCRATES: My dear Crito, your willingness to help is admirable – b
if there is any justification for it. Otherwise, the greater your
willingness, the more out of place it is. So we'd better look into
whether this is the right thing to do or not. It has been my
practice, not just now but always, from the resources at my
disposal, to trust only the principle which on reflection seems
most appropriate. I can't suddenly throw overboard principles
which I have put forward in the past, simply because of the
situation I now find myself in. Those principles seem to me to
be pretty much the same as ever, and I still esteem and value c
them the way I have done in the past. If we can't find any better
principle than these to put forward on this occasion, you can be
quite sure I'm not going to agree with you, however many
bugbears the power of the many produces to scare us – as if we
were children – letting loose on us its imprisonments, its death
sentences and its fines.

   Very well, what is the best way of looking into this question?
Why don't we start by going back to the argument you put
forward based on what people will think? Were we right or
wrong, all those times, when we said we should listen to some d
opinions, but not to others? Or were we right before I was
sentenced to death, only for it now to become clear that was a
waste of breath, spoken simply for the sake of having something
to say? Was it really all just juvenile fantasy? For my part, Crito,
I should very much like to carry out a joint enquiry with you,
to see whether the principle will seem rather different to me
now that I am in this situation, or whether it will seem the
same – and whether we're going to forget about it or follow it.
The principle so often put forward, I think, by those who

thought they knew what they were talking about, was the one I
was putting forward just now – that of the opinions held by
e men, we should regard some as important, but not others.
Seriously, Crito, don't you think this is a sound principle?
Barring accidents, you're not in the position of having to die
47 tomorrow, so you shouldn't be influenced by the present
situation. Examine the question. Don't you think it a sound
principle that we should not value all human opinions equally?
Shouldn't we value some highly, but not others? And the same
with the people who hold the opinions. We shouldn't value all
of them. We should value some, but not others. What do you
think? Isn't this is a sound principle?

CRITO: Yes, it is.

SOCRATES: We should value the good opinions, but not the bad
ones?

CRITO: Yes.

SOCRATES: Aren't good opinions the opinions of the wise,
whereas bad opinions are those of the foolish?

CRITO: Obviously.

SOCRATES: Well then, what was the kind of analogy we used to
b employ? If a man is taking physical exercise, and this is what he
is interested in, does he listen to just anyone's praise and
criticism and opinion, or only one person's – the person who is
in fact a medical expert or physical training instructor?

CRITO: Only one person's.

SOCRATES: So he should worry about the criticisms, and welcome the praises, of this one person, but not those of the many?

CRITO: Clearly he should.

SOCRATES: In what he does, then – in the exercise he takes, in
what he eats and drinks – he should be guided by the one man –
the man in charge, the expert – rather than by everyone else.

CRITO: That is so.

c SOCRATES: Well, then. If he doesn't listen to the one man,
doesn't value his opinion and recommendations, but does value

those of the many who are not experts, won't he do himself some harm?

CRITO: Of course he will.

SOCRATES: What is this harm? What is its extent? What part of the man who doesn't listen to the expert does it attack?

CRITO: His body, obviously. That is what it damages.

SOCRATES: Quite right. Well then, is it the same also in other situations, Crito, to save us going through all the examples – and especially with right and wrong, foul and fair, good and bad, the things we are now discussing? Should we follow the opinion of the many, and fear that? Or the opinion of the one man, if we d can find an expert on the subject? Should we respect and fear this one man more than all the rest put together? And if we don't follow his advice, then we shall injure and do violence to that part which we have often agreed is made better by justice and damaged by injustice. Or is this all wrong?

CRITO: No, I think it is right, Socrates.

SOCRATES: Very well. Take the thing which is made better by health and damaged by disease. If we ruin it by following advice other than that of the experts, is our life worth living once that is injured? This is the body, of course, isn't it?   e

CRITO: Yes.

SOCRATES: Is life worth living, then, if our body is in poor condition and injured?

CRITO: Certainly not.

SOCRATES: How about the thing which is attacked by injustice and helped by justice? Is our life worth living when that is injured? Or do we regard it as less important than the body, this thing – whichever of our faculties it is – to which justice and 48 injustice belong?

CRITO: No, we certainly don't.

SOCRATES: More important, then?

CRITO: Much more important.

SOCRATES: In that case, my dear friend, we shouldn't pay the slightest attention, as you suggested we should, to what most people will say about us. We should listen only to the expert on justice and injustice, to the one man, and to the truth itself. So you were wrong, for a start, in one of your suggestions – when you suggested we should worry about the opinion of the many on the subject of justice, right, good, and their opposites. 'Ah!' you might say, 'but the many are liable to put us to death.'

b CRITO: That too is obviously true. You might well say that, Socrates. You're quite right.

SOCRATES: All the same, my learned friend, I think the principle we've set out still has the same force as it did. And what about this second principle? Tell me, our belief that the most important thing is not to live, but to live a good life – does that still hold, or not?

CRITO: It does.

SOCRATES: And that good, excellent and just are one and the same thing – does *that* still hold, or not?

CRITO: It does.

SOCRATES: Well then, in the light of the points we've agreed, we must look into the question whether it is just or not just for me to attempt to leave here without the permission of the Athenians.
c If it becomes clear that it is just, let us make the attempt. Otherwise let us forget about it. As for the questions you raise – expense, public opinion, the upbringing of children – I suspect that in reality, Crito, these are the concerns of those who readily put people to death, and would as readily bring them back to life again, if they could, for no reason at all. In other words, the many. For us, though, the thing is to follow where the argument leads us, and I rather think the only question we need ask is the one we asked just now. Shall we act justly if we give
d our money and our thanks to those who will arrange my escape from here – or if we ourselves arrange the escape and allow it to be arranged? Or shall we in truth be acting unjustly if we do all these things? If doing these things is clearly unjust, then I'm pretty sure we shouldn't take into account the certainty either of

being put to death if we stay here and accept things quietly, or of suffering anything else at all, compared with the danger of acting wrongly.

CRITO: I'm sure you're right, Socrates. You'd better see what you think we ought to do.

SOCRATES: Let us look into it together, my good friend. And if you have an objection at any point to what I'm saying, then e object, and I'll listen to you. But if you don't, then for goodness' sake stop repeating the same thing over and over again – that I should leave here against the will of the Athenians. It's very important to me to act with your agreement rather than against your wishes. Now, think about the starting-point of our enquiry. Do you regard it as satisfactory? And when you answer 49 the question, mind you say what you really think.

CRITO: I'll try.

SOCRATES: Do we say we should never in any way deliberately act unjustly? Or are there some ways in which we should act unjustly, and other ways in which we should not? Or is acting unjustly, as has often been agreed among us in the past, never in any way good and right? Or have all those things we once agreed on become, in these last few days, so much water under the bridge? Did we, grown men and at the age we were, Crito, discuss things so enthusiastically with one another without b realising we were no better than children? Or is what we said then more true now than ever? Whether 'most people' agree or not, and whether we have to undergo hardships more severe even than these – or possibly less severe – isn't acting unjustly in fact, for the person who does it, in every way evil and bad? Is this what we say, or not?

CRITO: It is.

SOCRATES: In which case, we should never act unjustly.

CRITO: No, we shouldn't.

SOCRATES: And even if we are wronged, we should not act unjustly in retaliation, as most people think, since we ought not *ever* to act unjustly.

c CRITO: Apparently not.

SOCRATES: What about harming people, Crito? Should we do that, or not?

CRITO: I suppose not, Socrates.

SOCRATES: How about harming people in retaliation, if we are injured by them first – which is what most people say we should do? Is that just or unjust?

CRITO: Wholly unjust.

SOCRATES: And that, I imagine, is because injuring people is no different from treating them unjustly.

CRITO: That's right.

SOCRATES: In that case, we should neither act unjustly in retaliation, nor do any injury, to anyone in the world, no matter how we've been treated by them. And if you agree with that,
d Crito, make sure your agreement does not run counter to your true opinion. I realise not many people accept this view – or ever will accept it. There is no common ground between those who do accept it and those who don't. Each side necessarily regards the opinions of the other with contempt. So you too must think very hard about it. Are you on our side? Do you agree with us in accepting this view? Shall we base our argument on the premise that it is never right to act unjustly, or act unjustly in retaliation, or if you are injured, defend yourself by harming people in retaliation? Or do you disagree? Do you reject the original premise? Personally, I have held this view for
e a long time, and I still hold it now. If you have been holding some other view, tell me. Instruct me. But if you stand by what we said earlier, then listen to what follows from it.

CRITO: I do stand by it, and I agree with you. Tell me what follows.

SOCRATES: Very well, I'll tell you. Or rather, I'll ask you. If one person makes an agreement – a fair agreement – with another, should he do what he has agreed, or should he try and get out of it?

CRITO: He should do what he has agreed.

SOCRATES: See what follows, then. If we leave here without persuading the city to change its mind, are we or are we not injuring somebody or something – and those we have least cause to injure, at that? Are we standing by our agreement – our fair agreement – or not?

CRITO: I can't answer your question, Socrates. I don't understand it.

SOCRATES: Look at it like this. Suppose we were about to run away, or whatever we're supposed to call it, from here, and the laws and state of Athens came and appeared to me, and asked: 'Tell me, Socrates, what are you trying to do? Isn't your intention, in this action you are embarking on, simply to destroy both us, the laws, and the entire city, as far as lies within your power? Do you think it is possible for a city to continue to exist, and not be utterly overwhelmed, if the verdicts of its courts have no force – if they are rendered invalid and destroyed by private citizens?' What are we going to say, Crito, to these questions and others like them? There's a lot you could say, especially as public advocate, in *defence* of this law we're trying to do away with – the law which lays down that verdicts arrived at in the courts should be binding. Shall we say to them, 'Yes, but the city treated us unjustly. It did not reach its verdict fairly.'? Is that what we're going to say? Or what?

CRITO: Yes, that most emphatically is what we are going to say, Socrates.

SOCRATES: But then suppose the laws say, 'Was *that* what was agreed between us and you, Socrates? Or was it to abide by the verdicts the city arrives at in its courts?' And if we expressed surprise at their question, they might add: 'Do not be surprised by our question, Socrates. Answer it. You have had enough practice at question-and-answer. Come on, then. What principle do you appeal to, against us and the city, to allow you to try and destroy us? Did we not bring you into existence, for a start? Was it not through us that your father married your mother, and fathered you? Tell us, then, those of us who are the laws governing marriage, have you some criticism of us? Are we at fault in some way?' 'No, I have no criticism,' I should reply. 'And what about the laws to do with your upbringing, and the education you received after you were born? Did we not give your father the right instructions – those of us whose job it is to attend to this – when we told him to educate you in the arts and physical

e training?' 'No, they were the right instructions,' I would say.

'Well, then. Since you were born, brought up and educated under our protection, then for a start you were our offspring and our slave – you *and* your parents. Can you deny that? And that being so, do you think what is just for you is on a par with what is just for us? If we decide to do something to you, do you think it is right for you to do it to us in return? There was no equality of justice as between you and your father or master, if you had one, allowing you to do to him in return what he did

51 to you – to answer him back if he spoke abusively to you, or beat him in return if you were beaten, or anything like that. In which case, will it be permitted for you to do it to your country and its laws? If we decide to destroy you, because we think it right to do so, will you in your turn, to the best of your ability, set about destroying us, the laws, and your country, in return? And will you claim that in acting like this you are doing what is right, you who are so truly concerned about human virtue?

'Is this the extent of your wisdom, that you don't even realise that your country is something of greater value, something of greater divinity and holiness, and altogether more important –

b both among gods and among men, if they have any sense – than your mother, your father and all the rest of your ancestors put together? That your country should be revered, submitted to, placated when angry – more than your father – and either persuaded to think again, or obeyed? That you should quietly accept whatever treatment – beating, perhaps, or imprisonment – it decides you should receive? Or if it takes you to war, to be wounded or killed, that is what you should do, and that is what is right? That you should not give way, or retreat, or abandon your position, but that in war, in the lawcourts, or anywhere at all, you should do what your city and your

c country tell you, or else convince them where justice naturally lies? That the use of force against your mother or father is contrary to god's law – still more so the use of force against your country?' What are we going to say in answer to this,

Crito? Shall we say the laws are right, or not?

CRITO: Well, *I* think they are right.

SOCRATES: 'Consider, then, Socrates,' the laws might perhaps say. 'Are we right in saying there is no justification for the things you are now trying to do to us? We fathered you, brought you up, educated you, gave you and every other citizen a share in every good thing it was in our power to give. And even then, if d
there is any Athenian who when he comes of age takes a look at his city's constitution and at us, the laws, and finds we are not to his satisfaction, then by granting him permission we make a public declaration to anyone who wishes that he may take what is his, and go wherever he pleases. If a man chooses to go to one of your colonies, because we and the city are not to his liking, or to leave, emigrate to some other place, and go wherever he wants, with no loss of property, none of us laws stands in his way or forbids him. But we do say that anyone who chooses to e
remain after seeing how we reach verdicts in the courts and how we make our other political arrangements, has in effect come to an agreement with us to do what we tell him. We say the man who disobeys us is doing wrong in three ways. He is disobeying us who fathered him. He is disobeying those who brought him up. And having made an agreement to obey us, he is neither obeying nor trying to make us change our minds, if we are doing something which is not right. We make him a fair offer – not harshly demanding that he do whatever we order, but 52
allowing him a straight choice, either to make us change our minds or do as we say – and he does neither. These are the charges, Socrates, which we say you too will render yourself liable to, if you act as you are proposing to act. You in particular, not least among the Athenians.'

   And if I asked them why me in particular, they might perhaps have a legitimate complaint against me. They could say that I, more than any of the Athenians, really have made this agreement with them. 'Socrates,' they could say, 'we have convincing b
evidence that we and the city *were* to your liking. You couldn't possibly have spent more of your time living here in Athens than any other Athenian if the place hadn't been particularly to your liking. You wouldn't have refused ever to leave the city to see

famous places – except Corinth, once – or go anywhere at all,
except on military service. You never went abroad, as other
people do. You weren't seized with a desire to know any other
c city or any other laws. No, you were satisfied with us, and with
our city. In fact, so firmly did you choose us and agree to live
your life as a citizen under us, that you even produced children
in the city. You wouldn't have done that if it had not been to
your liking. Even at your trial it was open to you to propose a
penalty of exile, if you chose, and do then with the city's
permission what you are now proposing to do without it. You
put a brave face on it then, saying you didn't mind if you had to
die. You preferred death, you said, to exile. But now you feel no
shame at those words, and you feel nothing for us, the laws, as
you set about destroying us. In trying to run away in breach of
the contract and agreement by which you agreed to live your life
d as a citizen, you are acting as the meanest slave would act.
Answer us this, for a start. Are we right in saying that you have
agreed – not just verbally, but by your behaviour – to live your
life as a citizen under us? Or are we wrong?' What are we going
to say to this, Crito? Don't we have to agree?

CRITO: Yes, we're bound to, Socrates.

SOCRATES: 'Aren't you simply breaking contracts and agreements
e which you have with us?' they could ask. 'You didn't enter into
them under compulsion, or under false pretences. You weren't
forced to make up your mind on the spur of the moment. You
had seventy years in which you were at liberty to leave, if we
were not to your liking or you thought the agreement was
unfair. You didn't choose Sparta or Crete instead, places which
you have always described as well-governed. You didn't choose
52 *any* other city, inside or outside Greece. Even people who are
lame, or blind, or crippled in other ways, spend more time away
from Athens than you did. *That* is an indication, quite clearly, of
how you, more than any of the Athenians, found the city, and
us the laws, to your liking. After all, who could find a city to his
liking, and not like its laws? And will you not now stand by
what you agreed? You will if you take our advice, Socrates.
That way you will avoid making yourself ridiculous by leaving
the city.

'Think about it. If you break this agreement, and put yourself
in the wrong in this way, what good will you do yourself or
your friends? That your friends will probably have to go into   b
exile as well, be cut off from their city, and forfeit their
property, is reasonably clear. And you? Well, suppose you go to
one of the cities nearby – Thebes, say, or Megara, both of which
have good laws. In the first place, Socrates, you will come to
them as an enemy of their constitution. Those who care for
their city will look at you with suspicion, believing you to be a
destroyer of the laws. You will also reinforce the opinion of the
jury about you. They will decide they did reach the right
verdict. After all, there's a strong presumption that a man who   c
destroys the laws will be a destructive influence on people who
are young and foolish. Will you in that case avoid cities with
good laws, and the best governed among mankind? And if you
do, will it be worth your while going on living? Or will you
visit those cities? And will you have the nerve, in your
conversations with them – what sort of conversations, Socrates?
The ones you had here about virtue and justice being of the
greatest value to mankind, together with custom and the laws?
Don't you think this would seem a disgraceful way for Socrates
to behave? You certainly should.   d
'Or will you leave this part of the world and go to Crito's
friends in Thessaly? You'll find all sorts of anarchy and self-
indulgence up there. No doubt they'd love to hear the amusing
story of your running away from prison in some costume or
other – wearing a leather jerkin, perhaps, or one of the other
disguises people generally do wear when they're running away –
and altering your appearance. That you could bring yourself in
your old age, with but a small span of life in all probability
remaining to you, to cling so greedily to life by transgressing the   e
most important of the laws – will there be no one to say this?
Perhaps not, if you can manage not to annoy anyone. Otherwise,
Socrates, you will have to listen to a lot of humiliating comments
about yourself. Are you going to live by ingratiating yourself with
everyone, and being a slave to them? Oh, yes, you'll have a whale
of a time up there in Thessaly – as if you'd left Athens for a
dinner party in Thessaly. But all those conversations about justice
and other forms of virtue – what will become of those, pray?   54

'Oh, of course! You want to remain alive for your children's sake, so you can bring them up and educate them? By taking them to *Thessaly*? Is that any way to bring them up and educate them, turning them into foreigners, so you can give them that privilege as well? If you don't do that, if they are brought up here, will they be any better brought up and educated because you are alive and separated from them? Your friends are going to look after them. Will they look after them if you go and live in Thessaly, and not look after them if you go to Hades? If those b who claim to be your friends are worth anything at all, of course they'll look after them.

'No, Socrates, obey us who brought you up. Do not regard your children, or life, or anything at all, as more important than justice. When you come to the other world, you don't want to have to defend yourself on these charges to the rulers there. It does not seem better, more just or more righteous for you or your friends in *this* world if you act like this. Nor, when you come to the next world, will it be better for you there. As it is, c you are going there – if you do go – as one wronged. Not by us, the laws, but by men. If on the other hand you depart after so shamefully returning wrong for wrong, and injury for injury, breaking your own agreement and contract with us, and injuring those whom above all you should not have injured – yourself, your friends, your country and us – then we shall be angry with you while you are alive, and in the next world our brothers, the laws in Hades, will not receive you kindly, since they will know that you tried, to the best of your ability, to destroy us. So don't d let Crito persuade you to do as he says. Be persuaded by us.'

That, believe me, Crito, my very dear friend, is what I think I hear them saying, just as those gripped by religious fervour think they hear the pipes. The sound of their words rings in my head, and makes it impossible for me to hear any others. Be in no doubt. The way it looks to me at the moment, you will be wasting your time if you speak against them. But still, if you think it will do any good, by all means speak.

CRITO: Socrates, I have nothing to say.

e SOCRATES: Then forget about it, Crito. Let us act in the way god points out to us.

PHAEDO

ECHECRATES: Were you there yourself, Phaedo, in the prison 57
with Socrates, the day he drank the poison? Or did you hear
about it from somebody else?

PHAEDO: I was there myself, Echecrates.

ECHECRATES: What was it the man said before he died? And
what was the manner of his death? I'd very much like to hear.
Practically nobody from Phlius ever goes to stay in Athens these
days, and we haven't had a visitor from there for ages, to give us
a reliable account of what happened. All we heard was that he b
drank poison and died. Apart from that, no details at all.

PHAEDO: Didn't you even hear about the trial, then, and the way 58
that turned out?

ECHECRATES: Yes, that much we did hear, and we were surprised
that it was clearly such a long time after the trial that he was put
to death. Why was that, Phaedo?

PHAEDO: Quite by chance, Echecrates. The ship the Athenians
send to Delos had just had the wreath put on its stern the day
before the trial.

ECHECRATES: What ship?

PHAEDO: The ship, according to the Athenians, in which
Theseus once went to Crete with the 'seven youths and seven
maids', and saved their lives and his own life. They had vowed b
to Apollo, so the story goes, that if they escaped they would
send a mission to Delos every year in payment. And ever since
that time, right up to the present day, they've gone on sending
it to the god every year. Once they've started the mission, the
law says they shall keep the city free from bloodshed during this
period, and not carry out any official death sentence until the
ship has reached Delos and returned to Athens again. If the
winds hold them back, this can take a long time. The mission

c begins when the priest of Apollo puts a wreath on the stern of the ship. And as I say, this in fact took place on the day before the trial. That was why Socrates spent a long time in prison between his trial and his death.

ECHECRATES: All right, but what about his actual death, Phaedo? What was talked about? What was done? Which of his friends were there? Or would the authorities not allow them to be there? Did he die alone, without his friends?

d PHAEDO: No, there were friends there. A large number, in fact.

ECHECRATES: You must give us the most accurate account you can. Or are you busy?

PHAEDO: No, I'll try and tell you about it. I'm not busy. Remembering Socrates, whether I'm speaking myself or listening to someone else speaking, is always my favourite occupation.

ECHECRATES: In that case, Phaedo, you have an audience after your own heart. So try and tell us all about it in as much detail as possible.

e PHAEDO: Well then, I found it an extraordinary experience, being there. You'd expect me to have felt a wave of pity at the death of a close friend, but I didn't. He struck me as happy, Echecrates, both in his demeanour and in what he said, so fearlessly and nobly did he meet his end. And in consequence I got a strong feeling that he would not be going to the next world without some divine protection, and that if ever anyone was going to be all right when he got there, he would be. For

59 that reason I felt virtually none of the pity you'd have expected in someone present at such a tragic event. But then again, neither did I feel pleasure at our discussing philosophy in our usual way – though that is what our conversation was about. No, I just had this strange feeling, this unfamiliar mixture of pleasure and pain together, as I thought about the fact that he was shortly going to die. All of us there were in more or less the same state – now laughing, now crying – and one of us

b particularly so. Apollodorus. You know him, of course. You know how he is.

ECHECRATES: Of course I do.

PHAEDO: Well, he was acutely affected in the way I've described. But I was upset myself, and so were the others.

ECHECRATES: Who exactly was there, Phaedo?

PHAEDO: Well, of the Athenians, I've mentioned Apollodorus. Then there was Critobulus and his father, plus Hermogenes, Epigenes, Aeschines and Antisthenes. Ctesippus from the deme of Paeanis was there as well, and Menexenus, and some other Athenians. Plato was ill, I think.

ECHECRATES: Were there any foreigners there?

PHAEDO: Yes. Simmias the Theban, with Cebes and Phaedondas. c And from Megara Eucleides and Terpsion.

ECHECRATES: What about Aristippus and Cleombrotus? Were they there?

PHAEDO: No. They were in Aegina, apparently.

ECHECRATES: And was anyone else there?

PHAEDO: No, I think that was about all.

ECHECRATES: What about the conversation, then? How did it go?

PHAEDO: I'll try and give you a full account, starting from the beginning. We'd got in the habit of visiting Socrates – I and the d others – particularly during the last few days. We'd meet early, at the court-house where the trial had taken place, since it was close to the prison. We'd wait there every morning talking to one another until the prison opened, which wasn't very early. When it did open, we'd go in and see Socrates, and usually spend the day with him. This time we assembled rather earlier. We'd heard, when we left the prison the previous evening, that e the ship was in from Delos. So we passed the word to one another to come to the meeting-place as early as possible. When we turned up, the doorkeeper who generally answered the door came out and told us to wait, and not go in until he himself told us. 'The Eleven are releasing Socrates from his fetters, and making arrangements for him to be put to death today.' But it wasn't long before he came back and told us to go in. And as we went in, we found Socrates just released from his fetters, and 60 also Xanthippe – whom you know – sitting beside him holding their youngest child. When Xanthippe saw us, she urged us to be silent, and then said one of those things women will say: 'Socrates, this is the last time your friends will talk to you, or you to them.' Socrates glanced at Crito. 'Make sure someone sees her home,' he said.

b   She was taken home, crying aloud and lamenting, by some of Crito's people, while Socrates sat up on his bed, flexing his leg and rubbing it with his hand. And as he rubbed it, he said: 'What a strange thing it seems, gentlemen, this thing men call pleasure. And how surprisingly connected with its apparent opposite, pain. They won't come to a man both together, but if you go after one of them and get it, you're always pretty well bound to get the other as well – as if the two of them were
c   joined at the head. If he'd thought about it, I expect Aesop would have written a fable about god wanting to stop them fighting, but not being able to, and so joining their heads together for them, and that being the reason why anyone who experiences one of them finds the other following on after it as well. That's certainly what seems to have happened to me. The pain in my leg from the fetter seems to have been succeeded by the pleasure following on after it.'

Here Cebes intervened. 'Thank you, Socrates. Thank you for reminding me. Those verses you wrote, setting to music the
d   stories of Aesop and the Invocation to Apollo. Several people – notably Evenus, the day before yesterday – have been asking me your reasons for composing those pieces when you came here, though you'd never done anything like it before. So if you're at all interested in my being able to give Evenus an answer next time he asks me – and I know he *will* ask – tell me what I should say.'

'Tell him the truth, Cebes. Tell him I didn't write them out of any desire to compete with him or his compositions. I knew
e   that would be no easy task. No, I was interested in the meaning of some of my dreams, and I wanted to satisfy my conscience, in case those were the kind of works they had been telling me to produce all this time. I'll tell you about them. There's a recurring dream I've had all through my life. It appears in different forms at different times, but always says the same thing. "Compose music, Socrates. Make that your work." In the past

I've taken it to be encouraging me, telling me to do what I was already doing, in the way the crowd cheers on the runners in a 61 race. The same with my dream. I thought it was telling me to do what I was already doing – i.e. make music – since I thought philosophy was the finest form of music, and that was what I was doing. But then the trial took place, and the festival of the god prevented my being put to death, and I wondered if just possibly the dream had been telling me all those times to compose music in this popular sense. So to be on the safe side, I thought I had better not depart without first satisfying my conscience by doing what the dream said and writing some b poems. So I started off by writing one to the god whose festival it was. And after the god, I decided that a writer, if he was going to be a writer, should write fiction rather than fact. I had no talent for story-writing myself, and for that reason I took ready-made stories that I knew by heart – those of Aesop – and made poems out of the first ones I came across. That's what you can tell Evenus, Cebes. Say goodbye to him for me. Tell him, if he has any sense, to follow me as soon as he can. I am leaving today, apparently. That is the order of the Athenians.'   c

And Simmias said, 'That's a funny piece of advice to give Evenus, Socrates. I've met him several times, and from what I've seen of him, there's not the slightest chance of his doing what you suggest, if he can avoid it.'

'Really? Is Evenus not a philosopher?'

'I believe him to be,' said Simmias.

'Then he'll be happy to. Evenus and anyone else who is serious about being a philosopher. He probably won't do violence to himself, though. They say that's not permitted.' As he said this, he lowered his legs to the ground, and maintained d this sitting position through the rest of the conversation.

Then Cebes asked him, 'What do you mean, Socrates, by saying it is not permitted to do violence to yourself, but that all the same the philosopher would be very happy to follow in the footsteps of the dying?'

'Really, Cebes! Haven't you and Simmias learnt all about that in your time with Philolaus?'

'We haven't learnt anything for certain, Socrates.'

'Well, even I only know about it from hearsay, but I can't see

any objection to telling you what I have heard. After all, it may
e be especially appropriate for someone who is about to make the
journey to the other world to enquire and speculate about what
life in that world is like. Besides, what else is there for us to do
in the interval between now and sunset?'

'In that case, Socrates, why do they say it is not permitted for
a man to kill himself? In reply to your question a moment ago, I
have heard Philolaus say, when he was living in Thebes – and
I've heard it from other people as well – that it is wrong to do
this. But I've never heard anybody give a convincing reason
why.'

62   'Well, you must keep trying. You may yet find the answer.
But it probably will strike you as strange if this, unlike other
human situations, is uniquely clear-cut, if it never turns out that
at some times and for some people death is better than life. And
if death is better for them, it probably strikes you as strange that
it is wrong for them to do themselves this favour. They have to
wait for someone else to do it for them.'

Cebes laughed quietly in agreement. 'Aye, God knows,' he
replied in his own dialect.
b   'Yes, because looked at like that it would seem illogical. And
yet there may be some logic in it all the same. The argument
which is put forward for this view in mystery religions – that we
men are in a prison of some sort, and that a man has no right to
release himself from it, or escape from it – seems to me an
important one, and not easy to understand fully. However, part
of it at least I think is right, Cebes – the part which says that
those keeping an eye on us are gods, and that we men are
among the gods' possessions. Or don't you agree with that?'

'No, I do agree with it.'
c   'In that case, wouldn't *you* be angry if one of your possessions
did away with itself without you indicating your consent to its
death? Wouldn't you punish it, if you had any means of
punishment?'

'I certainly would.'

'On this argument, then, perhaps it is not illogical that a man
is not allowed to kill himself, but must wait for god to send
some unavoidable fate, such as mine now.'

'That seems fair enough,' said Cebes, 'as far as it goes. But you

also said a moment ago that philosophers would be quite happy
to die. That has a strange sound to it, if we were right just now d
in saying that the person keeping an eye on us is a god, and that
we are his possessions. It doesn't make sense that the wisest men
should have no objection to leaving this position in which they
are under the supervision of the gods, who are finest of all
supervisors. The wise man surely doesn't think he's going to
look after himself any better once he is free. A stupid man might
think that, and think he should try to get away from his master.
It might not dawn on him that it's a mistake to get away from a e
good one. Rather he should stay where he is as long as he can –
which is why it is irrational to try and get away. Anyone with
any sense, on the other hand, would presumably be keen to
spend all his time with one better than himself. On this
argument, Socrates, you'd expect it to be the opposite of the
view just put forward. It makes sense for the wise to be upset at
dying, and the foolish to be pleased.'

Socrates seemed to me to approve of Cebes's determination.
He glanced at us. 'Always looking for an argument, is Cebes. 63
He's not easily prepared to take anyone else's word for
anything.'

'Yes, but for once, Socrates,' said Simmias, 'Cebes has a point.
Even I think so. Why would truly wise men want to get away
from masters who are better than themselves? Why would they
be glad to leave them? I think Cebes's argument is directed at
you. You seem quite happy to leave us and your good rulers,
who are, as you yourself agree, gods.'

'That's a fair objection. What you're really saying, I take it, is b
that I should defend myself on this charge, just as I defended
myself in court.'

'Exactly,' said Simmias.

'Very well. I'll see if I can make a more convincing defence to
you than I did to the jury. My position, Simmias and Cebes, is
this. If I didn't believe, first that I am going to meet other good
and wise gods, and second that I shall join men – those who
have died – better than the ones here, then it would be wrong
of me not to be upset at the prospect of death. As it is, I can
assure you that I expect to find good men – though I would not c
state that as a certainty. But as for my belief that the gods I shall

encounter as my masters will be wholly good, all I can say is that if there is any belief of this kind which I *would* state as a certainty, it is this one. And that is the reason why I am not so very upset. I am confident that there is something in store for people after their deaths – something much better, as is traditionally said, for the good than for the bad.'

'Fair enough, Socrates,' said Simmias. 'But do you intend to keep this knowledge to yourself when you leave us, or can you
d share it with us? We all regard it as a good to be shared, and in any case it can be the defence you were talking about, if we find what you say convincing.'

'I'll do my best, then. But first let's see what Crito here wants. He's been trying to say something to me for some time now, I think.'

'It's nothing really, Socrates,' said Crito, 'just that the man who is going to administer the poison has been saying to me for a while now that I should advise you to talk as little as possible. He says people get heated if they talk too much, and this is not
e the best way to go about taking the poison. Those who do sometimes have to drink the poison two or three times.'

'Pay no attention to him,' said Socrates. 'He'll just have to be prepared to do his stuff twice – or even three times, if necessary.'

'I was pretty sure that was what you would say,' said Crito. 'But he's been pestering me for some time now.'

'Don't worry about him. Now, you people are my jury, so I'd like to try and defend my view that it is perfectly reasonable for a man who has truly spent his life in philosophy not to be afraid
64 at the approach of death, but to have high hopes that when he dies, he will win great rewards in the next world. How this can be, Simmias and Cebes, I will now try and explain. Most people probably don't realise that for those who have genuinely been engaged in philosophy in the truest sense of the word, dying and being dead are just exactly what they've been practising. That, and nothing else. And if that's the case, there would be some absurdity, I imagine, in spending your whole life looking forward to this one thing, and then when it came, getting upset at what you had been looking forward to and practising for.'

Simmias laughed. 'Dammit, Socrates. I wasn't feeling at all

like laughing a moment ago, but you've made me laugh now. I b think most people, hearing you say what you've just said, would regard it as a fair comment on philosophers – certainly where we come from, they couldn't agree more – to say that philosophers really might just as well be dead. As far as they're concerned, they say, it's quite clear that it would serve philosophers right if that's what did happen to them.'

'And they'd be right, Simmias, apart from the bit about it being quite clear to them. What isn't clear to them is *in what way* true philosophers might as well be dead, nor in what way death would serve them right, nor what sort of death they deserve. Still, never mind them. Let us pursue our own discussion, and c forget about them. Do we hold that there is such a thing as death?'

'Of course,' replied Simmias.

'Isn't it just the separation of the soul from the body? Isn't that what being dead is – the body being all by itself, separated from the soul, and the soul being all by itself, separated from the body? Surely death can't be anything other than this, can it?'

'No, that's exactly what it is.'

'In that case, my friend, see if perhaps you agree with me about this next question as well. I think it will help us to a better d understanding of what we are investigating. Do you think it is the mark of a philosopher to be enthusiastic about what are called pleasures – those of food and drink, for example?'

'No, Socrates.'

'What about the pleasures of sex?'

'Certainly not.'

'What about the rest of the body's needs? Do you think this sort of man regards them as important? I mean things like the possession of smart clothes and shoes, and the other things people use to improve their physical appearance. Does he value those, or does he regard them, beyond the bare necessities, with e contempt?'

'I think the true philosopher regards them with contempt.'

'In general, then, would you say a man like this is not concerned with the body – that as far as he can he has dissociated himself from it and turned towards the soul?'

'Yes, I would.'

'Aren't things like this one way in which the philosopher,
65 more than anyone else, releases his soul as completely as he can
from its partnership with the body?'

'It looks like it.'

'And do most people think, Simmias, that for the man who
takes no pleasure in those kinds of things, and has nothing to do
with them, life is not worth living? That the man who has no
interest in the pleasures which come from the body is only one
remove from being dead?'

'Absolutely right.'

'Now, what about the actual acquisition of wisdom? If you
take the body along with you as a partner in your search, is it or
b isn't it a hindrance? I'll give you an example of what I mean. Do
sight and hearing bring men any truth? Isn't it a constant theme
even in the poets that nothing we hear or see can be relied on?
And if these senses are not reliable or accurate, it is hardly likely
the other bodily senses will be, since they are all, I take it,
inferior to the first two. Don't you agree?'

'Yes, I do agree.'

'In that case, when does the soul make contact with the truth?
When it tries to look at something in partnership with the body,
it is obviously deceived by it.'

c 'True.'

'Isn't it in reasoning, then, if anywhere, that any of the things
that are become clear to it?'

'Yes.'

'And it reasons best, I take it, when none of those things
troubles it – neither hearing nor sight, neither pain nor
pleasure – when it is as much on its own as it can be, when it
pays no attention to the body, has as little to do with it as
possible, avoids touching it, and so reaches out for what is.'

'That is so.'

'So here too the soul of the philosopher treats the body with
d complete contempt, avoiding it and trying to get to be alone by
itself.'

'It looks that way.'

'What about this next point, Simmias? Do we say there is
something just, all by itself? Or is there no such thing?'

'We say there is such a thing. Most emphatically.'

'And again something right, and good?'

'Of course.'

'Have you at any time in your life seen one of them with your eyes?'

'No.'

'Have you ever grasped them by means of any other bodily perception? I'm talking about all of them, things like size, health, strength, about the being, to put it briefly, of all the rest of them – what each one actually is. Is it through the body that e the soul views what is truest in them? Or is it more like this? Won't those of us who are best equipped to think as long and as clearly as possible about each object of our enquiry just by itself, come closest in each case to knowing it?'

'Yes, that's exactly how it is.'

'Wouldn't this be done most purely by the man who approaches each one as far as possible with thought alone, without taking sight into account at all in his thinking, and not dragging in any other sense as a partner in his reasoning? He uses 66 thought in its pure form, all by itself, in an attempt to track down each one of the things that are, in its pure form, just by itself. He frees himself, as far as possible, from his eyes, ears, and to all intents and purposes from the whole of his body, in the belief that it is a distraction, and that when it is in partnership with the soul the body stops it acquiring truth and knowledge. Isn't this the man, Simmias, if anyone, who will grasp what really is?'

'What you say is absolutely right, Socrates.'

'The result of all these arguments, then, is that there comes to b be a widespread opinion among true philosophers of the kind which leads them to say to one another: "It looks as if there is some kind of short cut which can bring us out on the right track. As long as we keep the body, and our soul is contaminated by evil of that kind, we shall never really obtain the object of our desire – which we say is truth. The body's demands for nourishment create a hundred and one distractions, and if we are attacked by disease, then again we are obstructed in our search c for what is. The body fills us with all kinds of lusts, desires, fears, phantoms and a great deal of nonsense, with the result that we really and truly never ever, as the saying goes, get a chance to

think about anything at all. The body and its desires are entirely responsible for war, faction and fighting, since it is the acquisition of money which is responsible for all wars, and it is the body
d which compels us to acquire money. We are slaves in its service. So for all these reasons the body gives us no time for philosophy. Worst of all, if it does give us any time off, and we do get a chance to enquire into anything, the body keeps cropping up at every point in our enquiry, causing chaos and confusion, unsettling us, and so preventing us seeing the truth. No, it has been well and truly proved to us that if we are ever going to gain pure knowledge of anything, we must get rid of the body, and
e look at things themselves with the soul itself. It will be when we die, apparently – so the argument suggests – and not while we are alive, that we shall get the thing we desire and claim to be in love with, namely wisdom. After all, if it is impossible to gain pure knowledge of anything with the body, then we are left with two alternatives: either it is impossible to acquire knowledge anywhere, or it is possible only for the dead. Then, and only
67 then, will the soul be by itself, apart from the body. And while we are alive we shall be closest to knowledge, it seems, if as far as possible we refuse to associate with the body or have anything to do with it beyond what is absolutely unavoidable. We must not infect ourselves with the body's nature, but keep ourselves in a state of purity from it, until god himself sets us free. That is the way we can be pure, and freed from the body's foolishness. We shall be with others who are pure, in all probability, and we shall
b know through ourselves everything that is untainted. And this perhaps is truth. I suspect it is not permitted for what is not pure to have contact with what is pure." That, I think, Simmias, is what all true lovers of knowledge are bound to say and feel. Don't you agree?'

'I couldn't agree more, Socrates.'

'In which case, my friend, if that is true, there is good reason for anyone who goes where I am going to hope that there, if anywhere, he will fully possess that which so much of our energy has been directed towards in our past life. This means
c that the journey I am now required to make is cause for optimism – as it would be for anyone who thinks that his mind has been, as it were, purified.'

'Cause for optimism indeed,' said Simmias.

'And hasn't purification been agreed, a little earlier in our discussion, to be the fullest possible separation of the soul from the body, and its growing accustomed to assembling and gathering itself together, all by itself, completely removed from the body and living all on its own, as far as it can, both in this life and the next, freed from the fetters of the body?' d

'Yes, that is agreed.'

'Is this what we call death, then – the release or separation of soul from body?'

'Exactly that.'

'And in our view it's mainly – in fact, only – philosophers who are eager to release it. Isn't the practice of philosophy just this, the release and separation of soul from body?'

'It looks like it.'

'So as I said in the first place, wouldn't it be absurd for a man to be preparing himself during his lifetime to live in the closest e possible proximity to death, and to live his life in this way, but then to get upset when death came to him?'

'Yes, it would be absurd. Obviously.'

'In that case, Simmias, true lovers of wisdom really do practise dying, and being dead is less terrifying to them than to anyone else in the world. Look at it this way. If they are altogether opposed to the body, and want to keep their soul completely on its own, wouldn't it be highly irrational for them to be frightened and upset when this happens? Wouldn't they go gladly to the place where they can expect, on arrival, to find 68 what they desired all their lives – this being wisdom – and to be rid of the constant company of what they were opposed to? There have been plenty of people ready and willing to go down to Hades to follow their human loves – boyfriends, wives, children who have died – spurred on by the hope that there they will see, and be with, those whom they once desired. So will a true lover of wisdom, one who holds fast to the very same hope, that the only place he will come upon wisdom worth speaking of is in Hades, be upset when he dies? Will he not go b there gladly? Of course he will, my friend, if he really is a philosopher. He'll be convinced that this is the only place he's going to come upon wisdom in its pure form. And that being so, as I've just said, wouldn't it be highly irrational for a man like this to fear death?'

'Yes, indeed. The height of irrationality.'

'So if you see a man getting upset at the prospect of dying, isn't that a clear indication that he wasn't a lover of wisdom, c after all, but a lover of the body. And the same man turns out also, I imagine, to be a lover of money and reputation. One or the other of these – or maybe both.'

'Yes. It is exactly as you say.'

'Well now, Simmias, isn't what we call courage a distinguishing characteristic of people such as we have been describing?'

'It certainly is.'

'And self-control as well? Or even what most people call self-control? Not getting carried away with one's desires, but treating them with calm contempt? Isn't this a characteristic only of those who have an utter contempt for the body, and who live a philosophic life?'

d   'It's bound to be.'

'And that's because there's a paradox in the courage and self-control of other people, as you will see if you care to examine them.'

'What sort of paradox, Socrates?'

'You know how everyone who isn't a philosopher regards death as one of the great evils?'

'Of course.'

'So when brave men face death, they do so through fear of greater evils.'

'That is so.'

'In which case, it is through being afraid, through fear, that everyone apart from the philosopher is brave. But being brave as a result of fear and cowardice is a paradox.'

e   'Yes, it is.'

'And what about those of them who are well-ordered? Isn't it just the same with them? Isn't it lack of discipline which somehow makes them self-controlled? We say that's impossible, but all the same what happens to them, with their unphilosophical self-control, is very similar. They desire one set of pleasures, and are frightened of losing them, so they abstain from other pleasures because they are controlled by the first set. Being ruled

by pleasures is called lack of discipline, yet for these people the 69
situation is that they control some pleasures by being under the
control of others. That's roughly what we were saying just now
about people being in some way self-controlled through lack of
discipline.'

'Yes, that is the way it looks.'

'Really, Simmias! I do hope this is not the right kind of trade
in virtue, trading pleasure for pleasure, pain for pain, and fear for
fear – the greater for the lesser, like currencies. I hope there is
just the one true currency, namely wisdom, for which one
should trade all the others, and that with this currency, wisdom, b
come true courage, self-control and justice – true goodness, in
short, with or without pleasures, fears and everything else of that
sort. As for the exchange of these for one another, in the
absence of wisdom, virtue of this kind may be no more than an
optical illusion. Real slaves' virtue, in fact, possessing no health
or truth. The truth may be that in reality self-control, justice
and courage are a kind of purifying from things of that sort, and c
that wisdom itself is a kind of purification. It looks as if those
who established our mystic rites may not have been such fools
after all. What their riddles may really have been doing all this
time is showing us that anyone who arrives in Hades uninitiated
and without experience of the rites will be cast into the mire,
whereas the person who arrives there in a state of purification
and initiation will dwell with the gods. As the experts in the
rites tell us,

> Full many bear the novice wand, yet few
> Will wear the Bacchic crown.   d

And these, in my view, are simply the ones who have practised
philosophy correctly. What I have been doing, throughout my
life, is concentrate all my efforts on becoming one of them,
leaving nothing undone which was in my power to do.
Whether my efforts have been rightly directed, and whether we
have been getting anywhere, we shall know for certain, god
willing, when we get there. Pretty soon, I imagine.

'Well, Simmias and Cebes, that's my defence – that it is
reasonable for me to leave you and my masters here without
anger or distress, because I believe that there no less than here I e

shall encounter good masters and companions. And if you find my defence in any way more convincing than the Athenian jurymen did, so much the better.'

When Socrates finished speaking, Cebes replied. 'For my part, Socrates, I agree with most of what you say. But your views on
70 the soul are something people find pretty hard to believe. They're afraid that when the soul is separated from the body, it no longer exists anywhere; that it perishes and is destroyed on the day a man dies, the moment it is separated from the body; that it leaves the body like smoke or a breath of wind, taking flight and vanishing into thin air; and that it no longer has any existence anywhere. If it really did exist somewhere, collected together all by itself and freed from the evils you have just been describing, then there would be many good reasons, Socrates,
b for hoping that what you say is true. But this belief that the soul goes on existing after a man dies, that it goes on possessing some power and ability to think, is perhaps something which calls for a fair amount of reassurance and proof.'

'You're right, Cebes,' said Socrates. 'But what do you want us to do about it? Is this the question you'd like us to discuss — whether this is probably how things are, or not?'

'Well, I for one,' Cebes replied, 'would very much like to hear your opinion on the subject.'

'In which case, I don't think anyone listening to us now — not
c even a comic playwright — could say I was just chattering away, or that the things I am talking about are irrelevant. And if that's how you feel, we'd better examine the question. Let's look at it like this. Do the souls of people who have died exist in Hades, or don't they? There is an ancient tale we remember, that they do exist there after their journey from here, and that they come back here and are born again from the dead. If this is true, and the living *are* born again from the dead, surely our souls must
d exist there. They couldn't be born again, presumably, if they didn't exist. It would be a sufficient proof of this, if it really were clear that the living can only come from the dead. But if that isn't true, then we would need some other line of argument.'

'Indeed we would,' said Cebes.

'Very well. It will make it easier to see what I mean if you don't just confine your enquiry to humans. Take a look at the

animal and plant worlds as well, and in general at all those things
which come into being. Let's see if it's the same for all of them, e
that opposites can only come from opposites – those of them
that have opposites, that is. The beautiful, for example, is the
opposite of the ugly, I take it, and the just of the unjust, and the
same with any number of other things. So the question we are
to ask ourselves is this: is it necessarily true, for anything which
has an opposite, that it can only come into being from its own
opposite? When something becomes larger, for example, I
imagine it must necessarily first have been smaller, and only
become larger afterwards.'

'Yes.'

'And if it becomes smaller, will it first be larger, and then
become smaller afterwards?'   71

'That's right.'

'And does what is weaker come from something stronger, and
what is swifter from something slower?'

'Exactly.'

'How about something which becomes worse? Isn't that from
something better? And more just from something more unjust?'

'Of course.'

'Can we take it as established, then, that everything comes to
be in this way? Opposites come from opposites.'

'Indeed we can.'

'Now, the next step. Don't they also have another characteristic?
Something like this. Between every pair of opposites, since
there are two things involved, aren't there two processes of
coming to be? From the first to the second, and then again from b
the second back to the first? Between a larger thing and a smaller
thing, isn't there increase and decrease? And don't we
correspondingly call one process "increasing", and the other
"decreasing"?'

'Yes.'

'The same with separating and combining, cooling and
heating, and everything else. Even if we don't always use the
correct terms for them, must it not still be necessarily and
universally true in practice that they come to be from one
another, and that there is a process of coming to be of each into
the other?'

'Absolutely.'

c   'What about being alive? Does that have an opposite, in the way being asleep is the opposite of being awake?'

'It certainly does.'

'What is it?'

'Being dead.'

'Do they come to be from one another, then, if they are opposites? And since there are two of them, are there two processes of coming to be between them?'

'Naturally.'

'Now, I'm going to tell you about one of the pairs we were talking about just now – both the pair itself and its processes of coming to be, or becoming. You can tell me about the other. The pair I mean are being asleep and being awake. Being awake comes to be from being asleep, and being asleep from being

d   awake. As for their processes of becoming, one is falling asleep, and the other is waking up. Are you satisfied with that, or not?'

'I certainly am.'

'Now it's your turn to give me the same description of life and death. You agree, don't you, that being dead is the opposite to being alive?'

'I do.'

'And that they come to be from one another?'

'Yes.'

'What is it that comes to be from what is living?'

'What is dead.'

'And what comes to be from what is dead?'

'I have no choice but to agree that it is the living.'

'Is it from the dead, then, Cebes, that living things and living people come into being?'

e   'Apparently.'

'In which case our souls do exist in Hades.'

'It looks like it.'

'Very well. Of the two processes of becoming, one is in fact obvious. I would imagine dying is pretty obvious, isn't it?'

'It certainly is.'

'Now, what are we going to do? Are we going to refuse to allow the opposite process of coming to be in return? Is this an area where nature is going to be one-legged? Or must we necessarily allow some process which is the opposite of dying?'

'We certainly must, I imagine.'

'And what process is that?'

'Coming to life again.'

'In which case, if there is such a thing as coming to life again, would this coming to life be a process of coming to be from the 72 dead to the living?'

'Absolutely.'

'So here too we are agreed that the living have come to be from the dead no less than the dead from the living. And we decided that if this were so, it would surely be sufficient proof that the souls of the dead must necessarily exist somewhere, in a place from which they are born again.'

'I think, Socrates, from what has been agreed, that it must necessarily be so.'

'Look at it like this, Cebes, and I think you will see that our agreement was justified. If, as they come to be, one class of things were not constantly returning to the other, so that they b go round in a kind of circle, if the process of becoming were simply linear, from the one class to its opposite, if there were no curve, no turning back to the first class, can you see that in the end everything would present the same appearance and suffer the same fate? Things would stop coming to be at all.'

'What do you mean?'

'It's not difficult to see what I mean. If we had going to sleep, but no waking up to offer recovery from sleep in exchange, you can see that in the end everything would be asleep. It would make a mockery of Endymion. There'd be nothing at all c remarkable about him, because the same thing would have happened to everything else as well. Or if everything could combine, but not separate, then Anaxagoras' "unity of all things" would soon have turned into a reality. In the same way, my dear Cebes, imagine that everything which can share in life were to die, and that dead things, when they died, remained in that state and didn't come to life again. Isn't it inevitable that eventually everything would be dead, and nothing would be alive? If it were the case that living things come from some- d where other than the dead, and that living things do die, what is to stop them all being used up, and finishing up dead?'

'Nothing, I think, Socrates,' said Cebes. 'I entirely agree with you.'

'Yes, Cebes, in my opinion it is as true as anything can be, and we are not mistaken in our agreement on this point. There really is such a thing as coming to life again, the living really are
e born from the dead, and the souls of the dead really do go on existing.'

'And what's more,' put in Cebes, 'apart from the argument you have just put forward, there's also the argument you've often used in the past, Socrates – assuming it to be true – that learning for us is in fact simply recollection. It necessarily follows from both these, I imagine, that we must at some earlier time have learnt the things we are now reminded of. But this is
73 impossible unless our soul existed somewhere before being born in this human shape. So this too seems to point to the soul being something immortal.'

At this point Simmias intervened. 'What are the proofs of that argument, Cebes? Remind me. I can't quite remember them just at the moment.'

'One very convincing argument,' said Cebes, 'is that when you ask people questions, if you ask them in the right way, they can give correct answers quite spontaneously – though if the knowledge and the correct answer were not in fact present in them, they would be incapable of doing this. Secondly, the use
b of diagrams or visual examples of that kind provides an absolutely clear indication that the theory is true.'

'And if you don't find that convincing, Simmias,' said Socrates, 'see if you agree when you look at it in a slightly different way. Are you dubious about what we call learning in fact being recollection?'

'Not exactly dubious. It's just that I need the very thing we are talking about. I need to be reminded. I can more or less remember from hearing the way Cebes set about the proof, so I do accept it really. But I wouldn't mind hearing how you set about it, for all that.'

c 'The way I set about it is like this. I imagine we agree that if you're going to be reminded of something, you must at some earlier time have known it.'

'Yes.'

'Well then, do we also agree that knowledge which comes to us in a particular way is recollection, or being reminded? What way do I mean? If seeing something, or hearing it, or receiving some other perception of it, not only makes you recognise that thing, but also puts you in mind of something else — something which is the object of a different knowledge — aren't we justified in saying you have been reminded of the second thing you were put in mind of?'

'What do you mean?'

'Something like this. Knowledge of a man, I take it, is different from knowledge of a lyre.'

'Of course.'

'Good. Now, you know what lovers are like when they see a lyre or cloak or anything the boy they love generally uses. They recognise the lyre, and it puts them in mind of the boy the lyre belongs to. And that is recollection. When you see Simmias, for example, you are often reminded of Cebes. I'm sure you could find thousands of examples of the same kind.'

'Yes, thousands,' said Simmias.

'So are things like that some kind of recollection? Particularly when it happens with things which the passage of time — and not seeing them — has made you forget about?'

'Yes, they certainly are.'

'How about seeing a picture of a horse, or a picture of a lyre, and being reminded of a man? Or a picture of Simmias, and being reminded of Cebes? Is that possible?'

'Very much so.'

'Or seeing a picture of Simmias, presumably, and being reminded of Simmias himself?'

'That's certainly possible.'

'Doesn't it turn out, in all these examples, that the recollection can arise either from things which are similar or from things which are dissimilar?'

'Yes, it does.'

'When you are reminded of something by what is similar, isn't something else bound to happen as well? Don't you decide whether or not it in any way falls short, in point of similarity, of the thing you were reminded of?'

'Yes, that's bound to happen.'

'Now, see if the next thing I have to say is true. We talk, don't we, about an "equal" of some sort. I don't mean a stick being equal to a stick, or a stone equal to a stone, or anything of that sort. I mean something else, apart from all these, the equal itself. Should we say there is such a thing, or no such thing?'

b 'We should undoubtedly say there is,' said Simmias. 'No question about it.'

'Do we know just what it is?'

'We certainly do.'

'Where did we get our knowledge of it from? Wasn't it from what we were talking about just now – from seeing sticks or stones or other things which were equal? Wasn't it from those that we formed an idea of equal itself, although it is different from them? Or doesn't it seem to you to be different? Look at it like this. Take sticks and stones which are equal. Without changing themselves, don't they sometimes seem to be equal to one thing and not equal to some other thing?'

'They certainly do.'

c 'What about true equals? Do you think they are ever unequal? Do you think equality is ever inequality?'

'No, Socrates, never.'

'So those equal things are not the same as the equal itself.'

'Not at all the same, Socrates, as far as I can see.'

'Still, wasn't it those equal things, different though they are from the equal we've been talking about, that nonetheless put you in mind of it and gave you your knowledge of it?'

'That is quite true.'

'And is the equal either like those equal things or unlike them?'

'Yes.'

'In fact it makes no difference. Provided you see one thing,
d and the sight of it puts you in mind of another – whether like it or unlike it – then that, without question, is recollection.'

'Yes. That's right.'

'Now, what about this? When it's a question of sticks, and the equal things we were talking about a moment ago, do we find something like this? Do they strike us as being equal in the same way as the one which really *is* equal? Or do they to some extent fall short of it, in being *like* the equal? Or do they not fall short at all?'

'They fall a long way short of it,' he said.

'All right, then. Sometimes the sight of something can make you think, "What I am now seeing is trying to be like some other thing that is, but it falls short. It cannot be quite like it. It can only be an inferior version." Do we agree that when you think this, it necessarily follows that you have in fact previously known the thing you say it resembles, though it falls short of it?'

'Yes, necessarily.'

'And is this what we find with things which are equal and the equal itself, or isn't it?'

'Yes, that's exactly what we find.'

'In which case, it must follow that we knew about the equal before the time when seeing the equal things first suggested to us that they were all trying to be like the equal and failing.'

'True.'

'However, we also agree on something else. This was not suggested to us – nor could it have been – by anything other than sight, touch, or one of the other senses. I count all the senses as the same.'

'They are the same, Socrates – for the purposes of this argument, at any rate.'

'And it has to be the senses that suggested to us that all the objects of our senses are striving after the equal which really *is* equal, but falling short of it. Is that what we are saying?'

'Yes.'

'So before we even started to see, or hear, or use our other senses, we must in fact have gained from somewhere a knowledge of the equal itself – what it is. Otherwise we could not have referred the equal things perceived by the senses to it, or decided that they were all doing their best to be like it, but falling short of it.'

'That necessarily follows from the earlier steps in the argument, Socrates.'

'Was it at birth that we started seeing and hearing, and possessing the other senses?'

'Of course.'

'And we must have gained our knowledge of the equal before these, didn't we say?'

'Yes.'

'In which case, it seems, we must necessarily have gained it before we were born.'

'So it seems.'

'And if we gained the knowledge before birth, and were born with it, then did we have the knowledge – both before we were born, and the moment we *were* born – not only of the equal, the greater and the smaller, but also of all other things of the same kind? After all, our present argument is no more about the equal

d than about the beautiful itself, the good itself, the just and the holy – in fact everything, as I say, to which we could attach the description "what *x* itself is" when we ask our questions or give our answers. We must necessarily, therefore, have gained our knowledge of all these things before we were born.'

'That is true.'

'And unless, having gained this knowledge, we forget it each time, we must always be born possessing it, and must continue to possess it throughout our lives. After all, to know something is merely to have gained the knowledge and not lost it. Isn't that what we call forgetting, Simmias – the loss of knowledge?'

e   'Exactly that, I think, Socrates.'

'The other possibility, I imagine, is that we gained it before we were born, but have then lost it at birth, and that it's only later, through the use of our senses directed towards the things we were talking about, that we regain our former knowledge, the knowledge we once possessed in the past. If that's what happens, wouldn't what we call learning be the regaining of knowledge which is already ours? And would we be justified in calling this regaining "being reminded"?'

'We certainly would.'

76   'Yes, because we established earlier on that it was possible to perceive something – either by seeing it or hearing it or receiving some other perception – and from it, by association, to form an idea of something different which had been forgotten, something the first thing was either similar to, or dissimilar but related. So as I say, we have two alternatives: either we are all born with this knowledge, and go on possessing it throughout our lives, or else at some later stage, when we say people are learning, they are simply being reminded of it. Learning would then be this recollection, or being reminded.'

'That is exactly the position, Socrates.'

'Which alternative are you going to choose, then, Simmias? Are we born possessing this knowledge? Or are we reminded at b some later stage of things we once had a knowledge of in the past?'

'I don't know how to make a choice, Socrates, just at the moment.'

'How about a different choice? What is your view on this? If a man knows something, could he give an account of what he knows, or not?'

'He must necessarily be able to, Socrates.'

'And do you think everyone can give an account of the things we've just been discussing?'

'If only they could! But I'm afraid it's much more likely that this time tomorrow there will be nobody in the world capable of doing so properly.'

'So you don't think everyone has a knowledge of these things, c Simmias?'

'By no means.'

'Are they, in that case, being reminded of what they once learnt in the past?'

'They must be.'

'When did our souls gain this knowledge? Clearly not after we are born as human beings.'

'No.'

'So it must have been before.'

'Yes.'

'In which case, Simmias, our souls did exist even before their existence in human shape, separate from our bodies, and they did possess the power of thought.'

'Unless of course we gain the knowledge of these things at the actual moment of birth, Socrates. There still remains that period of time.'

'Fair enough, my friend. But our loss of this knowledge – when d does that happen, if not at birth? We're not born with it, we've just agreed that. Or do we lose it at the precise moment we gain it? Or is there some other period of time you can suggest?'

'No, Socrates. I didn't realise what I was saying didn't make sense.'

'So is this the position we have reached, Simmias? Let's assume that the things we keep going on about do exist – a beautiful, a good, and every reality of that kind – and that we refer everything which comes from the senses to this reality, rediscov-
e ering what was once ours, and that we compare the things which come from the senses with this reality. It follows that just as those things exist, so too must our souls exist even before we are born. And if those things don't exist, the argument we have constructed so far will have been a waste of time, won't it? Is that the position? Does the existence of our souls before we were born depend on the existence of those things? So that if those things do not exist, then neither can these?'

'I think it's overwhelmingly clear, Socrates,' said Simmias, 'that the one does depend on the other. So the final refuge of
77 the argument is the claim that our soul's existence before we are born is as sure as the reality you are now describing. Which is lucky for us, since for my part I find it as clear as anything can be that all these sorts of things – a beautiful and a good and all the other things you mentioned just now – do exist in the fullest possible way. As far as I'm concerned, the proof is satisfactory.'

'How about Cebes? We must convince Cebes as well.'

'He finds it satisfactory,' said Simmias, 'at least, I think he does, though he's the most obstinate man in the world when it comes to being sceptical about an argument. But I think he's fully
b convinced that our soul did exist before we were born. That it will go on existing after we die, however, does not seem – even to me, Socrates – to have been demonstrated. Cebes's objection of a short while ago still stands – the common fear that the soul may vanish into thin air at the moment when a man dies, and that this may be the end of its existence. After all, what is to stop it coming into being and being put together from somewhere else, existing before it arrives in a human body, but then after its arrival and separation from the body, itself dying and being destroyed as well?'

c 'You're right, Simmias,' said Cebes. 'In showing that our soul existed before we were born, we seem to have proved half of what we had to prove. For the proof to be complete, we must also show that it will go on existing after we die, no less than before we were born.'

'We *have* shown that already, Simmias and Cebes,' said
Socrates, 'if you care to combine this argument with the one
before it, which we all accepted – that every living thing comes
into being from what is dead. If the soul exists even before birth,
and if, when it enters life and is born, it cannot possibly come d
from anywhere other than death and being dead, the inescapable
conclusion must be that it goes on existing after it dies as well,
given that it has to be born again. So the proof you want has
been given already. All the same, I get the impression you and
Simmias would be glad to deal with this argument too in greater
detail. I think you have the fear children have, that as the soul
leaves the body, the force of the wind really may blow it away
in all directions and disperse it – especially if you're unlucky e
enough to die when there's a bit of a gale blowing, and not on a
nice calm day.'

Cebes laughed. 'Take it we *are* afraid, Socrates, and try to
reassure us. Or not so much that *we* are afraid, but perhaps
somewhere inside, even in us, there is a child with fears of this
kind. Try and make *him* change his mind, and not fear death as
some sort of bogeyman.'

'You will have to use enchantments. Sing them to him every
day, until you have charmed the fears out of him.'

'And where will we find an enchanter who is any good at 78
dealing with fears of this kind, Socrates, now that you are
leaving us?'

'Greece is a large place, Cebes. There must be good men in it,
surely. And there are all the foreign nations as well. You must
search every one of them in your quest for this enchanter you're
after. Don't worry about the expense or the work involved –
there's no better investment you could make. And you should
look for him by yourselves as well, in company with one another.
After all, you may not easily find anyone better at it than you are.'

'It shall be done,' said Cebes. 'But can we go back to the
point where we left off, if you've no objection?'   b

'Of course I've no objection. Why should I have?'

'Good.'

'Very well,' said Socrates. 'Aren't the sort of questions we
should be asking ourselves these? What kind of thing is liable to
have this happen to it – this being dispersed? For what kind of

thing can we be afraid that this might happen to it? And what kind of thing is not liable? After that shouldn't we go on to ask which the soul is, and depending on the answer, be optimistic or apprehensive about our soul?'

'You're right,' he said.

c 'Well then, isn't something which is compound, or naturally composite, liable to have this happen to it – this separation into the elements of which it is composed? And if something is not composite, isn't this the one object, above all others, which is not liable to have this happen to it?'

'I think that is so,' said Cebes.

'And things that are always constant and unchanging are most likely not to be composite, while those that vary from one time to another, and are never constant, are most likely to be composite.'

'I think so.'

'Let's take the things we were talking about in our previous
d argument. Is the actual reality whose existence we are giving an account of by our questions and answers always unchanging and constant, or does it vary from one time to another? Surely the equal itself, the beautiful itself, what any given thing itself is – that which is – surely these don't admit of any change at all? Since what each of them is, taken by itself, has a single form, isn't it always unchanging and constant, never anywhere, in any way, admitting any alteration at all?'

'It must necessarily be unchanging and constant, Socrates,' said Cebes.

'What about the many beautiful things – men, let's say, or
e horses, or cloaks, or anything else of that sort – or equal things, or any of the things which go by the same names as those things which are "what each is"? Are they constant? Or are they just the opposite of those things? Are they practically never in any way constant, either in relation to themselves or to each other?'

'You're right about them, too. They are never constant.'

79 'You can touch the many things, can't you, or see them, or perceive them with the other senses, whereas it is only possible to grasp the things which are constant by means of rational thought? Things of this kind are invisible, aren't they? They cannot be seen.'

'You are absolutely right,' he said.

'Do you want us to say, then, that there are two classes of things – one seen, the other invisible?'

'Yes.'

'And that the invisible is always constant, and the seen never constant?'

'Yes, let us say that as well.'

'Very well. Now, isn't one part of us our body, and another b part our soul?'

'Yes.'

'To which class of things, then, do we say the body would be more similar, more closely related?'

'It's obvious to anyone that it is more similar to the seen class.'

'What about the soul? Is that something seen, or something invisible?'

'Well, it's certainly not seen by men, Socrates.'

'Surely when we talked of things being "seen" and "not seen", we meant by human eyes. Or did you think we were talking about some other eyes?'

'No. Human.'

'All right, then. What is our view of the soul? Do we regard it as something seen or something unseen?'

'Something unseen.'

'Invisible, in fact?'

'Yes.'

'So the soul is more similar than the body to what is invisible, while the body is more similar to what is seen.'

'They must necessarily be, Socrates.'   c

'Well then, did we also say a little while back that when the soul makes use of the body for the purpose of looking into something, by means of sight, hearing or one of the other senses – after all, examining something using the body simply *means* examining it using the senses – it is dragged by the body into the realm of things that are never constant? That it becomes erratic, confused and dizzy – as if it had had too much to drink – through contact with objects which are like itself?'

'We did.'

'When it looks at things all by itself, on the other hand, the d soul departs from here to what is pure, always existing, immortal and unchanging. The soul is closely related to this, and is there with it all the time – when it is all by itself, that is, and it is allowed to. Its wanderings are over, and when it is with those objects it remains all the time constant and unchanging, because of its contact with things which are constant and unchanging. Isn't "wisdom" the name given to this state of the soul?'

'That's a good description, Socrates. And quite true.'

'Once again, then, on the strength of the previous discussion and this present discussion, which class of things do you think e the soul is more like? Which is it more akin to?'

'On this line of argument, Socrates, I think it would be agreed by anyone – however slow on the uptake – that the soul is in every way possible more like what is always constant than what is not.'

'What about the body?'

'The body is more like the other class.'

'And here's another way of looking at it. When soul and body 80 are united, nature ordains that the body should serve and be subject, the soul rule and be master. On that basis, again, which of them do you think is like what is divine? Which of them is like what is mortal? Don't you think the divine is a natural ruler and leader, and the mortal a natural subject and servant?'

'Yes, I do.'

'In that case, which of them is the soul like?'

'Obviously, Socrates, the soul is like what is divine, and the body is like what is mortal.'

'What do you think, then, Cebes? Is the conclusion of our b whole discussion so far that the soul is most like what is divine, immortal, the object of thought, of one single form, indestructible, and remaining ever constant and true to itself, whereas the body is most like what is human, mortal, of many forms, not the object of thought, destructible, and never remaining true to itself? Do we want to raise any objection to this account of things, my dear Cebes?'

'No, we don't.'

'Well then, if that is how things are, isn't it appropriate for the body to be easily destroyed and for the soul, by contrast, to be altogether indestructible – or very nearly so?'

c 'Of course.'

'Think what happens when a man dies. The visible part of him, his body, which is located in the visible world, and which we call the corpse, is liable to destruction, decay and dissolution. None of these things starts happening to it straight away, though. The corpse can easily last for a reasonable while, even if a man's body is in the peak of condition when he dies, and he is in the prime of life. And it *can* last for a very long time. If the body is shrunk and embalmed, the way people are embalmed in Egypt, it can remain more or less complete for an incredible time. And even if the body decays, still some parts of it – bones, d sinews, things like that – are virtually everlasting, aren't they?'

'Yes.'

'What about the soul, then, the invisible part of him? It goes to a different place, a place like itself – noble, pure and invisible, the house of Hades in the true sense of the word – to the good and wise god, which is where, god willing, my soul too is shortly going to have to make its way. Does this soul of ours, whose character and nature are as we have described, get blown in all directions and destroyed as soon as it is released from the body, as most people say? Don't you believe it, my dear Cebes e and Simmias. No, what really happens is much more like this. Either the soul is released in a state of purity, dragging nothing of the body after it, since it has no more to do with the body in its life than it can help; it avoids it and gathers itself together by itself, since this is what it is constantly rehearsing for. Its life amounts simply to the pursuit of wisdom in the right way, and a genuine rehearsal for dying without regret. Or wouldn't this be 81 a rehearsal for death?'

'It certainly would.'

'Does a soul in this condition, then, go to what is like itself, to what is invisible – the divine, everlasting and wise? And when it gets there, does it have the chance to be happy, now that it is free from its wandering and folly, its fears and wild desires, and other human evils? Does it, as they say of those who have been initiated, truly spend the rest of time in the company of the gods? Should that be our view, Cebes? Or something different?'

'That. Most emphatically,' said Cebes.

'On the other hand, the soul may be in a polluted state and b unpurified when it is released from the body. It has probably

spent all its time in the company of the body, serving it, in love with it, bewitched by it and by its desires and pleasures, with the result that only what is corporeal seems real to it – things it can touch, see, drink, eat, or use for sexual enjoyment. What is hidden from the eyes and invisible, what can be thought or grasped by philosophy, this it has come to hate, fear and avoid.
c Do you believe a soul in this condition will get away all by itself, pure and unalloyed?'

'Impossible.'

'Yes. I imagine it will have patches of what is corporeal, won't it, grafted on to it by the fellowship and company of the body, through constant association and the habits of a lifetime?'

'It certainly will.'

'Yes. We should think of the corporeal as a burden, my friend. Heavy, earthbound and visible. A soul of this type, with this corporeal element, is weighed down and dragged back to the visible realm, so we are told, by fear of the invisible and of
d Hades. It haunts tombstones and graves. That is where the shadowy phantoms of souls are actually seen, the kind of apparitions produced by souls of this type, souls which have not been set free in a pure state, but still have some element of what is visible – which is why they can be seen.'

'Quite likely, Socrates.'

'Extremely likely, Cebes. And it won't be the souls of the good, but those of the wicked. They are compelled to roam around places of that sort, paying the penalty for their evil way of life in the past. They carry on roaming like this until their
e desire for the thing which accompanies them, the corporeal, makes them go back and be chained to a body again. They are chained, as you'd expect, to characters which match their actual habits during their life.'

'What sort of characters do you mean, Socrates?'

'Well, for example, if they haven't been careful to avoid gluttony, lust and drunkenness, if they've made a habit of them, they may well be born in the shape of donkeys or some animal
82 like that. Don't you think so?'

'More than likely.'

'And those who have set the highest value on injustice, tyranny and robbery, in the shape of wolves, or hawks, or kites.

Where else can we say souls like this go?'

'Naturally,' said Cebes, 'that's the kind of shape they will take.'

'And is it obvious,' he asked, 'where every other class of soul will go, depending on what its previous way of life was like?'

'Yes, it is obvious. Of course it is.'

'In which case, aren't the most fortunate among them, and the ones who go to the best place, those who in public and political life have made a habit of excellence – what they call self-control b and justice – when these are the result of their disposition or way of life, but not of philosophy and reason?'

'In what way the most fortunate?'

'Because they will probably return as members of an organised, civilised species like themselves. Bees, I should think, or wasps, or ants – or even back again to the same human species, to become decent men.'

'They probably will.'

'But to join the company of the gods is not permitted to the man who has not practised philosophy and departed this life in a c state of perfect purity. It is permitted only to the lover of wisdom. And that, Simmias and Cebes, my dear friends, is why true philosophers abstain from all bodily desires. They stand firm, and do not give in to them. It's not because they have some fear of losing the family fortune, or being poor, as most people have, in their obsession with money. Nor again do they abstain from bodily pleasures through fear of notoriety or the reputation of living an evil life, like those who are eager for public office or public recognition.'

'No, that wouldn't be the right motive, Socrates,' said Cebes.

'Indeed it wouldn't. That's why those who care at all for their d own soul, and do not spend their life moulding it to fit the body, forget about all these others. They set out by a different route from people who seem to have no idea where they are going. Their duty, they believe, is not to oppose philosophy, or the release and purification it brings. And so, in their pursuit of it, they follow the direction in which it leads.'

'How do they do that, Socrates?'

'I'll tell you. Lovers of knowledge realise that philosophy finds their soul literally imprisoned in the body, glued to it, compelled e

to look at the things that are through the body as if through
prison bars, as it wallows in total ignorance, unable to look at
them all by itself. And it can see that the cleverness of the prison
is the way it uses desire to make the prisoner, as far as possible,
83 his own jailer. Well, as I say, lovers of knowledge realise that
philosophy, finding the soul in this state, gently encourages it
and tries to set it free. It points out that enquiry carried out
using the eyes is fraught with deception, and fraught with
deception likewise the ears and other senses. Philosophy persuades
the soul to withdraw from these, except in situations where it
has no choice but to use them. It urges the soul to collect and
gather itself together by itself, and have no confidence in
b anything other than itself and the thoughts which it has, by
itself, about any of the things that are, by themselves. Anything
it examines by different means, anything which is different in
different situations, it should regard as without truth. This kind
of thing is an object of perception, and seen, whereas what it
sees for itself is an object of thought, and invisible. And this
release, the soul of the true philosopher thinks, is not something
it should fight against. This is why it keeps away from pleasures,
desires and pains as much as it can. Its reasoning is that when
people experience too much pleasure, or fear, or desire, what
happens to them is not the kind of minor evil you might expect
c as a result – falling ill, perhaps, or wasting money on the
satisfaction of their desires. No, what happens to them, without
their thinking twice about it, is the greatest and most extreme of
all evils.'

'And what is that, Socrates?'

'The fact that no one's soul can feel extreme pleasure or pain
over anything without at the same time being compelled to
believe that the thing which occasions the pleasure or pain is
outstandingly clear and true, when in fact it is nothing of the
kind. This is particularly true of things which are seen, isn't it?'

'Yes.'

d   'Isn't it when this happens that the soul is most imprisoned by
the body?'

'Explain.'

'Every pleasure and pain attaches the soul to the body with a
kind of rivet, pinning it there and making it like the body, with

the result that whatever the body says is true, the soul believes
it. The inevitable result, I believe, of having the same opinions
as the body, and taking pleasure in the same things, is that the
soul is forced to adopt the same nature and nurture. It is no
longer capable of reaching Hades in a pure state, but must
always be imbued with the body when it leaves here. So it
quickly falls back into another body, like a seed being sown and e
growing again, and this stops it having any share in the company
of what is divine, pure and single in form.'

'What you say is absolutely true, Socrates.'

'That is the reason, Cebes, why true lovers of knowledge are
well-ordered and brave. It is not for the reasons given by most
people. Or do you think it is?'

'No, I certainly don't.'   84

'No, indeed. A philosopher's soul will reason in the way we
have described. It will not think both that it is philosophy's job
to free the soul from the body, and that while it is doing so, the
soul should of its own accord keep handing itself over again to
pleasures and pains, and so bind itself to the body again,
performing Penelope's endless task of undoing its own weaving.
No, it provides a calm retreat from all this by following reason,
and being always engaged in it. It keeps its eyes on what is true,
divine and not the object of opinion, and is sustained by that. It b
thinks that this is how it should live, for as long as it does live,
and that when it dies, it will come to what is akin to itself and
like itself, and be rid of human evils. With this kind of
upbringing, Simmias and Cebes, there is no danger of the soul's
being afraid that it will be torn to pieces in its separation from
the body, that it will be blown away, disappear into thin air, and
no longer have any existence anywhere.'

When Socrates finished speaking, there was silence for a c
considerable time. Socrates himself was absorbed in the argument
he had just put forward, as far as we could see. And so were
most of us. But Cebes and Simmias went on talking to one
another, just the two of them, in a low voice. Socrates looked at
them. 'What is it?' he asked. 'You don't think there's some flaw
in what we've just said, do you? I'm sure it's open to all sorts of
doubts and objections, for anyone who feels like going into it
properly. If it's something else the two of you are wondering

about, that's fine. But if it's something to do with our discussion that is bothering you, don't hesitate to say what *you* think, and
d give your own explanation, if you think it could be better expressed in some way. Or again, take me along with you as well, if you think you'll get on any better with my help.'

'All right, Socrates,' Simmias replied, 'I'll be honest with you. For some while now we've both been a bit unsure what to do. We've each been egging the other on, and telling one another to ask you something. We want to hear your answer, but we're worried about upsetting you. It may be a bit unwelcome in your present predicament.'

This brought a chuckle from Socrates. 'Oh dear, Simmias,' he said. 'I'd certainly have a job convincing the rest of the world
e that I don't regard my present situation as a predicament. I can't even convince you people. You're afraid I may start being all touchy now, in a way I've never been in the past. You must think swans have a much clearer idea of the future than I do, by the sound of it. Though they do sing during their lifetime as
85 well, swans reserve their longest and most beautiful song for when they realise it's time for them to die. They rejoice that they are about to depart and join the god whose servants they are. Mankind's own fear of death causes them to do the swans an injustice. They say it's a song of grief the swans are singing on their departure, in lament for their own death. They ignore the fact that no bird sings when it's hungry, or cold, or in any other kind of pain. Not even the nightingale, the swallow or the hoopoe, though people do say these birds are in distress, and singing songs of lamentation. But I don't think it's distress
b which makes them sing, any more than it makes swans sing. It's because they belong to Apollo, I imagine, and so they can see the future. They sing because they can foresee the good things which await them in Hades, and they are happier that day than they have ever been before. I regard myself as the swans' fellow-servant, devoted to the same god. I don't think the vision of the future granted me by my master is in any way inferior to theirs, or that I am any more dismayed than they are at parting with life. So as far as that goes, you should speak out, and ask any questions you want, while the Athenians' Committee of Eleven allows it.'

'That's very good of you,' said Simmias. 'In that case I'll tell you what's bothering me, and then Cebes here can tell you c where *he* doesn't accept what has been said. My view on things like this, Socrates, is perhaps the same as yours. In our present life, as I see it, to know for sure is either impossible or something extremely difficult. But not to test the things that are said on the subject in every possible way, refusing to give up until you have examined them to the point of exhaustion, shows a very feeble spirit. And in this inquiry you have to do one of two things. You can either be told how things are – or you can find out for yourself. Or if that's impossible, you can take the best and most irrefutable of human teachings and travel on that, making it the raft on which you hazard the voyage of d your life – unless anyone can make the journey more safely and with less risk using some divine teaching as a more reliable form of transport. And on this occasion in particular I make no apology for asking questions, since that's what you yourself tell me to do. That way I shan't have to reproach myself at some later date for not saying what I think now. In my opinion, Socrates, when I examine the things that have been said – either on my own or with Cebes here – the argument is not entirely satisfactory.'

'Perhaps, my friend,' Socrates replied, 'your opinion is correct. e But tell me in what way the argument is unsatisfactory.'

'Well, it's only a personal view, but it seems to me you could use exactly the same argument about the tuning of a lyre and its strings. You could say that in the tuned lyre the tuning is something unseen and incorporeal, a thing beautiful and divine, 86 whereas the lyre itself and its strings are material bodies, corporeal, composite, earthly and related to what is mortal. Suppose you then smash the lyre, or cut or break the strings. It would be open to anyone to maintain, using the same argument you used, that the tuning must necessarily still exist and not have been destroyed. After all, if the lyre and the strings, which are perishable, can go on existing after the strings have been broken, there's no possible way the tuning can be destroyed – and destroyed before what is mortal – since it is of b the same nature as what is divine and immortal, and akin to it. The tuning itself must necessarily exist somewhere, he would

say. The wood and the strings would rot away long before anything happened to that. I mean, as I see it, Socrates, you must be well aware yourself that this is pretty much the kind of thing we take the soul to be, as if our bodies were under tension, held together by hot and cold, dry and wet, and things like that. We think of our souls as a combination and
c attunement of just these things, properly mixed with one another and in the right proportions. Well, if the soul really is some kind of attunement, then obviously when the balance between relaxation and tension in our bodies is destroyed by disease or any other evil, the soul is bound to be destroyed immediately, however divine it may be – just like any other attunement, whether in musical notes or in the works of any skilled artist or craftsman – even though the remains of any particular body go on existing for a considerable time, until the
d body is burnt or rots away. There you are, then. You'd better see what we're going to say in reply to this argument, if someone claims that the soul is a mixture of the elements in the body, and so perishes first in what is called death.'

Socrates gave one of those wide, unblinking stares of his. Then he said, with a smile, 'It's fair enough, what Simmias says. So come on, those of you who are a bit quicker than I am. Why don't you answer him? He looks to have a pretty good grasp of the argument. Wait, though. I think, before answering him, we should first hear what fault Cebes here in his turn has to find
e with the argument. That will give us a little time to decide what our reply is going to be. Then after listening to what they have to say we can either agree with them, if they seem to be singing in tune, or if they don't, that will be the moment for us to put the case for the argument. So come on, Cebes, it's your turn now. Tell us what it was that was bothering *you*.'

'All right, I'll tell you,' said Cebes. 'In my view, the argument is still where it was, open to the same objection we put forward
87 earlier on. That our soul did exist before entering this human shape, I did not and do not dispute. That has been elegantly and, if it is not presumptuous to say so, conclusively proved. But that the soul goes on existing somewhere after we die – this has not, I think, been proved. I don't agree with Simmias' objection to the claim that the soul is something stronger and more long-

lasting than the body. I think that in all these respects it is far and away superior to the body. But when the argument asks, "Are you still not convinced when you can see that even what is weaker goes on existing after a man dies? Don't you think what is more long-lived must necessarily go on being preserved b during this time?", then see whether my reply to this makes any sense. I too need to use an analogy, I think, just as Simmias did. I think what is being said about the soul is like arguing, on the death of an old weaver, that the man has not perished, but still exists somewhere, safe and sound. You might offer as proof the cloak which the man had himself woven, and which he used to wear. "The cloak is safe enough," you might say. "That hasn't perished." And if anyone remained unconvinced, you could ask c him which kind of thing was more long-lived, a man or cloak which is in use and being worn. If the reply was that a man is much longer-lived, you would think it had been proved that the man was safer than ever, since the thing which was more short-lived had not perished.

'But the truth is otherwise, I think, Simmias. What I am saying is directed at you too. Anyone's reaction would be that this is a pretty naive argument. This weaver of ours has woven himself lots of cloaks like this one, and worn them out. He has perished later than all those other ones, admittedly – but *before* this last one, I take it. That doesn't in any way make a man d something worse or weaker than a cloak. This is an exact analogy, I think, of the soul's relationship to the body. You could say precisely the same things about them – with every justification, in my view. The soul is something long-lived, while the body is weaker and more short-lived. You might agree that each soul wears out many bodies, especially if it lives for a large number of years. Though the body may be in a state of flux, perishing while the man is still alive, yet the soul always weaves afresh what is being worn out. But it would necessarily e be true, for all that, that when the soul perished, it was in fact wearing its final garment. This one alone would outlive it. And when the soul had perished, then the body would reveal its natural weakness. It would swiftly decompose, and vanish. So we can't yet rely on this argument, and be confident that our soul continues to exist somewhere after we die.   88

'You can imagine someone going along with the speaker even further than you go. He might concede not only that our souls exist during the time before we are born, but also that when we die there is no reason why the souls of many of us shouldn't continue to exist now, and go on existing in the future, and be born and die again many times over – the object in question being naturally so strong that it can survive being born repeatedly. He might concede all this, but still refuse to allow that the soul suffers nothing in all these births, that it doesn't finally, in one of its deaths, perish completely. The particular death, he might say,

b the particular dissolution of the body, which brings destruction to the soul, is something no one can know, since it is impossible for any of us ever to perceive it. But if this is so, there is no reason for anyone to approach death with confidence, since his confidence may be misplaced – unless he is able to demonstrate that the soul really is something wholly immortal and imperishable. Otherwise, he might say, someone who is about to die is always bound to fear for his soul, in case it is utterly destroyed in this particular separation from the body.'

c   We were all discouraged by what they had to say – as we admitted to one another afterwards. We had been firmly convinced by the earlier argument. But now, we thought, they had thrown us into confusion again, casting doubt not only on what had been said so far, but also on what was going to be said from now on. Were our powers of judgement useless? Was the whole question of its very nature doubtful?

ECHECRATES: Heavens, Phaedo, I don't blame you. My own impulse now, hearing you tell the story, is to say something like

d this to myself. 'What argument *can* we any longer have confidence in? The argument Socrates was putting forward was extremely persuasive, and now that has been thrown into doubt.' The argument that our soul is a kind of harmony has an incredibly powerful hold over me. It always has, and it still does. Hearing it again served as a kind of reminder that it was something I myself already believed. Now I'm right back where I started. I need some different argument to convince me that when a man dies his soul does not die with him. So tell me, how exactly did Socrates pursue the discussion? Was *he* visibly

upset at all, as you say the rest of you were, or wasn't he? Did he e
calmly come to the defence of his argument? And was his
defence successful, or did it fail? Tell us the whole story in as
much detail as you can.

PHAEDO: Well, Echecrates, much as I had always admired
Socrates, I was never so impressed by him as I was at that
moment. That Socrates should find *something* to say was perhaps 89
not so very surprising. But what I found completely astonishing,
speaking for myself, was first the pleasure, courtesy and delight
with which he listened to the young men's arguments; second,
how quickly he realised the effect of their arguments on *us*; and
third, the skill with which he healed us, encouraging us and
rallying us in our defeat and headlong flight, and leading us back
to join in examining the argument.

ECHECRATES: How did he manage that?

PHAEDO: I'll tell you. I was sitting, as it happened, on his right –
on a kind of stool beside his bed. So he was a good deal higher b
than me. He stroked my head, gathering a handful of the hairs
on my neck – he used to tease me about my hair from time to
time – and said, 'I suppose tomorrow, Phaedo, you will have
this lovely hair cut off.'

'Probably, Socrates.'

'Not if you take my advice.'

'What *should* I do?'

'Do it today. You cut yours, and I'll cut mine, if that really is
the death of our argument, and we can't bring it back to life.
That's what I'd do if I were you, and the argument were getting c
away from me. I'd take an oath, the way the Argives did, not to
grow my hair again until I'd taken on the argument of Simmias
and Cebes again, and defeated it.'

'But even Heracles, so the saying goes, was not capable of
taking on two at once.'

'Appeal to me for support, then, while there's still light. I'll be
your Iolaus.'

'Very well. I do appeal to you, but not as Heracles. I am
Iolaus, and I call on Heracles.'

'It makes no odds. But first, there's one thing we have to
make sure doesn't happen to us.'

'What is that?'

d   'We mustn't become misologists, haters of argument. Like
misanthropists. It is impossible,' he said, 'for any greater evil to
befall a man than to find he has come to hate argument.
Misology and misanthropy both arise in the same way. Misanthropy grows out of placing a blind, uncritical trust in someone,
believing that person to be in every way true, healthy and
reliable, only to find a little later that he is evil and unreliable.
And then the same again with a second person. If this happens
to someone a lot of times, particularly with those he regarded as
e   his closest friends, then in the end, after repeated blows, he starts
hating everybody and thinking there is absolutely no good in
anybody. Or have you never heard of that happening?'

'No, I certainly have heard of it.'

'Isn't it an ugly thing when it does happen? And isn't it obvious
that someone like this was trying to deal with human beings
without having any real knowledge of human nature? If he had
any knowledge, he would presumably have realised – what is in
90   fact the case – that there are very few who are either very good or
very bad, whereas those in between are extremely numerous.'

'Can you explain that?'

'It's the same with the very small and the very large. Is there
anything more uncommon, do you think, than to find a man –
or a dog, or anything else – who is really enormous or really
tiny? Or again, swift or slow? Or ugly or beautiful? Or pale or
dark? Aren't you aware that in cases like this the extreme
examples at either end are rare and few, while the intermediate
examples are many and abundant?'

'Yes, of course.'

b   'In which case, if there were a competition in wickedness,
don't you think that there too the winners would be few and far
between?'

'Quite likely,' I said.

'It's very likely. However, that's not where the similarity
between arguments and people lies. I was following your lead
there. The point of similarity is this. When someone with no
real knowledge of arguments believes an argument to be true,
and then a little later decides it is false – sometimes when it is,
and sometimes when it isn't – and then a second argument, and

then a third: especially people who've spent their time on c
paradoxes. You know how they finish up. They think they've
grown immensely wise, and that they're the only people to have
realised that there's nothing healthy or trustworthy either in any
action or in any argument, but that everything that is ebbs and
flows as if floating in the Euripus, never remaining in one place
for any length of time.'

'How right you are,' I said.

'Well, Phaedo, it would be a pity if there really were some
argument which was true, reliable and within our grasp, but if
familiarity with the kind of arguments which seem to be true d
one moment and false the next led someone to put the blame
not on himself and his own lack of knowledge – if eventually, in
his distress, he was only too glad to shift the blame away from
himself and on to the argument, and then spend the rest of his
life hating and condemning arguments, and losing the true
knowledge of the things that are.'

'Heavens, yes. That would indeed be a pity.'

'That's one thing we have to be careful about, then. We
mustn't let the idea that there's probably nothing healthy in e
argument gain admittance to the soul. Much better to realise
that *we* are not yet healthy, and that we must make a brave and
determined attempt to become healthy. You and the others
because it affects the whole of the rest of your lives, and I
precisely because of my death. It may well be that at the 91
moment my approach to the question is not philosophical, but
competitive. Like someone with no education at all. When
people like that argue about something, they don't care how the
things the argument is about really are. All their energy is
devoted to getting those present to accept the opinion they
themselves put forward. I think that in my present situation I
shall differ from them in one respect only. My energy will not
be devoted – except incidentally – to getting those present to
believe that what I say is true, but rather to getting *myself* to
believe, as strongly as possible, that it is so. My reasoning, dear
friend, is as follows – and note how determined I am to have b
things both ways. If what I am saying is in fact true, then it is a
good idea to believe it. If on the other hand there is nothing in
store for a person after he dies, then at least during this actual

period before my death I shall make less of a nuisance of myself to you all with my lamentations. And my stupid mistake will not be very long-lived – which *would* be a bad thing – but will very soon come to an end.

'There you are, you see, Simmias and Cebes. I approach the argument with my position well worked out. As for you, if you
c take my advice, you'll be much less worried about Socrates than about the truth. If anything I say strikes you as true, you must agree with it. But if you don't think it is true, you must oppose it in every way, and make sure that in my eagerness I don't deceive both myself and you at the same time, and depart like a bee, leaving my sting still in you.

'On, then. Remind me first what you said, if it turns out I don't remember. Simmias is sceptical, I think, and afraid that the soul, despite being something more divine and more beautiful
d than the body, may nevertheless exist in the form of an attunement, and be destroyed before the body. Cebes, on the other hand, agreed with me, I thought, that the soul was more long-lived than the body, but said that no one could know whether the soul, after wearing out numerous bodies in numerous lives, might not finally be itself destroyed, leaving behind its last body, and that *this* might be what death is, the destruction of the soul, since the body is being destroyed continuously and unceasingly. Is that wrong, Simmias and Cebes? Or are those the questions you want us to examine?'

e   They both agreed these were the questions.

'Well then, did you reject *all* our earlier arguments? Or reject some and accept others?'

'We rejected some,' they both answered, 'and accepted others.'

'In which case, what is your view of the argument in which we said that learning was recollection, and that this being so, our soul must necessarily already exist somewhere else before its
92 imprisonment in the body?'

'Speaking for myself,' said Cebes, 'I found it wonderfully convincing when I heard it, and I stand by it now. More than any other argument.'

'The same goes for me, too,' said Simmias. 'On this question at least, I'd be astonished if I ever changed my mind.'

'Well, my Theban friend, you have no choice but to change it, if you want to keep this opinion that an attunement is something composite, and that the soul is a kind of attunement composed of the elements of the body under tension. You won't, I imagine, allow yourself to say that an attunement b existed as something composite *before* the elements from which it was going to be composed. Or will you?'

'No, Socrates.'

'Do you realise this is what you *are* saying, when you say both that the soul exists before it enters the form and body of a man, and also that it is composed of elements which do not yet exist? You see, an attunement isn't the kind of thing you are making it out to be. The lyre, strings and notes come into being first, untuned to start with. The tuning comes last of all, and is the c first to perish. So how is this theory of yours going to harmonise with your theory about recollection?'

'It isn't,' said Simmias. 'It can't possibly.'

'And yet if ever a theory ought to be in harmony, one about attunement ought to be.'

'Yes, it ought,' said Simmias.

'Well, this theory of yours is not in harmony. So you'd better see which theory you prefer – that learning is recollection, or that the soul is an attunement.'

'I much prefer the first, Socrates. The second was not the result of any proof. I believed it because it was plausible and d attractive – the same reason most people believe it. I am well aware that arguments which rely on plausibility to establish proofs are confidence tricksters. They can take you in completely, if you aren't extremely careful about them – both in geometry and in other disciplines. Whereas the argument about recollection and learning was based on a hypothesis which commands acceptance. What it says, I take it, is that the existence of our soul before it enters our body is as certain as the existence of the reality bearing the name "that which is". This hypothesis, I am in absolutely no doubt, I have fully and rightly accepted. And e therefore I must necessarily, as far as I can see, reject any claim made by myself or anyone else that the soul is an attunement.'

'And here's another way of looking at it, Simmias. Do you think it makes sense for an attunement, or anything else which is

93 composite, to be somehow different from the elements of which
it is composed?'

'No.'

'Nor for it to do anything, I imagine, or have anything done to
it, different from what those elements do or have done to them?'

He assented.

'So it doesn't make sense for an attunement to lead the
elements of which it is composed. It can only follow them.'

He agreed.

'It's out of the question, in that case, for an attunement to
make any movement or sound in opposition to its own parts –
or be opposed to them in any way.'

'Absolutely out of the question.'

'Again, isn't it the nature of any attunement to be an
attunement just as it has been tuned?'

'I don't understand.'

'Well, if it is tuned more fully and completely – assuming such
b a thing to be possible – wouldn't it be a fuller and more
complete attunement? And if it has been tuned less fully and
completely, wouldn't it be a less full and complete attunement?'

'Of course.'

'Does the same apply to the soul? Can one soul be just this
very thing – a soul – even very slightly more fully and
completely, or less fully and completely, than another?'

'No, not in the least.'

'But then surely there's another objection. Is one soul
described as possessing intelligence and virtue, and being good,
while another is described as possessing folly and wickedness,
c and being bad? And are these descriptions correct?'

'Yes, they are correct.'

'In which case, what is any of these people who maintain that
the soul is an attunement going to say these qualities of goodness
and badness in the soul are? A further attunement and non-
attunement? Has one soul – the good one – been tuned? But it
is already itself an attunement. Does it contain a second
attunement within it? And the soul which has not been tuned?
Is *that* itself an attunement, but one which does *not* contain a
second attunement within it?'

'I don't have an answer to that,' said Simmias. 'But anyone

putting forward that theory would obviously have to say something like that.'

'But it has already been agreed that one soul is no more or less d a soul than another soul. And this is the agreement, is it not, that one attunement is no more full and complete, or less full and complete, than another attunement?'

'Absolutely.'

'And what is no more or less an attunement cannot have been either more or less tuned. Is that right?'

'It is.'

'Does what has not been more or less tuned have any greater or smaller share in attunement? Or does it have an equal share?'

'An equal share.'

'In which case, since one soul is just this thing − a soul − neither more nor less than another soul, then neither has it been e any more or less tuned?'

'That is so.'

'In which case, it couldn't have any greater share in non-attunement or attunement, could it?'

'No, it couldn't.'

'And in that case, could one soul have any greater share in badness or goodness than another − if badness is non-attunement and goodness is attunement?'

'No.'

'Or rather, to be strictly accurate, Simmias, I take it that no 94 soul, if it is an attunement, will have a share of badness. Presumably an attunement which was altogether just this − an attunement − couldn't ever have any share in non-attunement.'

'No, it couldn't.'

'Nor, presumably, could a soul which was altogether a soul have any share in badness.'

'How could it, on what has been agreed so far?'

'On this argument, therefore, we shall find that all souls, of all living creatures, are equally good, if it is the nature of all souls equally to be just this − souls.'

'I think we shall, Socrates.'

'Do you find this a satisfactory conclusion? And do you think this would have happened to our argument if our hypothesis b that the soul is an attunement were correct?'

'No, I don't. Not for a moment.'

'And another point. Can you point to anything apart from the soul – particularly a wise soul – which is in control of all the elements in a man?'

'No, I can't.'

'Because it agrees with what the body is feeling, or because it opposes it? I mean, for example, if there is heat and thirst in the body, but the soul drags it in the opposite direction, towards not drinking? Or if there is hunger in the body, and the soul drags it towards not eating? And I imagine we can see any number of
c other ways in which the soul is opposed to the body's feelings, can't we?'

'We certainly can.'

'But didn't we agree earlier on that if it was an attunement it could never sound a note which was out of keeping with the elements of which it was in fact composed – their tensions and relaxations, the striking of the strings, or anything else that happens to them? Didn't we say it followed them, and could never lead them?'

'Yes, we did agree that. Of course we did.'

'So what are we to make of the fact that the soul is now clearly doing the exact opposite? It acts as the leader of all those
d elements of which it is said to be composed, and opposes them in virtually everything throughout its life. It acts as their master in every way, being sometimes more harsh in its punishments – using the pain of physical training and medicine – and sometimes more gentle. Sometimes it threatens, at other times it advises, addressing desire, anger and fear as things quite different from itself. Rather like what Homer says about Odysseus in the *Odyssey*, I imagine:

> But smiting on his breast, thus he reproved
> The mutinous inhabitant within:
e > 'Heart, bear it. Worse than this thou didst endure.'

Do you think that when he wrote this he thought of the soul as an attunement, capable of being influenced by the body's feelings? Didn't he rather think of it as capable of being the leader and master of those feelings, and being itself something much too divine to be thought of as an attunement?'

'I'm sure he did, Socrates.'

'In that case, my friend, it is quite wrong for us to say that the soul is some sort of attunement. We would apparently be 95 contradicting not only the divine poet Homer, but also ourselves.'

'That is true.'

'Very well,' said Socrates. 'It looks as if we have more or less made our peace with our lady of Thebes, the goddess Harmonia. How about the objection of Cadmus, Cebes? How shall we make our peace with that? What argument shall we use?'

'You'll find one,' said Cebes. 'I'm sure of it. Certainly the argument you've just put forward against attunement was wonderfully unexpected. When Simmias was in difficulties, and explaining what bothered him, I really couldn't see how anyone was going to find a way of dealing with his argument. So I was b very surprised when it couldn't withstand the very first onslaught of your argument. I wouldn't be at all surprised if exactly the same thing happened to the argument of Cadmus as well.'

'Don't tempt Providence, my friend. We don't want our next argument defeated because we've put the evil eye on it. That's all in the lap of the gods, though. Our job is to come to close quarters, like true Homeric heroes, and find out if there really is anything in what you say. What you're after, to put it in a nutshell, is this. Imagine a philosopher on the point of death, c who believes with some confidence that after his death he will fare better in the other world than if he were dying at the end of any other kind of life. You think that if his confidence is not to be irrational and foolish, it must be demonstrated that our soul is indestructible and immortal. Showing that the soul is something strong and godlike, and that it was already in existence before we were born as human beings, can perfectly well point, you say, not to immortality but to the fact that the soul is long-lived, that it existed somewhere previously for an incredibly long time, and that it knew and did all sorts of things. But it was no more immortal, for all that. Indeed, the very fact of entering a d human body at all was the beginning of its destruction. Like catching a disease. It lives this life in pain, and it finally perishes in what we call death. As for the fears we all of us have, you say it makes no difference whether the soul enters our body once or

many times. You'd be a fool not to be afraid if you don't know,
and can't prove, that it is immortal. That's roughly your
position, I think, Cebes. I've deliberately gone over it more
than once, to make sure we didn't leave anything out, and give
you the chance to add or subtract anything, if you want to.'

'No, there's nothing I want to subtract or add just at the
moment,' Cebes replied. 'That *is* my position.'

Socrates paused for a considerable time, thinking something
over to himself, before saying: 'It's no small thing you're asking,
Cebes. It involves dealing with the whole question of the cause
of coming to be and being destroyed. What I *can* do, if you like,
is explain my own experience of those things to you. Then if
you find any of what I say useful, you can use it to settle the
questions you are asking.'

'Yes,' said Cebes, 'that is what I would like.'

'Listen, then, and I'll tell you. When I was young, Cebes, I
was incredibly keen on the branch of knowledge known as
natural science. I thought it was a wonderful thing to know the
causes of everything – why each thing comes to be, why it is
destroyed, why it exists. And I used to be constantly shifting my
ground. I'd start with questions like: "Is it when hot and cold
cause some sort of putrefaction, as some people used to say, that
living creatures are formed? Is it the blood which enables us to
think? Or is it the air, or fire? Or is it none of these? Is it the
brain which provides the sensations of hearing, sight and smell?
Do memory and opinion arise from these? And as memory and
opinion become fixed, is that how knowledge arises?" Then
again I'd start asking questions about the destruction of all these
things, and about the behaviour of the heavens and the earth,
until finally I decided I was uniquely unfitted for this sort of
enquiry. I can give you convincing proof of this. Things I had
once known for certain, so I and everybody else thought – well,
I was now so utterly blinded by all this enquiry that I had
unlearnt even the things I previously thought I knew: in
particular the answer to the question "What makes a man
grow?" Until then I had thought it obvious to anyone that the
answer was eating and drinking; that when food added flesh to
flesh, and bones to bones, when in this way, following the same
principle, the appropriate substance grew on to the other

individual parts of the body, that this was when a small mass became in time large, and how the small man becomes a large one. That's what I used to think. Not unreasonably, wouldn't you say?'

'I would indeed,' said Cebes.

'How about one or two other examples? If a tall man standing by a small man seemed to be taller just by a head, I found no difficulty with that. Or a horse being larger than a horse. And it was clearer still, I thought, that ten was more than eight by the addition of two, and that a two-cubit measure was bigger than a one-cubit measure because it exceeded it by half of its own length.'

'And now?' Cebes asked. 'How do you feel about those things now?'

'I feel I couldn't be further from even beginning to think I know the reason for any of these things. I can't even believe my own account of what happens when one is added to one. Has the one which was added to become two? Or is it the one which was added? Or have the one which is added and the one it was added to become two because of the addition of one to the other? I'm puzzled by the fact that when each of them was apart from the other, then each of them was one, and the pair of them were not then two, but that when they came near one another, this was the cause of their becoming two – this union which consists in being put beside one another. Nor can I any longer be persuaded, if you divide one, that this is the cause – this division – of its becoming two, since the cause of two coming into being now seems the opposite of what it was before. Then it was because they were brought close to one another, and one was added to the other. Now it is because one is being removed and separated from the other. I can't even persuade myself any more that I understand why one comes into being, nor why anything else, to put it briefly, comes into being or is destroyed or exists. Not pursuing this manner of enquiry, at any rate. I now pursue a different method, having lost all interest in the other, and make a cheerful confusion of my own.

'Then one day I heard someone reading from a book which he said was by Anaxagoras, and saying that intelligence was in fact the organising principle and cause of all things. Now this was the kind of cause or reason I really liked, and I decided it was in some way right that intelligence should be the reason for all things. If it is true, I thought, then intelligence, being the organising principle, must organise everything and arrange each individual thing in the way that is best. So if you want to find the reason for any particular thing coming to be or being destroyed or existing, the question you have to ask about it is how it is best for it to be, or act, or be acted upon in any way. d And it follows from this that what is best and finest, whether in relation to himself or anything else, is the only proper subject of study for a man – though the same person would necessarily have to know the worse as well, since the same knowledge applies to both. That was my reasoning, and I was delighted to think that if I wanted a reason for the way things are, I had found in Anaxagoras a teacher after my own heart. I thought he would start off by telling me whether the earth is flat or round, e and after telling me that go on to explain in detail the reason and necessity for its being so. I thought he'd talk about what was better, and say that it was better for it to be the way it was. And if he said the earth was at the centre, then he'd explain in detail how it was better for it to be at the centre. If he could make 98 those things clear to me, I was quite prepared to stop yearning for some other kind of reason.

'The same with the sun, the moon and the rest of the heavenly bodies – their velocities relative to one another, the solstices, and everything else about them. I was all set to ask the same question about them: how it was better that each of them should act and be acted upon in the way that it was. Since he claimed that these things had been organised by intelligence, it never occurred to me that he would bring forward any reason for them other than that it is better for them to be the way they b are. I thought that when he gave the reason for each of these things individually, and for them all collectively, he would explain in detail what was best for each individual thing and what was good for them all together. I wouldn't have parted with my hopes for a fortune. Eagerly I got hold of the books and read them as quickly as I could, so that I could find out what was best – and what was worse – as quickly as possible.

'It was a wonderful dream, my friend. But it was soon dashed.

As I read on, I found a man making no use of intelligence at all, and not attributing the organisation of things to its causality in any way. Instead he found causes in air, ether, water, and all c sorts of extraordinary things like that. I decided his position was just like that of someone who says that Socrates does all the things he does as a result of intelligence, and who then tries to give the reasons for the particular things I do. He might start by saying that the reason I'm sitting here now is because my body is composed of bones and muscles. The bones are hard, and separated by joints, whereas the muscles can be tensed or relaxed. They enclose the bones, along with the flesh and skin d which hold them together. When the bones pivot in their sockets, the muscles relax or contract, and somehow or other make it possible for me to bend my legs. And that's the reason why I'm sitting here all bent up.

'Then again, he could give another set of reasons of the same kind for my conversation with you. He could explain it in terms of sounds, air currents, hearing sensations, and any number of things of that sort, without ever bothering to mention the real e reason, which is that the Athenians decided it was better to condemn me, and that is why I, in my turn, have decided that it is better to sit here, and more just to remain here and submit to the penalty they have decreed. God knows, these muscles and bones would have been in Megara or Boeotia ages ago, 99 following their opinion of what was best for them, if I hadn't thought it better and more just to submit to the penalty the city imposes, rather than running away and taking to my heels. Calling those sorts of things reasons is quite absurd. You might say that if I didn't possess those things – bones, muscles, and all the things I do in fact possess – I'd be quite incapable of doing what I've decided to do. And that would be true. But given that my actions are the result of intelligence, to say that these things, rather than my choice of what is best, are the *reason* why I do the things I do, would be a thoroughly sloppy use of language. b Fancy being unable to distinguish between the reason for what is and the thing without which the reason couldn't possibly be a reason!

'It seems clear to me that most people are groping around in the dark and using the wrong name when they call this the reason. That's why one person puts a vortex round the earth, and has the earth kept in place by the heaven, while another treats the air as a base and the earth as a kind of flat lid pressing

c down on it. As for the force which keeps these things arranged in the best possible way they could be arranged, they never look for it. They have no idea of its incredible power. They expect to find some Atlas who is stronger and more immortal than ours, and more capable of holding everything together. It doesn't occur to them that what is good and binding is, quite literally, what binds and holds things together. For the truth about that sort of reason I'd have been only too glad, speaking personally, to have been anyone's student. Disappointed in that, and unable to discover it for myself or learn it from anyone else, I have

d adopted a different route in my search for the reason. Do you want me to give you a demonstration of it, Cebes?'

'Yes, I'd like that more than anything.'

'Very well. My next decision, after I'd abandoned my enquiry into things, was to be careful not to let the same thing happen to me as happens to people who watch and study the sun during an eclipse. As you know, they can ruin their eyesight, some of them, unless they look at the sun's reflection in water or

e something like that. The same kind of thought occurred to me. I was afraid I might completely blind my soul by looking at objects with my eyes and trying to grasp them with each of my senses. So I thought it would be a good idea to take refuge in propositions, and look for the truth of things in them. Mind you, in one way I don't think the analogy is a very good one,

100 since I don't for one moment accept that the person who studies things using propositions is studying them in images more than the person who studies them using solid objects. But at any rate that was my starting-point. In any given case I assume to be true the proposition which I judge to have most validity. Whatever agrees with this I take to be true – whether it's a question of causes or anything else – and what doesn't agree I take to be false. But I'd like to tell you what I mean a bit more clearly, since I suspect that at the moment you don't understand.'

'No, I certainly don't,' said Cebes. 'Not really.'

b 'What I mean is this. It's nothing new. I've been saying it for years, and saying it again today in the discussion we've just been having. I'm going to try and show you the kind of causation I've developed, and I shall go back to those things I keep going on about, and start with them. I shall assume that beautiful, just by itself, is something. Likewise good, large, and all the rest. If you grant me those, and agree that they exist, I hope to use them to give you an explanation of causality, and discover that the soul is something immortal.'

'Well,' said Cebes, 'you can take it I do grant them. So go c right ahead, by all means, and draw your conclusions.'

'Think about what follows from those things,' he said. 'See if you agree with me. As far as I can see, if there is something else beautiful, apart from the beautiful itself, there can be no reason for its being beautiful other than that it shares in that beautiful. And I would say the same of all the others. Do you accept a reason of that kind?'

'I do,' he said.

'In which case,' he said, 'I can no longer understand or recognise all those other clever reasons. If somebody tells me the reason something is beautiful is because it is brightly coloured, d or because of its shape, or anything of that sort, I have no time for all that. I get confused by all those other things. In my simple, unsophisticated, possibly naive way I cling to the fact that the only thing making it beautiful is that beautiful I've just mentioned – its presence or communion, or whatever exactly the connection is. It isn't any longer something I'm prepared to be dogmatic about. All I know is that it is the beautiful which makes all beautiful things beautiful. That seems to me to be the safest answer to give myself or anyone else. If I hold on to that, I don't believe I shall ever come to grief. The safe answer to give e myself or anyone else will be that it is the beautiful which makes beautiful things beautiful. Don't you agree?'

'I do.'

'And is it largeness that makes large things large, and larger things larger? And smallness that makes smaller things smaller?'

'Yes.'

'So you wouldn't allow it if someone said that one person was larger than another by a head, and that the smaller was smaller by the same thing. You'd maintain that the only thing you 101 personally could say was that any one thing which was larger than any other thing was larger as a result only of largeness, and that this thing – largeness – was what made it large. Likewise that the smaller was smaller as a result only of smallness, and that this thing – smallness – was what made it smaller. You'd be afraid, I imagine, that if you say someone is larger or smaller by a head, you will run into a paradox. In the first place, what is larger is larger, and what is smaller is smaller, by the same thing. And in the second place, the person who is larger is larger by – or as a result of – his head, which is small. And that's an absurdity, for someone to be large as a result of what is small. Or would you not be afraid of those things?'

Cebes laughed. 'No, I certainly would.'

'In which case, would you be afraid to say that ten is more than eight by two, and that this is the reason why ten exceeds eight, rather than saying ten exceeds eight by quantity and as a result of quantity? Or that two cubits is greater than a cubit by half of itself, rather than by greatness? There'd be the same fear, presumably.'

'Indeed there would,' he said.

'How about when one is added to one? Wouldn't you be a bit hesitant about saying the addition was the cause of two coming into being? Or the division, when one is divided? You'd proclaim that you know no way for any given thing to come into being other than by sharing in the particular being of each thing it does share in, and that in these instances you can allow no cause of two coming to be other than its sharing in twoness. Things which are going to be two must share in this, and anything which is going to be one must share in oneness. You'd have no time for these divisions and additions, and other subtleties of that sort. You'd leave those answers to wiser heads than yours. For your part, you'd be afraid of your own shadow, as the saying goes, and your own lack of experience, and you'd stick to the security of your hypothesis in giving your answer. If anyone fastened upon the hypothesis itself, you'd pay no attention to him, and refuse to answer until you'd investigated the things which followed from it, to see if they were consistent or inconsistent with one another. And when you were required to account for the hypothesis itself, wouldn't you account for it in the same way, framing in its

turn another hypothesis — whichever of the higher-level
hypotheses seemed best — until you came to something
adequate? You wouldn't get your argument mixed up, the way e
lovers of paradox do, by talking about the starting point and
the things that follow from it at the same time — not if you
wanted to find out any of the things that are. To them, this
may not be a matter of any great interest or concern. They're
quite capable, such is their wisdom, of confusing things
completely and still being well pleased with themselves. You,
on the other hand, if you are among the number of the
philosophers, would presumably follow the procedure I am 102
describing.'

'Absolutely right,' said Simmias and Cebes.

ECHECRATES: Heavens, yes, Phaedo. I should think so too. He
made it all incredibly clear, I think, to anyone with even a grain
of intelligence.

PHAEDO: That's certainly what everyone there thought, Echecrates.

ECHECRATES: And what we think, who weren't there and are
hearing it now. But what were the things that were said after
that?

PHAEDO: As I recall, when he had gained agreement on these
points, and it was agreed that each of the forms was something, b
and that it was just from the forms that anything else which
shared in them took its name, the next thing he went on to ask
was this: 'Very well, if that is your view, then when you say
Simmias is taller than Socrates and shorter than Phaedo, aren't
you saying that both these things — tallness and shortness — are
present in Simmias?'

'Yes, I am.'

'And do you agree that the statement "Simmias is taller than
Socrates", as it is normally expressed, does not give the truth of
the matter? It isn't Simmias' essential nature to be taller, c
presumably, simply by being Simmias. You say he is taller
because of the tallness which he just happens to possess. Nor is
he taller than Socrates because Socrates is Socrates, but because
Socrates possesses shortness in comparison with his tallness.'

'True.'

'And again, you wouldn't say Phaedo is taller than him because Phaedo is Phaedo, but because Phaedo has tallness in comparison with his shortness?'

'That is correct.'

'In which case, this is how Simmias can come to be called short *and* tall. It's because he is midway between the two. To d the tallness of the one he can submit his shortness, so that it can be surpassed. To the other he can present his tallness, which surpasses the other's shortness. I'm probably starting to sound like a book,' he said with a laugh, 'but I'm sure it is as I say, for all that.'

He agreed.

'The reason I'm talking like this is that I want your agreement. As I see it, not only is tallness itself never prepared to be tall and short at the same time, but even the tallness which is in us never admits of shortness, and is not prepared to be surpassed. One of two things must happen. At the approach of its opposite, shortness, it can either take to its heels and make way for it, or e be destroyed when shortness approaches. But it refuses to tolerate and admit shortness, and so be something different from what it was before. So I, for example, can admit and tolerate shortness, and remain this same short person. But tallness, because it is tall, has never been able to bring itself to be short. It's just the same with the shortness which is in us, which refuses ever to become tall or be tall. Nor is anything which has an opposite, while still remaining what it was, prepared at the same time to become its opposite or be its opposite. When this 103 happens, it either departs or is destroyed.'

'Yes, that's exactly how I see it,' said Cebes.

This brought an interruption from one of the people there – I've no clear recollection who it was. 'In heaven's name, didn't we just agree, in our earlier discussion, the exact opposite of what we're saying now? We said the greater came into being from the smaller, and the smaller from the greater. Wasn't the coming to be *of* opposites precisely this, a coming to be *from* opposites? Whereas what is being said now, as far as I can see, is that this is something which can never happen.'

Socrates turned his head to listen. And when the speaker had b finished, 'It must have taken a bit of courage,' he said, 'to

remind me of that. But you're forgetting the difference between
what we're saying now and what we were saying then. What
we were saying then was that opposite *things* come into being
from opposite *things*. What we're saying now is that the opposite
itself – whether the opposite which is in us or the opposite
which is in nature – cannot ever become its own opposite.
Then, my friend, we were talking about things which *have*
opposites, and calling them by the names of those opposites,
whereas now we're talking about the opposites themselves
whose presence in the things gives them the name they are
called by. It's those opposites themselves we say would never be   c
prepared to admit coming to be from one another.' He glanced
at Cebes. 'How about you, Cebes?' he asked. 'You're not
troubled by anything he's said, I don't suppose.'

'No, not this time. Which is not to say there aren't a lot of
things troubling me.'

'That's one thing we're agreed on, then,' he said, 'without
reservation. What is opposite will never be opposite to itself.'

'Exactly,' he said.

'In which case, please think about the next step, and see if
you're going to agree with that. Is there something you call hot,
and something you call cold?'

'There is.'

'Are they the same as the things you call snow and fire?'

'Heavens, no. Of course they're not.'   d

'The hot is something different from fire, and the cold is
something different from snow?'

'Yes.'

'But I imagine you also think that while it remains snow, as
we were saying earlier, it can never admit heat and go on being
what it was – i.e. be snow *and* hot. At the approach of heat it
will either give way to it or be destroyed.'

'Exactly.'

'The same with fire. At the approach of cold it will either
make way for it or be destroyed. What it will never bring itself
to do is admit the coldness and go on being what it was – i.e. be
fire *and* cold.'

'True.'   e

'In which case, it is true of some of these things that not only can the form itself rightly be called by its own name for all time, but so also can something else – something which is not the form, but which whenever it exists always has the character of the form. Here's an example which may possibly make it clearer what I mean. The odd must always, I take it, have this name we now give it. Or does it not always have to have it?'

'No, it certainly must.'

'And of the things that are, is it the only one – this is my
104 question – or is there something else which is not the same as the odd, but which must nevertheless be called by this name along with its own name, because its nature is such that it can never be separated from the odd? An example of what I mean is the kind of thing which happens with the number three, and lots of other numbers. Take the number three. Don't you agree that it should always be called both by its own name and by the name "odd" – though the odd is not the same as three? Yet for all that the nature of three, five, and half the entire set of
b numbers, is such that each of them, while not being the same as the odd, always is odd. Then again two, four, and the whole other series of numbers, are not the same as the even, and yet each of them always is even. Do you agree, or not?'

'Of course,' he said.

'In that case, look carefully at the point I am trying to make. It is this. Not only do the opposites we were talking about clearly not admit one another, but even the ones which, while not being opposites to one another, still contain the opposites within them – even these show no sign of admitting that form which is opposite to the one which is in them. On its approach
c either they are destroyed, or they give way. Or are we not going to say that three will be destroyed, or allow anything to happen to it, rather than tolerate becoming even while still continuing to be three?'

'No, we certainly *are* going to say that,' said Cebes.

'And of course,' he said, 'two is not the opposite of three.'

'Certainly not.'

'So it's not only opposite forms which cannot tolerate one another's approach. There are other things as well which cannot tolerate the approach of the opposites.'

'Absolutely right.'

'Do you want us then, if we can, to define what kind of things
these are?'

'Yes.'

'Well then, Cebes, wouldn't they be the ones which are d
compelled by whatever occupies them to contain not only its
own form, but also always the form of some opposite as well?'

'What do you mean?'

'What we've just been saying. Obviously you accept that
things which the form of three occupies must necessarily be odd
as well as being three.'

'Yes, of course.'

'Well, what we're saying is that something like three can
never be approached by the form which is the opposite of the
form which makes it what it is.'

'That's right. It can't.'

'Is it the odd which makes it what it is?'

'Yes.'

'And the opposite to that is the form of the even?'

'Yes.'

'In which case, the form of the even will never come near e
three.'

'Certainly not.'

'So three has no part in the even.'

'No, no part.'

'So three is uneven.'

'Yes.'

'Now, the definition I was talking about just now, the kind of
things which, without being the opposite of something, nevertheless refuse to admit that thing – that opposite – as just now
three, without being the opposite of the even, was still no more
prepared to admit it, since it always brings up its opposite against
it, as two brings up its opposite against odd, and fire against
cold, and any number of other examples – well, see if your 105
definition is this. Not only does the opposite refuse to admit its
opposite, but so also does what brings up an opposite in its
support against the thing it is attacking. The thing which brings
up the support never admits the quality which is opposite to the
support being brought up. Let me remind you again. There's no
harm in hearing it more than once. Five will never admit the

form of the even, any more than ten, which is twice five, will admit the form of the odd. Double is itself the opposite of something different, yet it will not admit the form of the odd.

b Nor will one and a half, and the series of halves, or a third, and the whole series of thirds, admit the form of the whole, if you follow and agree with what I am saying.'

'I entirely agree,' he said. 'And I do follow.'

'Then let's go back to the beginning,' he said. 'Tell me again. And please don't just give me back my question as your answer. Follow my example. What I mean by this is that apart from the original answer I gave, the "safe" answer, I can now see safety of another kind, arising out of what we've just been saying. Suppose you were to ask me what has to be present in a thing's body to make that thing hot, the answer I shall give will not be

c the safe, stupid one – namely "heat" – but a more subtle answer arising out of the discussion we've just had – namely "fire". And if you ask what has to be present in a thing's body to make that thing ill, I shall not say "illness", I shall say "fever". And to the question, what has to be present in a number to make it odd, I shall not say "oddness" but "oneness". And so on. Think about that. Do you fully understand now what I'm after?'

'I do indeed,' he said.

'In that case,' he said, 'here's a question for you. What has to be present in a thing's body for that thing to be alive?'

'Soul.'

d 'Is that invariably true?'

'Of course.'

'Does soul, in that case, always bring life to whatever it takes possession of?'

'Yes,' he said.

'And does life have an opposite, or not?'

'It does.'

'What is it?'

'Death.'

'And soul will always refuse to admit the opposite to the thing it brings up in its support, won't it? We've already agreed that.'

'It most certainly will refuse,' said Cebes.

'Now, what about the thing which refuses to admit the form of the even? What name did we give that just now?'

'Uneven.'

'And what refuses to admit the just, or things which refuse to admit the musical?'

'Unmusical,' he said. 'And unjust.'   e

'Very well. Now, what do we call things which do not admit death?'

'Immortal.'

'And soul is something which does not admit death?'

'It is.'

'In which case, soul is immortal.'

'It is.'

'Very well,' he said. 'Can we say this has been demonstrated? What do you think?'

'I think it has been demonstrated quite satisfactorily, Socrates.'

'How about this, Cebes?' he asked. 'If the uneven were necessarily indestructible, would three have to be indestructible?' 106

'Of course.'

'And if the un-hot were also necessarily indestructible, then when someone brought hot against snow, would the snow withdraw, and remain intact and unmelted? It couldn't be destroyed, but then nor again could it tolerate and admit the heat.'

'True,' he said.

'In the same way, I imagine, if the un-coolable were indestructible, then when something cold came up against fire, the fire would never be extinguished or destroyed, but would depart and go away intact.'

'Necessarily,' he said.

'Well then,' he said. 'Aren't we bound to talk about the   b immortal in the same way? If the immortal is also indestructible, then it's impossible for the soul to be destroyed when death comes against it. What we've just been saying suggests that it will not admit death, nor will it be dead, just as we say three will not be even, any more than the odd will. Nor will fire be cold, any more than the heat in the fire. You might say "What is to stop the odd, when the even comes against it, not from becoming even – we've agreed about that – but from being destroyed itself, and allowing even to come into being in its   c place?" We couldn't defend ourselves against this objection by saying that the odd is not destroyed, because the uneven is not indestructible. If this *were* something we had agreed on, we could easily defend ourselves by saying that when the even comes against it, the odd and three depart and go away. And we could make the same defence in the case of fire, heat and the other examples, couldn't we?'

'We certainly could.'

'So too in this present example of the immortal. If we are agreed that the immortal is also indestructible, then soul, in addition to being immortal, would be indestructible as well. If d we aren't agreed on that, then we need a different argument.'

'Well, we certainly don't need one as far as that goes,' he said. 'If the immortal, which is everlasting, is going to admit destruction, then it's hard to see how there can be anything else which doesn't admit destruction.'

'Yes,' said Socrates. 'I imagine it would be agreed by everyone that god, and the actual form of life, and anything else which is immortal, can never be destroyed.'

'Heavens, yes,' he said. 'That would be agreed by all men. Still more, I should think, by the gods.'

e   'So given that the immortal is also indestructible, must not the soul, if it is indeed immortal, be indestructible as well?'

'Yes, it must necessarily be indestructible.'

'So when death comes against a man, it looks as if it is the mortal part of him which dies, while the immortal part departs and goes away, intact and undestroyed, giving ground before death.'

'Apparently.'

'In which case, Cebes,' he said, 'it is absolutely certain that 107 soul is something immortal and indestructible, and that our souls really will go on existing in Hades.'

'For my part, Socrates,' he said, 'I have nothing more to add to the discussion, and I can find no way of doubting the argument. But if Simmias here, or anyone else, has anything to say, now is not the moment to keep silent. For anyone wanting to speak about this subject, or listen to others speaking about it, I can't imagine a better time than the present.'

'No, I certainly don't have any grounds for doubting either,' said Simmias. 'Not on the basis of our discussion, at any rate.

Though when I think about the importance of the things
we're talking about – and having no great faith in human b
weakness – I'm bound to harbour some doubts still about the
things which have been said.'

'There's more to it than that, Simmias,' said Socrates, 'though
you're quite right. No matter how certain the original hypotheses may seem to you people, they still need more detailed
examination. If you analyse *them* fully, then I think you will
pursue the argument as far as is humanly possible to pursue it.
Make sure of doing that, and your search will be over.'

'True,' he said.

'But there's another point, gentlemen,' he said, 'which we c
ought to give some thought to. If the soul is immortal, then it's
not just the time during which what we call life lasts, but the
whole of time, which demands that we take care of it. And now
the danger for anyone who neglects it really would seem to be
very great. Suppose death were a release from everything. It
would be a stroke of luck for the wicked, when they died, to be
released at once from the body and also, along with the soul,
from their own wickedness. But as it is, since the soul clearly *is*
immortal, there can be no escape for it from evil – no d
salvation – other than becoming as good and wise as possible.
The soul arrives in Hades with nothing more than its education
and upbringing – things which are said to be the greatest help to
the dead, or do them the greatest harm, from the very beginning
of their journey to the other world.

'The story goes that when each individual dies, his own
guardian spirit, assigned to him by lot while he was alive, duly
takes him to a place where those assembled must submit to
judgement, and then journey to Hades with the guide whose e
job it is to conduct people from this world to that one. There
what must happen to them does happen, and they remain as
long as they must, until in the course of many long cycles of
time another guide brings them back here. So the journey is not
as Aeschylus' Telephus describes it. According to him, there is a
direct path leading to Hades, whereas in fact it seems to me to 108
be neither direct nor a single path, since there would then be no
need for guides. If there were just one path, there would
presumably be nowhere anyone could go wrong. No, to judge

by people's sacrifices and worship in this world, it looks as if the road has a large number of branches and forks.

'The well-ordered, wise soul follows its guide. It is familiar with its surroundings. But the soul which is full of desire for the body, as I mentioned earlier, hovers around the body and the
b visible world for a long time, with many struggles and sufferings, before being dragged off, by force and with great difficulty, by its appointed guardian. When it reaches the place where the others are, the soul which is unpurified, which has done something impure – taking part in wrongful killing, perhaps, or doing some similar deed akin to this, the work of kindred
c souls – this soul is shunned by them all. They turn away from it and refuse to be its companion or guide on the journey. This soul wanders on its own, in utter confusion, until certain periods of time have elapsed, at the end of which it is borne against its will to the dwelling appropriate to it. Meanwhile the soul which has lived out its life in a pure and well-ordered way finds gods to be its companions and guides on the journey. Each soul inhabits the place appropriate to it. The earth contains many wondrous places, and is itself, in its nature and size, not at all how it is imagined to be by those who spend their time talking about it. Or so I have been led to believe.'

d   'What do you mean, Socrates?' Simmias asked. 'I too have heard many accounts of the earth, but not this one that has won your acceptance. I'd be very glad to hear it.'

'Well, Simmias, I certainly don't think it needs the art of Glaucus to tell you what they are, these things I believe. Showing that they are true, on the other hand, does seem to me too difficult even for Glaucus. For a start, I probably wouldn't be capable of it. And secondly, Simmias, even if I did know how to, I think my life is now too short for the explanation. But
e my beliefs about the shape of the earth and the places in it – there's nothing to stop me telling you those.'

'That will do well enough,' said Simmias.

'Very well. The first thing I believe is that if the earth is spherical, and in the centre of the heavens, it has no need of air
109 or any other force of that kind to stop it falling. The uniformity of the heaven with itself in every direction, together with the earth's own equilibrium, is enough to support it. An object in

equilibrium, placed in the centre of something uniform, will have no reason to be inclined in one direction rather than another. Its uniformity will keep it free from any inclination. That's the first thing I believe.'

'And quite correct too,' said Simmias.

'Further, I believe it is something vast, and that we who live between Phasis and the Pillars of Heracles inhabit one small part b of it. That we live round our sea like ants or frogs round a pond, and that there are many other peoples in many other places like ours. All over the earth there are numerous hollows, of every shape and size, into which water, mist and air have collected. The earth itself is set in the heaven, a pure object in a pure medium. The heaven contains the stars, and most of those who spend their time talking about these things call it the aether. The c water, mist and air are the sediment of this aether, and they are forever flowing into the hollows of the earth. We don't realise we are living in the hollows of the earth. We think we live up above, on the surface of the earth. Like someone living in the very depths of the ocean, and yet thinking he lived on the surface of the sea. Seeing the sun and the other stars through the water, he would think the sea was the heaven. Because of his slowness and weakness, he would never have reached the d surface of the sea, or seen, as he emerged and stuck his head up out of the sea into the region in which we live, how much purer and more beautiful it is than his own. He would never even have heard about it from someone who had seen it.

'Our position is exactly the same. We live just in one hollow of the earth, and yet we think we live on the surface of the earth itself. We call the air the heaven, as if this were the heaven through which the stars move. But it's the same for us as for those people in the sea. Our weakness and slowness make us e incapable of getting through to the furthest limit of the air, though if anyone *could* get to the end of it, or grew wings and flew there, if he lifted his head and had a look, in the way that the fishes in our sea can stick their heads up and have a look at things here – well, in the same way someone could see the things there. And if his nature were strong enough to endure the sight, he would realise that was the true heaven, the true light and the true earth. This earth of ours, these stones and the 110 whole region here, are corrupted and eaten away, just as things in the sea are eaten away by the salt. There's nothing to speak of growing in the sea, and to all intents and purposes nothing perfect. Just eroded rocks, sand, and where there is any earth as well, indescribable mud and slime. It bears no comparison with the beauties of our world. The beauties of that other world, in its turn, would clearly be superior to ours by an even greater

b margin. If telling a story is in order, Simmias, it is worth hearing what things are actually like above the earth and below the heavens.'

'We'd very much like to hear your story, Socrates,' said Simmias.

'Very well, my friend,' he said, 'this is what they say. First, its appearance. If you could look at it from above, the true earth is like one of those balls made from twelve pieces of leather – variegated, and picked out in different colours, of which the colours we have here are merely samples such as painters use.

c They say that there the whole earth is made up of colours of this sort – and indeed far brighter and purer than these. One part is a purple of astonishing beauty, another gold. The part which is white is whiter than chalk or snow. And the earth is made up of the other colours likewise – and colours more numerous and more beautiful than we have ever seen. Even those very hollows we were talking about, being full of water and air, and gleaming

d amid the variety of the other colours, give a kind of appearance of colour.

'As a result the earth presents the appearance of a single unbroken, multi-coloured surface. And this character is reflected in the plants that grow there – trees, flowers and fruit. The same again with the mountains and rocks the earth has, which are correspondingly more beautiful in their smoothness, transparency and colour. The precious stones which are so highly prized here – cornelian, jasper, emerald and so on – are

e fragments of these. But there everything is of this kind – and even more beautiful than these. The reason for this is that those stones are pure, not like the ones here, eroded and damaged by mildew and salt from the elements which have flowed together, causing ugliness and disease in stones and the earth as well as in animals and plants. They say the earth itself is adorned with all these stones – and with gold, silver and the other precious metals besides. They are clearly visible, all over the earth, being 111 very numerous and large. It makes the earth a sight for blessed eyes to see.

'There are all sorts of living things on the earth, including humans. Some dwell inland, some on the shores of the air – as we live on the shores of our sea – while others dwell on islands in the air, close to the mainland. In short, what water and the sea are to us, for our purposes, the air is to them. And what air is to us, the aether is to them. Their seasons are so temperate that b the people are free from disease and live much longer than people here. In purity of eyesight, hearing, intelligence and every other faculty of that kind they are as far superior to us as air is to water, or aether to air. What is more, they have groves and temples belonging to the gods, which the gods really do live in. They have divine utterances, prophecies, visions of the gods, and face-to-face contact of that kind. The sun, moon and stars c are visible to them as they truly are, and their happiness in other ways is in accord with the things I have mentioned. Such is the nature, they say, of the earth as a whole and and its surroundings.

'There are many regions in it, corresponding to the hollows all round it. Some of these regions are deeper and more open than the one in which we live, some deeper but with a narrower opening than our region, and some shallower than the d one here, and broader. They are all connected with one another by a variety of underground passages – some narrower, some broader – and they have channels by means of which water gushes from one to another, like wine into mixing-bowls. There are underground rivers, ever-flowing and of unimaginable size, hot waters and cold waters, a tremendous fire, with huge rivers of fire and many rivers of liquid mud – be it clearer or more murky – like the rivers of mud which flow before the e lava, and the lava flow itself, in Sicily. Every region is filled with these rivers, depending in each case on the nature of the circular stream at that point. The whole thing is kept in motion, up and down, by a kind of pulsation inside the earth.

'The nature of the pulsation is something like this. One of the openings in the earth is particularly large, penetrating right through the earth from one side to the other. It's the one 112

Homer has in mind when he says:

> Far off, where deepest lies beneath the earth
> The pit.

Elsewhere both he and many other poets have given it the name Tartarus. All the rivers flow together into this opening, and from it they flow out again, the character of each individual river depending on the nature of the earth through which it
b flows. The reason why all the streams flow out of it and into it is that the mass of water has no bottom or resting-place. Hence the pulsation, as it surges up and down. The air and wind which surround it behave in the same way. They follow it as it washes over to the far side of the earth and back to this side, and just as the breath of people breathing is constantly in flux – out and in – so in the earth the "breath" which pulsates with the water creates incredibly severe winds on its way in and out. When the
c water retreats to the region which is called "down", it flows through the earth into the beds of the streams there, and fills them. Like an irrigation system. When it leaves that region and flows back here, it fills the streams here in their turn. And as they fill up, these flow through the channels and the earth until they reach the individual regions into which a course has been made for each. In this way they form seas and marshes and rivers and springs.

'From here they plunge again beneath the earth, some
d encircling regions more extensive and more numerous, others fewer and shorter, before they discharge once more into Tartarus, some at a point much lower than where they were drawn off, others only slightly lower. But they all flow in at a point lower than they flowed out – some on the opposite side from their point of outflow, others on the same side. And there are some which go round in a complete circle, winding themselves once or many times round the earth like snakes, going as low as they can before discharging into Tartarus. The
e lowest they *can* go, in either direction, is the centre. No further, because for both sets of streams the part on either side is uphill.

'There are many rivers, large and varied. And among these many rivers there are four in particular, of which the greatest,

flowing in a circle round the perimeter, is the one called
Oceanus. Diametrically opposite to this, and flowing in the
opposite direction, is Acheron, which flows through barren
countryside, and then flowing underground comes out into the   113
Acherusian lake. This is where the souls of the dead come to,
most of them, and after waiting their appointed time – some
longer, some shorter – are sent back again for the births of living
creatures. The third river issues from a point between these first
two. Near where it issues it flows into a vast expanse blazing all
over with fire, where it creates a lake bigger than our sea, a
boiling mixture of water and mud. From there it comes round
in a circle, foul and muddy, and as it winds itself round inside   b
the earth, it passes a number of places, among them the margin
of the Acherusian lake, though it does not mingle with the
water. And when it has wound itself round many times, it
emerges underground at a lower point in Tartarus. This is the
river they call Pyriphlegethon; its streams of lava belch forth
fragments at various places on the earth's surface. Opposite this
river, in turn, issues the fourth river – at first into a land which is
strange and wild, so the story goes, and which is entirely the
colour of lapis lazuli. They call this the Stygian land, and the   c
lake created by the river's outflow they call the Styx. As it falls
into the lake, the river acquires strange properties in its waters.
Finally it disappears below the ground, and winds about,
flowing in the opposite direction to Pyriphlegethon and meeting
it at the Acherusian lake, coming from the other side. Nor does
the water of this river mingle with any other, but it too goes
round in a circle and comes out into Tartarus opposite
Pyriphlegethon. The name of this river, according to the poets,
is Cocytus.

'That is the nature of the landscape there. When the dead   d
arrive at the place to which the spirit conveys each one, they
first submit themselves to judgement – those who have lived a
good and holy life, and those who have not. Those found to
have lived a middling sort of life make their way to the river
Acheron. Embarking in the transport provided for them, they
travel to the lake. There they dwell and are purified, being
absolved from their wrongdoings by paying the penalty for
them – those who have done any wrong – while for their good

e deeds they win reward, each according to his deserts. Those
judged to be beyond redemption because of the enormity of
their crimes – those who have carried out wholesale robbery
from holy places, or numerous unjust and unlawful killings, or
other crimes which are really the equivalent of these – meet the
fate they deserve. They are hurled into Tartarus, whence they
nevermore emerge.

'Those found guilty of crimes which, though great, are
redeemable, committing an act of violence in a fit of anger
114 against a father or mother, for example, or becoming a killer in
some similar way, but then living out their lives in a state of
repentance – these too must of necessity be thrown into
Tartarus. But after they have been thrown in and remained
there a year, the flood washes them back again – those guilty of
homicide down Cocytus, those who have killed a father or
mother down Pyriphlegethon. In their journey they pass the
Acherusian lake, where they cry out, and call upon those they
have killed or treated with violence. They call out in supplication,
b begging to be accepted and allowed to escape into the lake. If
they can persuade them, they do escape and are released from
their punishment. Otherwise they are borne once more to
Tartarus, and from there back again to the rivers. This goes on
happening to them unceasingly, until they do persuade those
they have wronged, since this is the penalty imposed on them
by the judges.

'Those whose lives are found to have been distinguished by
their holiness are the ones who are released and set free from
c these places below the ground, as if from prison. They rise and
come to the pure dwelling-place, where they live above the
ground. And of these people, those who have fully purified
themselves by means of philosophy live entirely without their
bodies for all time thereafter, and come to dwellings finer still
than those I have mentioned. It is not easy to give you a clear
idea of them, nor is there time enough now. But for the reasons
we have described, Simmias, we should do everything we can to
share in human excellence and wisdom during our lives. Fair is
the prize, and great our hope.

d 'It is not for a man of any intelligence to state dogmatically
that the underworld is precisely as I have described it. But that

this or something like it is the way things are for our souls and their dwellings, since the soul clearly *is* something immortal – that I do think he can say, and take a chance on believing, with every likelihood of being proved right. He should sing himself tales, like enchantments, of the kind we have just been telling – which is why I have been telling my story at such length. Anyway, those are the grounds for optimism about his soul, for anyone who in his life has rejected the pleasures of the body and its adornments as things which are alien to him, in the belief that they do more harm than good. Instead he will have embraced the pleasures of learning, adorning his soul with beauties which are not alien, but its own: self-control, justice, courage, freedom and truth. Thus prepared, he waits, ready to make his journey to the underworld when destiny summons him. You will all journey there one day, Simmias and Cebes and the rest of you. As for me, "Now is the hour", as a man in a tragedy might say. "I hear my destiny." And it's about time for me to be thinking about a bath. I'm sure it's better to have had a bath before drinking the poison, and save the women the trouble of washing the corpse.'

When he said this, Crito asked him, 'Well, Socrates, what instructions do you want to give these people here, or me – either about your children or anything else? What can we do for you that would most please you?'

'What I always say, Crito. Nothing new. Take care of yourselves, and whatever you do will be pleasing to me, to my family and to you yourselves, even if you make no promises here and now. If you take no care of yourselves, and refuse to spend your lives on the trail of the things we've been talking about today and in the past, then however many solemn promises you make today, it will get you nowhere.'

'Very well,' said Crito, 'we shall do our best to follow your advice. But what about burying you? How do you want us to do that?'

'However you like. Provided you can catch me, that is, and I don't get away from you.' He glanced at us, laughing to himself, and said, 'Gentlemen, I cannot convince Crito that I am Socrates, here, the person discussing things with you and setting out all these arguments. He thinks I'm that body he's d shortly going to see. And he asks how he is to bury me! This whole argument I have spent so much time putting together, to show that when I drink the poison I shall not remain with you, but depart – leaving I trust for that happy region of the blessed – all this encouragement, of you and of myself, was wasted on him, I think. So you must give Crito an undertaking on my behalf – the opposite to the undertaking he wanted to give the jury. His was that I would certainly remain. Yours must be that when I die I shall certainly *not* remain, but depart and go away.

e Then Crito will be able to bear it more easily, and won't get upset on my behalf when he sees my body being burnt or buried, as if something terrible were happening to me. He won't say, at my funeral, that he is laying out Socrates, or carrying him out, or burying him. Take my word for it, my good friend Crito, inaccurate use of language is not only objectionable in itself. It is positively damaging to the soul. You must cheer up. Tell yourself you are burying my body, and

116 bury it in whatever way you please, and think most in keeping with tradition.'

With these words he got up, and went into a room to take a bath. Crito followed him, telling us to wait. So we waited, discussing among ourselves the things which had been said, examining them closely, and then again going over the great misfortune which had befallen us. We thought, quite simply, that we were losing a father, and that we would be spending the rest of our lives as orphans. After he had had his bath, his

b children were taken in to him – he had two young sons, and one who was grown-up – and the women of his household went in. You probably know them. He spoke to them with Crito there, telling them his last wishes, and then told the women and children to leave, while he himself came back to us.

It was now close to sunset. He had spent a long time inside. He came and sat down, fresh from his bath. There was not much conversation after this. Then the officer of the Eleven

c arrived. He came up to him and said, 'Socrates, I'm sure I shall not have the same complaint against you that I have against others. They get angry with me and curse me when I tell them to drink the poison – though I am only carrying out the orders of the magistrates. But you, as I have known you during your

time here, are altogether the most generous, the most gentle and
the best man of all those who have ever come here. And now in
particular, I'm sure you are not angry with me, but with the
people responsible. You know who they are. So now, since you
know what I have come to say, farewell. Try to endure what d
must be as easily as possible.' With this he burst into tears,
turned, and left us.

Socrates looked after him. 'Farewell to you too. We will do as
you say.' And then to us, 'What a charming man. He has kept
coming to see me all this time, and sometimes he has stopped to
chat. In fact, he has been altogether the best of men. See how
generously now he sheds tears for me. Come, Crito, let us do as
he says. Let someone bring in the poison, if it has been ground.
If it hasn't, let the man get on with grinding it.'

'If you ask me, Socrates,' Crito said, 'the sun is still above the e
mountains. It hasn't set yet. Besides, I know of people who have
drunk the poison long after they were told to. They have had
dinner, and plenty to drink. Some of them have even had sex
with the people they most desired. There's no hurry. We still
have some time.'

'It makes sense for them, Crito – the people you are talking
about – to act as they do. They think they gain something by it.
And it makes sense for me not to act like that, since I don't
think I shall gain anything by drinking the poison a little later – 117
apart from making myself ridiculous in my own eyes by
clutching on to life, and trying to save the last drops when the
cup is already empty. Go on. Believe me. Do as I say.'

Hearing this, Crito nodded to his slave who was standing
nearby. The slave went out, and after some time came back
with the man who was going to administer the poison. He was
carrying it, already ground, in a cup. When Socrates saw the
man, he said, 'Well, my good fellow, you know about these
things. What is the procedure?'

'Just drink it and walk about,' he replied, 'until you feel a
heaviness in your legs. Then lie down. If you do that, it will b
work of its own accord.' As he said this, he handed the cup to
Socrates.

He took it quite cheerfully, Echecrates, with no hesitation,
and no change in his colour or facial expression. Giving the

man one of his usual quizzical looks, he asked him, 'What are your rules about this drink – I mean about pouring a libation to someone? Is that permitted, or not?'

'Socrates, we grind only as much as we think is right for the person to drink.'

c   'I see. But I imagine a prayer to the gods – that the move from this world to the next may be a happy one – is both permitted and the right thing to do. That is my prayer, and may that be how it turns out.' Saying this he raised the cup to his lips and drained it, quite unperturbed and with every appearance of enjoyment. Most of us, up to that point, had been reasonably successful in controlling our tears, but when we saw him drinking, saw that he had drunk, we could do so no longer. I found the tears coming despite myself, in a flood, so that I covered my face and wept for my loss. Not for him, but for my d own misfortune and the kind of man I had lost as a friend. Crito, unable to hold back his tears any longer, had got up and moved away already. Apollodorus had been crying incessantly even before this, but now he started howling aloud. In his grief and distress he made everyone there break down – apart from Socrates himself.

'Really!' he said. 'What an extraordinary way to behave! The main reason I sent the women away was so they wouldn't e disturb us like this. I have heard it said one should die in silence. So keep quiet, and be brave.'

This made us ashamed, and we stopped crying. As for Socrates, he walked around, and when he said his legs were getting heavy, he lay down on his back, as the man had told him to. As he did so, the man who had given him the poison put his hands on him, and after a little time tried his feet and legs. Then he squeezed his foot hard, and asked him if he could feel it. He 118 said he couldn't. After that, again, the man tried his shins. Moving his hand up, he showed us that he was growing cold and numb. The man went on touching him, and said that when it reached his heart, then he would be gone.

The chill had just about reached his abdomen when he uncovered his face, which he had covered up, and said – and these were the last words he uttered – 'Crito, we owe a cock to Asclepius. Pay the debt. Don't forget.'

'It shall be done,' Crito replied. 'Is there anything else you want to say?'

To this question Socrates made no reply, but shortly afterwards he gave a start, and the man uncovered his face. His gaze was fixed. Seeing this, Crito closed his mouth and eyes.

Such, Echecrates, was the end of our companion. He was the finest man, we would say, of all the people of that time whom we knew – and in general the wisest and most just.

WORDSWORTH CLASSICS

General Editors: Marcus Clapham & Clive Reynard

JANE AUSTEN
Emma
Mansfield Park
Northanger Abbey
Persuasion
Pride and Prejudice
Sense and Sensibility

ARNOLD BENNETT
Anna of the Five Towns

R. D. BLACKMORE
Lorna Doone

ANNE BRONTË
Agnes Grey
The Tenant of
Wildfell Hall

CHARLOTTE BRONTË
Jane Eyre
The Professor
Shirley
Villette

EMILY BRONTË
Wuthering Heights

JOHN BUCHAN
Greenmantle
Mr Standfast
The Thirty-Nine Steps

SAMUEL BUTLER
The Way of All Flesh

LEWIS CARROLL
Alice in Wonderland

CERVANTES
Don Quixote

G. K. CHESTERTON
Father Brown:
Selected Stories
The Man who was
Thursday

ERSKINE CHILDERS
The Riddle of the Sands

JOHN CLELAND
Memoirs of a Woman of
Pleasure: Fanny Hill

WILKIE COLLINS
The Moonstone
The Woman in White

JOSEPH CONRAD
Heart of Darkness
Lord Jim
The Secret Agent

J. FENIMORE COOPER
The Last of the
Mohicans

STEPHEN CRANE
The Red Badge of
Courage

THOMAS DE QUINCEY
Confessions of an English
Opium Eater

DANIEL DEFOE
Moll Flanders
Robinson Crusoe

CHARLES DICKENS
Bleak House
David Copperfield
Great Expectations
Hard Times
Little Dorrit
Martin Chuzzlewit
Oliver Twist
Pickwick Papers
A Tale of Two Cities

BENJAMIN DISRAELI
Sybil

THEODOR DOSTOEVSKY
Crime and Punishment

SIR ARTHUR CONAN
DOYLE
The Adventures of
Sherlock Holmes
The Case-Book of
Sherlock Holmes
The Lost World &
Other Stories
The Return of
Sherlock Holmes
Sir Nigel

GEORGE DU MAURIER
Trilby

ALEXANDRE DUMAS
The Three Musketeers

MARIA EDGEWORTH
Castle Rackrent

GEORGE ELIOT
The Mill on the Floss
Middlemarch
Silas Marner

HENRY FIELDING
Tom Jones

F. SCOTT FITZGERALD
A Diamond as Big as the
Ritz & Other Stories
The Great Gatsby
Tender is the Night

GUSTAVE FLAUBERT
Madame Bovary

JOHN GALSWORTHY
In Chancery
The Man of Property
To Let

ELIZABETH GASKELL
Cranford
North and South

KENNETH GRAHAME
The Wind in the
Willows

GEORGE & WEEDON
GROSSMITH
Diary of a Nobody

RIDER HAGGARD
She

THOMAS HARDY
Far from the
Madding Crowd
The Mayor of Casterbridge
The Return of the
Native
Tess of the d'Urbervilles
The Trumpet Major
Under the Greenwood
Tree